Power, Politics and Rural Development

ESSAYS ON INDIA

Power, Politics and Rural Development

ESSAYS ON INDIA

G.K. LIETEN

MANOHAR
2003

First published 2003

© G.K. Lieten, 2003

All rights reserved. No part of this publication may be reproduced or transmitted, in any form or by any means, without prior permission of the author and the publisher

ISBN 81-7304-475-9

Published by
Ajay Kumar Jain for
Manohar Publishers & Distributors
4753/23 Ansari Road, Daryaganj
New Delhi 110002

Typeset by
Guru Typograph Technology
New Delhi 110045

Printed at
Lordson Publishers Pvt. Ltd.
Delhi 110007

Contents

List of Tables   7

List of Figures   9

List of Abbreviations   11

Introduction   13

1. Decentralization in India: Learning from Old and New   17
2. Caste, Gender and Class in *Panchayats*: The Case of Barddhaman, West Bengal   33
3. *Panchayats* in Western Uttar Pradesh: Namesake Members   55
4. *Panchayats* and Natural Disasters: Floods in Jalpaiguri, West Bengal   78
5. Land Reforms at Centre Stage: The Evidence on West Bengal   91
6. West Bengal after a Quarter Century of Land Reforms   112
7. Human Development in Kerala: Structure and Agency in History   132
8. Development Priorities: Post-Modernist Assumptions and Pre-Modernist Aspirations   147
9. Women, Caste and Religion in a North Indian Village   165
10. Hindu Communalism around Ayodhya between Caste and Class   187
11. Rural Development in West Bengal: Development of the Weak   209
12. The Rural Discourse on Child Labour and Education   227

Glossary   255

Bibliography   261

Index   277

Tables

2.1	Occupational Distribution of *Panchayat* Members in Memari	49
4.1	Opinions on the *Panchayat* Councillors in Jalpaiguri Villages	84
4.2	Assessment of the Economic Position in the Flood-affected Villages in Jalpaiguri	88
5.1	Indices of Repeasantization: Barddhaman and Medinipur	96
5.2	Ranking of West Bengal Districts in Terms of Land Redistribution, Technological Inputs, and Productivity Changes	104
5.3	Irrigation Expenditure during Seventh and Eighth Plan	107
6.1	Changes in Rural Poverty in Major Indian States	124
6.2	Poverty and Social Indicators in Indian States	130
7.1	Some Social Indicators for South Indian States, 1991	134
7.2	Trends in Literacy Rate in Kerala by Gender and by District, 1961–71	138
8.1	Village Status Groups	157
8.2	Class-wise Development Priorities	161
10.1	Correlation of Caste and Class in a Jaunpur Village	197
10.2	Class-wise and Caste-wise Political Preferences, 1993	198
12.1	Literacy and Fertility Rate of Some Selected States, 1991	233
12.2	Age-wise Work and School Involvement of Boys, District Faizabad, 1981	235
12.3	Age-wise Work and School Involvement of Girls, District Faizabad, 1981	235
12.4	Current Use of Contraceptives by Number of Living Children in Selected States	249

Figures

2.1	Caste Composition of *Panchayats*, Memari, 1978–93	47
2.2	Landownership of *Gram Panchayat* Members in Barddhaman District, 1993–8	49
6.1	Rice and Potato Production in West Bengal, 1960–2000	120
6.2	Regional Comparison of Rural Literacy, 1970–95	130
7.1	Demographic Transition in Kerala, 1930–90	137
7.2	Literate Persons in Kerala, three regions, 1941–91	139
11.1	Perception of Economic Changes. Class-wise Appreciation in Barddhaman and Muzaffarnagar	217

Abbreviations

BAES	Bureau of Applied Economics and Statistics
BDO	Block Development Officer
BJP	Bharatiya Janata Party
BKD	Bharatiya Kranti Dal
BKU	Bharatiya Kisan Union
BLD	Bharatiya Lok Dal
BSP	Bahujan Samaj Party
CBR	Crude Birth Rate
CDR	Crude Death Rate
CPI(M)	Communist Party of India (Marxist)
CRP	Central Reserve Police
EPW	*Economic and Political Weekly*
GATT	General Agreement of Trade and Tariffs
GNP	Gross National Product
GOI	Government of India
HDI	Human Development Index
HYV	High-Yielding Variety
ICFTU	International Confederation of Free Trade Unions
ILO	International Labour Organization
IMF	International Monetary Fund
IMR	Infant Mortality Rate
INC	Indian National Congress
IRDP	Intergrated Rural Development Programme
KARB	Kerala Agricultural Relations Bill
LFG	Left Front Government

NABARD	National Bank for Agriculture and Rural Development
NGO	Non-Governmental Organization
NSDP	Net State Domestic Product
NSS	National Sample Survey
OBC	Other Backward Caste
PR	*panchayati raj*
PSP	Praja Socialist Party
RLEGP	Rural Labour Employment Guarantee Programme
RSP	Revolutionary Socialist Party
SAP	Structural Adjustment Policy
SC	Scheduled Caste
ST	Scheduled Tribe
SNDP	Shree Narayana Dharma Parishad
UF	United Front
UNDP	United Nations Development Programme
UP	Uttar Pradesh
USA	United States of America
VLW	Village-Level Worker
WB	West Bengal
WTO	World Trade Organization

Introduction

After having worked as an historian and as a political scientist, i.e. basically culling information from written sources, I took my first step as an anthropological fieldworker in 1988 in West Bengal. An anthropologist has the privilege and the joy to get his information, in a very rough form, from living people, but also has the encumbrance and the anxiety of a physically and mentally taxing job.

I still remember vividly the many doubts and pains during my first stint, from late winter into the hot summer on the plains of Birbhum district, but since I have continued this type of work in the years to come, the rewards must have been more tangible than the discomfort. Not only the personal rewards: through anthropological fieldwork I have understood that much of what we earlier had written in our learned academic treatises is not always and not fully (to put it euphemistically) in line with the views of the poor people in the villages. These people, however poor and illiterate, however much repressed by gender, caste and class, have a richness of thought that needs to be tapped much more than has been done so far. They are both the agents and the victims of history and have a knowledge of how the local structure of power and powerlessness operate. Much academic insight can be learned by listening to them.

When P.C. Joshi in 1952 approached his supervisor D.P. Mukerji to ask him to be his fieldwork guide, Mukerji, who did not consider it useful to go into the field is reported to have said: 'The fieldworker receives from fieldwork what he himself puts into it. There is no observation if the observer has no theory or point of view to guide him in his investigation.' One cannot have much qualms with such an observation (the fieldworker has his or her set of ideas and values) but Joshi soon found out that 'the real world of peasants as it unfolded itself before me day by day in all its richness was far removed from my mental picture of "rural idiocy", stagnation and backwardness which I had received from books' (Joshi 1979: 84). Joshi realized that peasants behave differently and express themselves differently according to the circumstances. In a scarcity-stricken agrarian setting, the concern for survival was perennial and imposed the primacy of community, patronage and compliance from which there was no escape. In the villages more exposed to the forces of commercialization and urbanization, tenants had become responsive to the ideology of exploitation and class conflict. Above all:

The idea that rural communities have a fixed set of beliefs and are indifferent or hostile to their being disturbed is false. [Villagers] discussed important matters, both practical and philosophical. A continuous process of reorientation of outlook and re-evaluation of personal and collective experience went on among them, and their acceptance or rejection of ideas and things had a logic of its own. (Joshi 1979: 88)

This is the spirit I have tried to emulate. My search for local development stories has taken me from Jalpaiguri, close to Assam to Muzzafargarh bordering Baluchistan and the Lower Sindh provinces in Pakistan. The commonness of the local voices has impressed. Differences did not emerge along the religious or regional divide but rather along the class divide and, to a lesser extent, along the gender divide.

One day I was sitting in a rural homeopathic hospital somewhere in Jaunpur district in north-eastern Uttar Pradesh. The hospital that probably was to serve a cluster of small villages was a clear sign that the government was serious on developing its extension services so as to reach out to the poor and remote hinterland. The homeopathic approach had my sympathy and I was pleased to realize that not everything was bad in this out-of-the-way place in the cow-belt area. The hospital was rather spacious, although badly kept and, I was disappointed to realize before long, hardly functioning. There were hardly any patients attending the hospital during a couple of weeks I resided in the village. The doctor lived in the city 20 km away and he showed up incidentally a couple of times. On one day that he had come and since only one patient had come, he had ample time to entertain me on various aspects of rural live. As a doctor he boasted of knowledge in different fields. He told me the facts and provided me with one or two explanations for the rather sad state of affairs. He was particularly appalled by the ignorance of the local people and by the shameless prorecreation in the midst of poverty. Especially the Muslims as a group drew his attention: with 4 wives and with at least 5 children per wife they were stated to have only one object in mind: to overtake the Hindu population as soon as possible. The good man spoke with the conviction of a Kshatrya. As a good Kshatrya, it turned out, he was proud of his manly powers, as he told me later, since he had produced 7 children himself.

During encounters as this one, I usually felt less comfortable than in the various meetings I had with the poor men and women in the villages, with poor Muslims and lower castes. I felt I was pontificated by persons who had distorted views of the reality around and yet claimed to be the guardians of local culture and Indianness. Yet the episode in a nutshell clarified a number of things about social relations and government structures in the particular area. It is through encounters like these that I got a perspective on rural India. The articles included in this book are based on around 18 months of effective village fieldwork in the 1990s. The aim was to look into social relations through the eyes of the actors involved. Social relations spans the entire gamut of economic changes, labour relations, power structures, politics and caste/class/gender identities. Through the self-perception of the actors involved, I intend to draw the local reality of what usually is looked at from macro-data or from survey data, which, in the best of cases, produces approximations without much qualitative insight into how and why.

The development of agriculture is not the subject of this study. It forms the background to it. Except for one chapter on Kerala, all cases refer to West Bengal and Uttar Pradesh. That choice was informed by a different trajectory of agrarian relations and economic development in both states.

Some of the research on which the findings in this book are based forms part of a wider project in collaboration with Ravi Srivastava (in Uttar Pradesh) and Ratan Khasnabis (in West Bengal). I have developed a warm friendship with both of them and with their families. The project was financially supported by the Indo-Dutch Programme on Alternatives in Development (IDPAD), and by the Amsterdam School of Social Science Research at the University of Amsterdam. Some of the finances were provided by the Amsterdam Institute for Research on Working Children (IREWOC). In the collection of the data, I was assisted by Devipriyo Datta, Santosh Kumar, Pradip Kumar Barman, Pronesh Chondra Roy and Sushil Srivastava. I am particularly greatly indebted to Harish Pande for his assistance during a long stint in Uttar Pradesh.

Fruitful suggestions and directions as well as logistic support I received from Madan Gopal Ghosh, Biplab Das Gupta, Sukumal Sen, George Mathews, Nagesh Kumar and Prabhat Dutta, as well as from the various districts and development block officials in Uttar Pradesh and West Bengal.

Jan Breman, Mario Rutten, Michele Leclerq, Neil Webster, Otto van den Muyzenberg, Ashwani Saith, Dick Kooiman, Patricia Jeffery and Ben White helped me to sharpen my argument and to modify my approach, not always successfully. They have offered useful suggestions on the papers and pointed out inaccuracies.

Some of the papers have been published earlier and have been reproduced here with some stylistic modifications but with a minimum of updating. Chapter 8 has been published in the *Southeast Asian Journal Of Social Science*. Chapter 10 was earlier published in German and, in a modified from, in the *Journal of Contemporary Asia*, which also carried Chapter 11 (*JCA* 1996, No. 2). Chapter 5 has earlier been published in *Development and Change*. Chapter 1 was presented in Paris and in modified forms was published in the IDPAD Bulletin and in *Cahiers du Gemdev*. Chapters 2 and 6 have not been published before. Chapter 9 was previously available as part of a bigger working paper published by IDPAD. Some of its material has also been made use of in Lieten and Srivastava (1999). The other chapters (3, 4, 7 and 12) in one way or the other have been published in *Economic and Political Weekly*.

I hope the chapters, which deal subsequently with the effects of decentralization on poverty, the alternatives in development and the views from below, in a small way will advance the knowledge of rural development, particularly of the mechanism behind it.

Amsterdam, June 2002

CHAPTR 1

Decentralization in India: Learning from Old and New

The idea of decentralization has a modern ring. It has become associated with 'good governance', with participatory development, with localization against the backdrop of globalization, and with the synergy of 'civil society' and the state. Neither the idea nor the policy, however, are new and the present policy interest would benefit from the lessons to be learnt from the past. In doing so, we shall compare two areas in India that have developed along different trajectories. While one trajectory is associated with land reforms and resistance from below, the other is been associated with the continuing hold of the landholding elite on economic and political developments.

Decentralization has for long been a buzzword in development debates. The idea of decentralization of government administration is in fact not a new concept. India was one of the pioneers in implementing it, at least on paper. It had been introduced during the late nineteenth century by the colonial administration, with the aim of inducing the 'intelligent class of public-spirited men' into the management of rural areas under British rule. The local councils were conceived as appendages of the central administration. Decentralization in fact was a function of the ultimate subordination of the villages under the dominance of the state. The legitimization for introducing 'village democracy' was partially based, in a truly Orientalist fashion, on a coloured reconstruction of the past by a colonial historian, Charles Metcalfe who had depicted the Indian village as a place of cordiality, tranquillity, simplicity and unchangeability. The idea of the oriental village was later carried on to the modern period by Mahatma Gandhi and his school of thought.

In the policy approach of the Government of India after Independence, it was recognized right from the 1950s onwards that the strategy of rural development should be pursued with local rural communities as the subject and the object. This formed the rationale behind the

Community Development Programme of the 1950s, which sought to promote local self-government and participatory development through a reactivation of the *panchayats*.

The *panchayats* were supposed to have been an ancient institution, but the programme, in financial and managerial terms, had a USA trademark.[1] Uttar Pradesh especially became a laboratory of community development initiatives, and the first reports were encouraging. In practice, however, it soon turned out that the *panchayats* failed to function, and the development structure remained very much dominated by the centralized departments. These departments provided the access to infrastructure and finances, and little power was delegated. From the late 1970s onwards, many attempts were made to reactivate the *panchayats*. In some provinces, these attempts were successful, but in general, as aptly noted by Jain (1985), the attempts to revitalize grass roots democracy showed feeble results. In 1994, the 73rd Amendment to the Constitution of India recognized the *panchayats* as the lowest rung of self-government, and gave them a greater share of financial resources.

In a sense, this new departure and the high hopes it has engendered are in line with the changing appreciation of the role of the state in the wake of the acceptance of neo-liberal policies in most countries. It is now widely argued that the centralizing and affirmative state is too costly and too inefficient. The new call for localization at the turn of the century, this time supported by the World Bank, may not be more successful than previous attempts have been. The idea of 'locality' as opposed to globalization operates under the assumption that states in the Third World, and the governments representing them, are bureaucratic, rent seeking, inflexible, and aloof from the real needs of the people, and therefore have to be sized down to their optimal sizes.

The arguments to opt for lower levels of government (and for market-driven regulation) moreover make use of a series of dichotomies between the state and civil society, which the non-governmental organizations (NGO) world also has been keen to stress. The state is considered as exploitative of rural interests, a Leviathan intruding into the uniqueness of the moral economy of the village. Especially within

---

[1] Alice Thorner, in an interesting article on this first post-Independence Indo-American cooperation, has argued that the project reflected a deep anxiety to check political upheavals and agrarian unrest which were expected to be imminent: village community development was considered as 'a necessary antidote to rural unrest' (Thorner 1981: 120).

the post-modernist paradigm, the centralizing states are seen as colonizing the rural and indigenous hinterland, just in the way the colonial masters did before. Pleading for village and community values and localized decision making therefore appears as a defiance of all that is alien, colonizing and exploitative, and as the panacea to all the problems that centralized states have been accused of.

Decentralization is also a method of governance by the modern state. It can encourage democratic participation, but it can also reinforce elitist control. Rajni Kothari, one of the foremost Indian political scientists and a strong believer in civil society, was rather ambivalent on the decentralization of powers to elected village councils: 'Panchayats, local cooperatives and their like can be used for both democratic and elite-dominated ends. By themselves they are not decentralizing' (Kothari 1989: 19). This chapter reviews the discussion between the protagonists and the antagonists of the devolution of more state powers to the village level. The debate, and its long history of implementation, extend over more than a century, from the initiatives of the colonial administration and later the Gandhian attempts at the construction of village life to the 73rd Constitutional Amendment enacted in 1994. An examination of the evolution and implementation of these initiatives until the present stage will help to clarify why the *panchayats* have not really worked and why, given the existing socio-economic structure, they are likely not to not work, notable exceptions notwithstanding. Since the formal leadership at the village level can be expected to mirror the prevailing power relationships, it is not likely to foster a development process that will benefit all sections of society, including the poor and the weak. In this context, the emergence of an environment in which these sections can participate actively is vital. There is therefore a need to ask whether and how the needs of 'participatory development' and 'development for the poor' mesh with the emerging socio-economic and political realities of the rural countryside.

This chapter intends to trace the reasons for the failure of decentralization in the past, and how it continues to fail in the present, except in those states, like West Bengal, where the power configuration in the villages has been altered in the wake of land reforms. Decentralization is not a panacea. The net effect will depend on the absence or presence of a supportive environment. The contrast between the situation prevailing in West Bengal and Uttar Pradesh is used to illustrate this understanding.

Early Approaches

The idea of the decentralization of administration had been introduced during the late nineteenth century by the colonial administration (Maddick 1970: 17; Matthai 1915; Zamora 1990: 20–4). The local councils were conceived as appendages of the central administration. Their legitimization was based on a reconstruction of the ancient villages by Charles Metcalfe:

> They seem to last where nothing else lasts [and] the village communities, each one forming a separate little state in itself, has, I conceive, contributed more than any other cause to the preservation of the people of India . . . and is in a high degree conducive to their happiness, and to the enjoyment of a great portion of freedom and independence. (quoted in Maddick 1970: 23)

As elected bodies, they were given the responsibility for road maintenance, tree planting, hospitals, schools, drainage, health, etc., but the bare reality was that the devolution of finances and responsibilities remained constricted within the centralized framework. Nevertheless, the idea of a modern type of village councils in place of the traditional village *panchayats* had been introduced. After Independence, the voices within the Indian National Congress (INC) calling for a re-alignment of India with its historical roots were responsible for the introduction of the idea of *panchayati raj* (PR). Ideologically, they were operating in the shadow of Mahatma Gandhi, the by then assassinated leader of the nationalist movement.[2] The ideological assumptions led the PR protagonists to strive for a partyless democracy aimed at self-sufficiency and self-government. They succeeded in inserting Article 40 in the Constitution of the new Republic of India. The article envisaged the *panchayati raj* institutions to function as units of self-government. PR came to be regarded, in rather bombastic words, as a 'process of democratic seed-drilling in the Indian soil, making an average citizen more conscious of his rights than before' (Bhargava 1979: 19).

These high expectations were not shared by all politicians in the Constituent Assembly. The messages, born from a Gandhian tradition, were confronted head—on by B.R. Ambedkar, the Westernized and

---

[2] These voices stood by the appropriateness of the ideas of Mahatma Gandhi for the future of India, and actually also confirmed the reading of the Orientalists. The eulogy of Indian tradition, and therefore the defence of the self-governing and self-sufficient little republics, found many ideological advocates in the tradition of Mahatma Gandhi. Movements like Sarvodaya and the movement for PR achieved both an intellectual respectability and a sentimental attachment.

urbanized leader of the then untouchables. As one of the main architects of the Constitution, he was initially unwilling to insert a clause on village *panchayats*. While introducing the Draft Constitution in 1948, he remarked sarcastically that villages may have survived, as the Orientalists had argued, but that within those so-called village republics suppression and archaism were the rule:

That they have survived through all the viscitudes may be a fact. But mere survival has no value.The question is on what plane they have survived. Surely on a low, on a selfish level. I hold that these village republics have been the ruination of India. I am therefore surprised that those who condemn provincialism and communalism should come forward as champions of the village. What is the village but a sink of localism, a den of ignorance, narrow-mindedness and communalism? (Constituent Assembly, Vol. VII: 39)

Ambedkar's statement roused the ire and anger of many members, but was also supported by many who argued that the influential classes in the villages would appropriate all the powers and finances and would misuse the process of decentralization. Since the village *zamindars* and *taluqdars* had unrestricted political, economic, and social power, they could not be expected to allow democracy of the many against the few to function. Since India had embarked on the path of modernization and state building, it was better, the argument continued, to have enlightened intervention by the centralizing state.The state has an enlightened vision and a developmental mission, and has to intervene at local levels against the prevailing power structures. If the intervention in local hegemonies of high caste landlords, with their bent for archaic cultures and suppressive economies, is permissible, decentralization has to remain guided from above.

It appears thus that, half a century ago, at the very start of the construction of the legal and administrative framework of the Republic of India, there was a clash between the two extreme views on state formation.The next section traces the practical experience with decentralization over the next half a century.

The Failure of Community Development

The *panchayat* structure was preceded by a honeymoon with the philosophy of the Community Development Programme funded by the USA. The programme entailed the training and despatch into rural India of a huge army of local administrators and extension workers. The expectations were high and western and Indian scholars hinted at an imminent revolution: 'This army is to awaken village India—by encouragement, by demonstration, by offers of material help to those who will stir to help themselves' (Morris-Jones 1971: 113–14). The Planning Commission, in the First Five Year Plan, described community development as the method 'to initiate a process of transformation of the social and economic life of the villages' (Planning Commission 1952: 223). A committee under the chairmanship of Balvantray Mehta was asked to develop ideas for a system of democratic decentralization that would form the core of rural development efforts. The committee in its report, in 1957 came, with up a number of recommendations, which in the following years were incorporated in the *panchayat* legislation of the various states, but also expressed concern about the democratic potentials of the village *panchayats* itself. Factionalism and suppression associated with power politics continued in the villages: 'we are genuinely concerned about this aspect of village public life and apprehend that unless a suitable and effective solution is found, it will spell ruin to all schemes for community development' (Balvantray Mehta 1957: 236).

In the extract we find some of the doubts which had been expressed by the minority in the Constitutive Assembly. The honeymoon with village republics, self-rule, etc., was soon to dissipate since it emerged that there was neither community nor much development in the Community Development Programme. The village *panchayats* more often than not were captured by autocratic and invariably corrupt leaders from among the male village elite.[3] According to Berreman (1979: 32 and 38) the inegalitarian social stratification, particularly the political, social, and economic ramifications of the caste system, made democratic play on a level field a near impossibility:

Since people in the village are aware of this, stress is inherent in the system; stress which under most circumstances is covert. Overt expression of it is held in check partly by the threat of physical, economic, social and religious sanctions, and partly by the fundamental necessity for continued social interaction which overt expression might impair or destroy. . . . The contemporary rural community in India is simply not structured for democratic, egalitarian self-administration.

[3] A team of American scholars has made a detailed report of what happened with this first foreign-supported attempt at decentralization. Another general finding was that the *panchayats* hardly ever met and gradually went into oblivion 'owing to a number of reasons, such as illiteracy, caste discrimination, factionalism, ineffective communication, poverty, etc.' (Zamora 1990: 122; see also Mertin 1962; Etienne 1968; Kantowsky 1970)

Personal relations in the villages were not face to face, but back to back. Small peasant and landless families were kept powerless under the dominance of the landed elite, led by the Brahmins and other high castes. These very same households had their family members in the civil service, and thus had direct access to those officials who were in charge of decentralization. It was a foregone conclusion that decentralization would not work. The failure prompted Barrington Moore (1973: 394) to conclude that the real source of change lies outside the village boundaries, and that structural changes in land ownership structure were a necessary precondition for village democracy:

Fundamentally, the notion of village democracy is a piece of romantic Gandhian nostalgia that has no relevance to modern conditions. The pre-modern Indian village was probably as much of a petty tyranny as a petty republic; certainly the modern one is such. To democratise the village without altering property relationships is simply absurd.

PR as a means of development and as an instrument of democracy was the God that failed, and especially in the late 1960s when the INC of Indira Gandhi started with a progressive agenda, including land reforms, the *panchayats* were clearly seen as the fiefdoms of the local reactionary classes. These powerholders were considered as inimical to economic development and to economic justice. The PR accordingly was left in hibernation. The central government created its own administrative hierarchy for rural development with a plethora of special programmes that all bypassed the PR institutions. India was on its way to having a strong rural administration but not a rural government. By the second half of the 1970s, the governments in New Delhi and in the state capitals had become indifferent to the PR mechanism and most councils had become defunct: elections were postponed and the sitting councils were dissolved or superseded. This state of affairs continued until the process of rejuvenation started with the reconstitution of the *panchayats* in West Bengal and with the appointment of the Asoka Mehta Committee by the first non-INC federal government in the late 1970s.

By the late 1970s, the Green Revolution in various areas in the country had created a rich and middle peasant segment. These peasants were interested in having the wherewithal needed for modern farming at their doorsteps. The decentralization of the government machinery, particularly of its delivery system, would help to assure a direct access by the new rural elite, the enterprising rich farmers. In line with their newly acquired economic power, and their interest in state funded programmes, came the motivation to occupy the relevant echelons in the political structure. The village councils were the easiest to conquer. Rich farmers whose tentacles directly and indirectly, through power networks, stretched to the district and state administrations could directly lay their hands on the village delivery system.

PR was again given the central place as a delivery system. Two decades after the Balvantray Mehta report, the Asoka Mehta Committee noted that the *panchayats* had failed for various reasons, but expected that the democratization process as a component of modernization would tend to destabilize traditional leadership in the long run. The committee stated that PR had engendered 'a process of democratic seed-drilling in the Indian soil', and that 'it helped rural people cultivate a developmental psyche' (Mehta 1978: 1.11). The first non-INC government gave way to Indira Gandhi, and then to Rajiv Gandhi. For more than a decade nothing happened. Then, after a long period of inactivity, the Constitutional Amendment Bill, based on the Asoka Mehta Committee recommendations, was suddenly introduced in 1993. By and large, the 73rd Amendment called for the formation of a three-level *panchayat* system, with the elected *gram sabha* (village assembly) as the lowest tier. The recommendations of the committee broke new ground in a number of ways.[4]

The adoption of the Constitutional Amendment, making *panchayats* mandatory, led to a wave of intellectual and political enthusiasm, comparable to the enthusiasm that the Community Development Programme had generated in the 1950s. The eulogies are rather inappropriate. Prior to the Constitutional Amendment Act, the *panchayat* institutions had been functioning with varying degrees of success in a number of states. The reasons for the varying degree of success and failure were to a large extent the same as those reported by scholars and committees in the 1950s and 1960s, and which formed the rather longish introduction to this chapter. The sceptical reading had identified the

---

[4] The report had argued that elections were expected to help to upturn the social soil: with greater awareness and organization among the poor, their numerical strength can get translated into political power. The new legislation accordingly made reservation for the ex-untouchable castes in proportion to their population mandatory and earmarked one-third of the seats and of the mayors for women. The panchayats were uniformly set to last for five years, after which the council would automatically stand dissolved unless new elections were conducted. Accountability and linkages with higher level political processes were expected to be facilitated by allowing political parties to participate in the PR elections.

socio-economic structure (polarized landownership, the hierarchical caste system, and the traditional *panchayats*) as an insurmountable impediment in the democratic process. Decentralization within such a system would amount to putting the horse behind the cart.

New Push and New Questions

The problems that have hijacked the good intentions in the past are still at work. Any call for a decentralization of government (the currently fashionable 'localization') may derive beneficial lessons from a study of those problems in the past. Localization in the end may turn out to be as romantic a notion as the PR in India, and may not help to transfer power to democratic institutions unless the socio-economic conditions are changed.

The debates of half a century ago, between the followers of the 'decentralizing' line of Mahatma Gandhi and the centralist school around Ambedkar, are still with us. The decentralizing approach has got a new push in recent years. The new push is thought to be associated with the concern for agency, civil society, empowerment, locality, and other such exalted concepts. There is, however, reason for a critical reflection, and for more research in this area. These concerns are elaborated below, before some of the findings from an earlier study on West Bengal and Uttar Pradesh are introduced.

One concern pertains to the ambiguity of civil society. There is a tendency in the Anglo-Saxon world to construct state and society as a dichotomy, the former representing the bad and the latter representing the good. The state is increasingly constructed, both in neo-liberal theory and in post-modernist discourse, as a Leviathan, a predator on indigenous culture and agency. On the other hand, the various associations constituting civil society are assumed to be close to the people, flexible in their operations, and attuned to the local environment.[5] Decentralization, to the extent that it empowers the people below and reduces the centripetal tendencies inherent in the post-colonial state, then tends to obliterate the dichotomy between state and society.

There is a predicament, however, village councils are still institutions of the state, and as such are quasi untouchable for the champions of civil society, particularly for the NGOs. Typical of the distance between *panchayats* and NGOs is the fact that no significant study on their

[5] For a critical reflection from an unexpected corner, see Hoeber Rudolph (2000).

relationship, and their complimentarity, has been undertaken. We hence do not know whether NGOs are really more efficient, less corrupt, and more developmental than the elected village councils and the state under which they resort. My inkling is that the performance of private institutions such as NGOs, which by definition are closed to public scrutiny, will depend on the local environment, just as the *panchayats* do. A large-scale research programme could offer some useful insights.

Village councils are located at the interface between the state and society. They are also located at the interface between traditional autocratic decision making (the *panch* male elders of the dominant castes) in connivance with the bureaucratic and economic elite on the one hand and the democratic procedures that ideally are guaranteed by the state institutions and the other hand. The dire conditions that Ambedkar had painted have not disappeared and access to public space remains highly unequal and undemocratic.

Village councils are also located at the interface between the local and the global, in a number of ways. The agenda of decentralization fits another agenda, namely the agenda of globalization and the rolling back of the state. Globalization actually sucks the local into a centralizing process of the free-market. Nation-states are somewhat receding and are ceding sovereign power to (international) market forces. The delegation of power to the locality may then serve the purpose of exonerating the central government for not spending enough resources on local development efforts and human capital building. It may saddle the local authorities with responsibilities for which they do not have the financial wherewithal. The reducing activities of the state, it is legitimate to assume, given the grim state of government finances, especially of the state governments, will curtail the activities of state governments and the lower organs.

What is the meaning of decentralization (and *PR*) in such a context? We of course are entering a grey area of assumptions, but in general a lower state support and a higher reliance on market forces is most likely going to help the already powerful and rich. The targeted interference by state and local governments in the past has somewhat enabled a countervailing power to the powerful. In the process of liberalization, the pro-poor policies and rural good governance may be the first victims.

Village councils, finally, are also at the interface between government policies and local implementation. Let me quote Akbar Zaidi (1999: 70) writing on Pakistan, a country that despite all rhetoric bears many analogies to India, states that the fault for malfunctioning local governments lies at a higher level: 'Local government also suffers the consequences of the ills of higher levels of government.... Hence reform of local government, or its institutional strengthening, becomes a non-starter, unless broader issues are addressed at higher levels of government.'

Decentralization that Works

A summary comparison of two major Indian states, West Bengal (WB) and Uttar Pradesh (UP), will help us to understand the differences between a decentralization that works and a decentralization that is still embedded in the structural constraints on which the *panchayats* foundered early in the 1950s. Both these states, WB in the east, with a population of 60 million bordering Bangladesh, and UP in the north with a population of 150 million, have been intensively studied.[6]

The findings presented below are based on studies that covered around fifty villages in both states and made profiles of around 1000 elected council members. We shall limit the enumeration of characteristic features to a minimum. Although the fieldwork predates 1997, there are no indications that the general picture has changed since then. While it can be assumed that the cases studied are an indication of the overall situation in each state, it is also true that the picture may show wider variations than observable in four big *panchayats* in West Bengal and thirty odd small *panchayats* in Uttar Pradesh.

All members of the *panchayats* (even the female members in Uttar Pradesh although that access was severely restricted by the male intermediaries) were extensively interviewed, and a complete census of a number of villages and in-depth interviews with hundreds of villagers were undertaken. The outcome of these interactions, certainly when summarized in a few statements, sounds like a caricature of extremes.

The first remarkable feature is the difference in knowledge of the local population in the two states about the mere existence of the *panchayats*. In West Bengal, the *panchayats* have become a household name.

[6] Studies were conducted in two districts in West Bengal (Barddhaman and Medinipur) and in three districts in Uttar Pradesh (Muzaffarnagar, Rae Bareli, and Jaunpur). I worked in close association with my colleagues Professor Ratan Khasnabis of the University of Calcutta and Professor Ravi Srivastava, then of the University of Allahabad and now at the Jawaharlal Nehru University in New Delhi. Two separate publications have come out (G.K. Lieten 1996a; G.K. Lieten and Ravi Srivastava 1999). See also an earlier publication: G.K. Lieten 1992a.

The villagers know where the *panchayats* office is located, who the mayor is and who the members are. In Uttar Pradesh, the councils are constituted on the basis of the village as a geographical unit, unlike in WB where they represent a cluster of villages. Members, therefore, represent a smaller number of villagers, not uncommonly only a cluster of houses. It is, however, difficult to enter a village and attempt to find out the identity of the member of the council. Usually, a *panchayat* office does not exist. The only person known by the villagers to be associated with the *panchayat* is the *pradhan*.[7]

A second difference exists in the personal attributes of the members. Members in UP, since they represent small wards, each with their own class/caste identity, automatically span the various classes, but power is restricted to the village elite. The *pradhan* in a number of cases was the scion of an established landed family. Invariably, he was associated with the dominant faction in the village. In some cases, the mayor was a rather poor villager who acted as the rubber stamp of the dominant landlord who, due to various reasons, could not stand for election to the post of mayor. The members were usually not active on the public stage, and as a rule were not engaged in any organization, movement, or institution. In fact it was the less capable villagers rather than the better equipped who had been asked by the prospective mayor to join his team. A poor widow with six young children would stand a better chance of being invited to join the *panchayat* than an upright and educated young women.

In West Bengal, a remarkable change took place since the mid-1970s. Until then, the *panchayats* had been functioning in the manner they still function in UP, and the majority of the members came from rich peasants, landlords, and the professional classes such as school teachers. Since then, the composition has changed radically, so much so that today the majority of the members belong to the poor strata, such as agricultural labourers and poor peasants. From among the poorer classes, active people have been recruited into public work. They function not only as members of the *panchayats* but in addition, they are active in various other organizations such as school committees, womens' organizations, peasant movements, cultural clubs, etc. Their involvement in various

---

[7] The unawareness is partially because of the absence of elections in quite a number of villages. Quite often, there is only one candidate for the seat. The concerned person in that case had been requested by the strong man of the village who aspired to become the mayor and who needed members to support him.

activities is the reflection of the emergence of what is now fashionably referred to as *civil society*.

The hold of the village elite has been tempered and the lower class people have been made to realize, and have come to realize that they can come forward and organize village affairs. A number of these lower class people, before joining the *panchayat*, had not been very active on the public stage, but their membership galvanized them into action in various fields and made them into public figures. This was particularly the case with women. In terms of gender, a transformation has taken place in West Bengal. The women who entered the *panchayats* had been requested by party leaders or by neighbouring friends and family members to stand for election. They had not always been organizationally active before, but in most cases they were females who had an enterprising and concerned spirit, and had been solving social problems in their neighbourhood. This latter function was now combined by these women with an active participation in the decision making process and in supervising the programmes that were executed by the *panchayats*. In a short time, they learned to understand the intricacies of the programmes that the village councils were dealing with, and they eagerly participated, as learners to start with, in the technical sub-committees of the council. They went around the village to enquire about the problems, to check on the implementation of the programmes, and also to gave a patient hearing to the women in the village who now could talk to somebody of their own gender in authority and whom they could approach for typical gender questions. During interviews, the female members often said that since women numbered half of mankind, they should also be active in large proportions in the *panchayats*.

Not many decades ago, WB was as restrictive and oppressive to its women as UP used to be, and as UP continues to be. In UP, during the course of the fieldwork occasionally one did meet village women who had the same enterprising and concerned spirit as their counterparts in WB, but they happened to not be members of the *panchayats*. The female members of the *panchayats* were usually, as mentioned before, infirm and socially marginalized. A large number of them could not even be met for an interview. They were kept under *pardha* (seclusion), and although it was possible to speak to some of them from behind a wall, it was obvious that they would not venture to go out and become active members of the *panchayats*. If any work had to be done, the husband, son, father, or brother would be in charge. In some cases, a female had been appointed as the mayor, but here too she was a mere proxy for a male relative. When the male member of a dominant family, being too young or being a government servant, was not in a position to function directly as the village chief, he could do so indirectly by proxy of his wife, his unmarried sister, or his mother.

A third difference relates to the functioning of the councils. The minimum requirement for democratic institutions from below to be qualified as such is their mere functioning. This, surprisingly, was hardly ever the case in UP. The official line is that they are functioning in accordance with the law and in the spirit of village harmony. Behind this facade, however, emptiness prevailed. No meetings were held, and all decisions were taken by a few dominant people. In WB on the other hand, the *panchayat* has developed into a smoothly functioning institution, with meetings taking place twice a month. Sub-committees also meet on a regular basis. The meetings are fairly transparent and well-managed affairs. Even the village assembly, which is meant to assemble all the villagers twice a year for a public scrutiny of the village council, has been fairly successful. Although only a minority of people turn up, this novel initiative has helped to increase transparency and efficiency.

A fourth difference lies in the range of activities undertaken. On the basis of the official mandate there should not be a difference, because the basket of tasks that have been decentralized is more or less similar in both states. The councils in both states have been provided with a small staff and finances and with an assigned share in the programmes of the federal government. Whereas West Bengal has gone quite far in devolving the state finances and the political responsibility to the elected *panchayat* level, in Uttar Pradesh the government administration has kept the control intact. It must be added that even in WB, a substantial share of rural development finances is being routed through the line departments of the ministries, and that an overall devolution of financial responsibilities still remains an incomplete and problematic task.

A fifth difference between both states relates to the effectiveness of the programmes. The Government of India has introduced a number of targeted programmes, and has put in place an administrative machinery and extension services that have been somewhat successful but that also have been plagued by distortions. A sizeable chunk of the finances has gone down the drain in terms of leakage to non-target groups and in terms of internal financial misappropriation. The close supervision of the civil servants by the village councils and the public knowledge of the distribution of benefits in West Bengal have created a situation of transparency and accountability. The poverty alleviation and development programmes have by and large reached the target groups, and, in general, have left no opportunity for the people in authority to appropriate part of the money as bribery charges. In Uttar Pradesh, leakage in the targeted poverty alleviation programmes was common, and in hardly any case did a transaction occur without a considerable bribe changing hands. Control from below was a non-issue in Uttar Pradesh since the programmes were run by the bureaucrats in conjunction with the big men in the villages.

Increasing popular involvement appears to be associated with higher efficiency. A comparison of government expenditure on minor irrigation, for example, showed that Uttar Pradesh had a much higher outlay per capita but that West Bengal had a more pronounced increase in agrarian productivity, indicating a higher efficiency. A sixth difference indeed, although not strictly related to the process of decentralization, relates to the overall variation in development. The degree and direction of development do depend on various factors that are outside the mandate of the *panchayats*, and as a matter of fact, do relate to extraneous factors that in no small measure have become outside the regulatory powers of government institutions. Nevertheless, *panchayats* potentially have various functions that impact on development and on the spread of entitlement over various groups. Village councils in West Bengal have played a crucial role in land redistribution and in the registration of sharecroppers, as a consequence of which millions of small families graduated to being independent peasants with an increasing income.[8]

Conclusion

In the development discussion, it has become fashionable to bandy around such concepts as good governance, civil society and decentralization. The power of these concepts hides in their seductive character and in their elusive meaning. Devolution of power indeed occupies the high ground of political ethics, but many crucial questions surrounding the concept still have to be researched. Decentralization relates to issues have already, since Independence has been addressed, and tackled in

---

[8] The process of decentralization and the initiation of structural reforms went hand in hand. It is interesting to know that in terms of rural head count poverty ratio, West Bengal by 1997, according to one classification, had moved into the second best position (after Punjab), up from the eleventh rank among major states that it occupied in 1974, while during the same period, Uttar Pradesh dropped from the second rank to the ninth rank. A more detailed treatment is available in the chapter 'West Bengal after a Quarter Century LFG', later on in the book.

policy initiatives. It seems that many of the pitfalls of the past are still with us, and that further policy reforms should draw on an analysis of these past pitfalls. This chapter has tried to create such a perspective through an analysis of two Indian states.

As stated before, the short summary reads as a caricature of differences. In a more detailed picture, in studies at the micro-level, deviations from the mean would emerge. The intense political battle in Uttar Pradesh in the 1990s for example in a number of villages has shifted the balance of power from the upper caste and *ashraf* elite to the (upcoming elite of) the *bahajut* (majority) castes. The overall conclusion would nevertheless be that whereas West Bengal has done extremely well in working decentralized governance, UP has failed in doing so. The process of decentralization and the initiation of structural reforms went hand in hand in West Bengal, explaining the success in the state. The absence of this joint operation explains why decentralization in Uttar Pradesh, despite much social, political, and economic dynamism, is still imbued with weaknesses similar to the ones already encountered half a century ago.

CHAPTER 2

Caste, Gender and Class in *Panchayats*: The Case of Barddhaman, West Bengal

An emancipatory movement, which the Communist Party of India (Marxist) in West Bengal claims to represent, should be expected not only to provide a sufficient and equitable access to economic resources, but also to strive at emancipation from oppressive social and political forces. A more equitable share of basic economic assets and access to credit, inputs, and markets may allow for economic development, but, as Anisur Rahman has noted, poverty alleviation programmes tend to transfer the dependence of poor households from one source to another. Such programmes often remain 'a narrow management notion subject to manipulation by those who would enjoy the monopoly of social knowledge' (Rahman 1984: 11). A truly emancipatory movement, therefore, would require a continuous process of political and social change. Such a process has been variously labelled as empowerment, conscientization, and self-reliance. The various concepts are overlapping and interdependent. The overlap can be referred to as enfranchisement. In this contribution we shall highlight one aspect of this enfranchisement, namely at the level of the functioning of the *panchayats* as the basic unit of village democracy. Empirical material from one block in the district of Barddhaman (the new name for Burdwan) is used as the main reference, and additional material from a block in Birbhum district as the secondary reference. The material on Barddhaman is particularly useful since it allows for a dialogue, and a dispute, with the analysis in Webster (1990).

Local Power

West Bengal has a long history of local self-government institutions. By the Local Self-Government Act of 1885 and the Village Self-Government Act of 1919, District Boards and Union Committees were constituted on the basis of limited electoral franchise; the:· were dominated by the landowning *zamindari* class. The Pancha ..i Act of 1957 did not help to undermine this stranglehold. The impact of the new Act, although envisaging elections based on universal franchise, was diluted by the existence of well-established local leaders of the old order who controlled all resources (M. Bhattacharya 1977). They, after the last round of elections in 1964, remained in power until the arrival of the Left Front Government (LFG). A democratic system of self-government, Buddhadeb Ghose (1971) argued, was incompatible with the dependence of the rural masses on the trinity of landowners, traders, and money lenders: 'Panchayati Raj has been introduced in such a background. Without breaking antiquated economic institutions, we have sought to introduce a new social and economic order which seeks to liberate all individuals and create a society of equals.'

The revitalization and democratization of the *panchayat* system was one of the first initiatives taken by the LFG after it was voted into office in 1977. It made use of the *panchayat* legislation as it had been enacted in the previous thirty years,[1] but gave it a new meaning by organizing the contest, and the accountability, on the basis of party politics. At the same time, the LFG accompanied the constitution of the new *panchayats* with a massive campaign of land redistribution and tenancy reforms which mutated the agrarian power structure in a way that weakened the dominance of the landed elite and strengthened the position of the poor villagers. The necessity of land reforms had been a consistent strand in Indian agricultural studies (see Joshi 1975) and in the policy approach (Frankel 1978; N. Bandyopadhyaya 1988). The dominant themes underlying the pleas for land reforms have been considerations of social justice and efficiency, but also the strategic necessity of breaking the socio-political and economic semi-feudal power bloc of landlords-cum-moneylenders. The position of the CPI(M) in respect of the second aim reads as follows:

So long as local power is concentrated in the hands of the rural rich, so long will they enjoy the political clout and see to it that no developmental plan benefiting the rural poor is either conceived or accepted or implemented. . . . Unless this process is reversed, panchayats do not have a chance to survive and flourish. (Harkishen Singh Surjeet in *People's Democracy*, 11.06.1999: 7)

[1] On the *panchayat* system and its historical genesis, see Mukhopadhyaya (1977), and Mukherjee (1974).

The West Bengal *panchayat* elections of 4 June 1978 were deliberately mounted to break this stranglehold. It was, as Bhabani Sen Gupta observed, one of the most massive electoral operations ever mounted and 'unique' in all aspects: 'For the first time in this republic's history, there was a keen *political* contest for the roots of power. It was an *open, democratic and peaceful* contest. . . . Never in the history of Indian politics did a political party penetrate so deeply and methodically the ancient vastness of the village' (Sen Gupta 1979: 118 and 131).

Soon after the 1978 elections, the state government in Calcutta decided to extend the functions and resource base of the local elected bodies. Since then, the three levels of local administration—*gram panchayat* at the village level, the *panchayat samiti* at the block level, and the *zila parishad* at the district level—have played an increasingly important role in rural development. Their activities impinge more and more on the planning of developmental and infrastructural works, especially after the state government in 1988 decided to make the *panchayats* directly responsible for various development works which were hitherto looked after by the respective departments in Writers' Building in Calcutta. The elected leaders at the village, block, and district level have therefore now a say in earmarking not only the district plan funds, but also, at least theoretically,[2] the funds which were earlier handled by the red-tape infected departments in distant Calcutta. In addition, as elsewhere in India, they had to handle the resources provided by the different national special programmes such as the Integrated Rural Development Programme (IRDP) and the Rural Labour Employment Guarantee Programme (RLEGP). They have been assigned the responsibility for selecting the beneficiaries of the production loans schemes under the central IRDP, and for implementing the scheme in collaboration with the commercial banks.

Advances in Agriculture

The ultimate assessment of the system of decentralization of power has to be addressed against the backdrop of the overall economic development, particularly the development of agriculture. The decreasing farm size, as a consequence of the allocation of small portions of land to the

[2] In practice, it turns out to be difficult to effectively decentralize such departments as for example education, health, power and agriculture and remove the funds and the power from the direct control of ministers and bureaucrats at the higher echelons.

rural underclass, Sanjib Baruah has argued, necessarily means that the land reform process has been exhausted. Land reforms in West Bengal, instead of being a programme capable of bringing about a regime of viable peasant proprietorship, has amounted to 'the de facto abandonment of the concern with viability' (Baruah 1990: 143). The empirical evidence for such statements is, however, lacking. Detailed analysis shows that not only has the pie been enlarged, but that it has been more equitably distributed as well (Lieten 1992a). West Bengal has, over the last decade, witnessed a sustained growth in agrarian production and productivity. The increase, as illustrated elsewhere, is fairly impressive.

The policy of betting on 'a little for everyone', as Baruah has subtitled one of his paragraphs, if accompanied by supportive measures, can positively deliver the goods of agrarian development: after barely fifteen years of post-land reform agriculture, by the early 1990s, rice production had virtually doubled! The dramatic increase in production was hardly due to a change in physical factors (land endowment, irrigation), and therefore may be attributed to the changing political environment. Both the increase in the supply of credit, minikits, and fertilizers and the various measures to make sure that they reached the poor households as well, in combination with redistribution of land and security of tenancy, can be isolated as the factors behind the increase in productivity. Webster, who studied three villages in 1977–8, before the *panchayat* elections, and one village again ten years later, noted the difference:

In all the villages [in 1977] the allocation of loans and inputs from Block level agencies favoured the economically and politically strong and their clients. . . . These patron-clients relations clearly served to reproduce the structure of agrarian relations and the underlying structures of exploitation. . . . The structural changes [in 1987–8] openly benefited the weak at the expense of the strong. The change might be marginal in economic terms but that did not detract from its political significance in challenging the status quo. It was openly seen as helping those at the base of the village at the expense of those above and this was important. (Webster 1990: 211)

Class and Management

In India, the policy of waging on the strong has by and large been the practice of rural development programmes. In its policy of waging on poor and middle peasants, the LFG seems to have achieved two objectives at one go: a fair degree of development and a more equitable distribution of the fruits of development. The debate is thus whether it has also brought enfranchisement to the rural poor. From Webster's statement it would appear that it has, but in his article, he repeatedly questions its full realization. He argues that the further consolidation of political power has been achieved by a shift away from structural reform towards mere development. In this shift, the LFG has brought development programmes and improvements to the villages, but at the same time, it has avoided the danger of alienating the middle peasantry, and of further alienating a section of the rich peasants. This has led to what he calls a managerial approach: 'It is a change that has defused tensions in agrarian relations and directed activism into institutional works' (Webster 1990: 41). The goals have shifted away 'from radical activism towards consensual politics', and have increasingly become non-antagonistic. The significance of the *panchayats* should therefore be assessed as an institution which shifts politics from class to management:

The current decentralization of development planning under Panchayati Raj is a crucial step in this process. On the one hand it seeks to create institutions based upon popular participation in which those who were previously excluded or marginalized can now assert their interests, but on the other hand the panchayats' principal function is the management of development programmes funded from above, whose overall nature is determined at the state or all-India level, and in which the panchayats' role as initiators is limited to the proposal of specific works to which they attach priority within the framework of these programmes. (Webster 1990: 41–2)

The shift from 'class struggle' to 'institutional management' not only means that the redistribution of the surplus and of the means of production (further land reform measures) is removed from the political agenda. It also entails the danger of the benefits being cornered by a select group, the politically organized minority, which, Webster adds, in objective class terms continues to be different from the landless and marginal population, and which has a tendency to retain their seats in the *panchayats*. The holding on to power and the incarnation of bureaucratic procedures then reinforces their separation from those below whom they seek to serve. Kirsten Westergaard (1987: 109–10) had earlier come to the conclusion that by and large the representation of the poor villagers 'has not resulted in any significant increase in their control over these institutions'. She stated that in terms of the popular participation framework, the poor are represented in the institutions of power, but that devolution of power was lacking: 'Compared to the pre-Left Front, the changes set in motion as regards rural power structure are considerable. Certainly, the first steps necessary for a process of increased popular participation have been taken. However, there are very few indications that the Left Front parties give priority to furthering this process.'

The reading of the functioning of the *panchayat* system in West Bengal by Webster and Westergaard can be summarized as follows. On the positive side, it is recognized that the system has delivered the goods, and has contributed to the welfare and involvement of the economically and socially most disadvantaged groups. On the negative side, it is argued that the system is tending towards emphasis on management, obliterating its mobilization function, and that the system is being cornered by the political key men from rich and middle peasant stock. The latter point is also made by Baruah (1990) and particularly by Olle Tornquist who goes one step further. Everywhere in WB, he perceives a top-down approach by organizations that include not only the weak and poor peasants ('who are not entrusted and empowered') but also middle peasants and petty landlords who have sustained their position of power and influence. He assumes that the poor villagers have even been excluded from the *panchayats* for not being sufficiently knowledgeable and enlightened: 'Emphasis is more on representation and enlightened leadership than on the participation or even consultation of those who are affected by various measures. Therefore it is a serious problem that very few of these who are elected are landless peasants and sharecroppers' (Tornquist 1991: 68).

We intend to take on these negative assessments. The reference material has been obtained from an ongoing study on the functioning of the *panchayats* in Memari II block in Barddhaman district, and shall occasionally be supplemented with material from an earlier research stint in Muhammad Bazar block in Birbhum district (Lieten 1992a).

Barddhaman

Barddhaman district, in terms of economic and social development, is a fairly developed district. Lying in the centre of West Bengal, it extends in the form of a smoking pipe from the extensive industrial and mining belt along the Durgapur-Asansol axis in the West to the rice-bowl of the state in its central and eastern parts. Burdwan, as it used to be called, became the cradle of the Green Revolution after it was chosen in 1962 as the pilot area for the new *Intensive Agricultural District Programme* (See Frankel 1971: 157–90). Despite the combined blessings of nature and of preferential access to technological inputs, productivity increased only marginally between the mid-1960s and the mid-1970s. It was only after the ascent of the LFG in 1977 that yield figures started to climb sharply (see Lieten 1996a).

The *mofussil* (provincial) town of Memari lies 50 km to the east of Barddhaman on the main railway line connecting the major cities in northern and western India with Calcutta. Administratively, Memari has been bifurcated into two Development Blocks. Satgachia, the market centre of Memari II, lies 20 km north of Memari, on the road-crossing of the Barddhaman-Kalna road and the Memari-Manteswar road. Memari II is one of the 33 blocks in the district. The block is divided into 12 *onchals* (*panchayat* sections) and counts approximately 1,25,000 inhabitants. It is overwhelmingly rural and agricultural. In the past, as observed by Danda and Danda (1971) in a village 50 km to the west of Memari, there were basically two groups: the *manib* (master) and the *munish* (dependent worker). The agrarian families were equally divided among the categories of peasant ownership, landless labour, and *bargadar* (sharecropper). The dependence of the latter two categories on the bigger landowners until the mid-1960s was unmitigated. Their position was so vulnerable that efforts to organize them had largely failed (Frankel 1971: 177).

The predominant position of the CPI(M) in Barddhaman has nevertheless been of a long standing. Unlike most other districts where the break towards leftist politics came after the late 1960s, Barddhaman, already in the 1950s, registered a majority vote for the left parties. In Memari, the electoral support base of the Communist Party of India (CPI) has been extensive since the days of the *tebhaga* (three shares) movement. The high tide in CPI support continued after the 1964 party split, when the CPI(M) took over the mantle of the CPI. Its electoral fortunes were abruptly reversed in 1972. Rigging of elections in that year was fairly widespread, and even Field and Franda (1974: 19), who otherwise take the results of the elections in the state at their face value, make an exception for Barddhaman. In Memari, CPI(M) votes dwindled from almost 40,000 in 1969 to 11,000 in 1972. An observer commented in the *Economic and Political Weekly* (25 March 1972) that the results looked 'more like the product of *indrojal* (jugglery) than *indirajal* (Indira charm or wave)'. With the next elections, in 1977 after the overthrow of Indira Gandhi's authoritarian

Emergency rule, the trend of a gradual shift towards the CPI(M) got reasserted. The INC retained hardly one-third of the votes; the rest of the electorate opted for the CPI(M) candidates.

Composition of the Panchayats

The electoral system in India implies that for each seat only the candidate with the highest number of votes gets elected. The Congress party in Memari, after its drubbing in the 1977 polls, realized that it had become pointless to participate in the *panchayat* elections. Many seats during the election round for local bodies in the subsequent elections hence fell unopposed into the hands of CPI(M) candidates.[3] Most observers agree that the elections were as fair as elections in a politically sensitive state can be. Skirmishes in the villages in West Bengal occasionally do occur, but it is a far cry from the widespread violence in the early 1970s. The semi-fascist tremors which Congress *goondas* or hoodlums in those days let loose over the countryside are vividly recalled by practically all the *panchayat* members in Memari. A large number of them were actually driven into the fold of the CPI(M) by the acts of these *goondas* who unnerved and mauled them to the point of no return during the years after the rigged 1972 elections. Many have a tale to tell about themselves. Some of them were attacked in broad daylight in the bazaar (market) area and were left behind struggling for life. Others had to leave their village and go in hiding elsewhere inside and outside the district; they lost cattle and houses, and court cases were lodged against them. Some had seen how a mother or a sister got raped, how an uncle or a brother was killed. Others were not directly affected but had witnessed the atrocities in the village. They then decided that they were finished with Congress. One of them was AH, a school teacher and a middle peasant, who in class terms had nothing to gain from the Communist Party:

Murder, arson and loot, that is what our village had been reduced to. A couple of years earlier, there had been an attempt at land reforms, and there had been some tension, but it remained within the bounds of decency and respect for the law. Then this all changed. The Congress people, led by the Youth Wing and the Chhatra Parishad, in connivance with the police and the CRP [Central Reserve

---

[3] This was more often than not the case in strong support districts like Barddhaman, Bankura, and Hooghly where the CPI(M) romped home with four-fifths of the *panchayat* seats. In other districts also, the party achieved a majority in most of the *panchayats*.

Police], started organizing resistance squads. They claimed to be sent to maintain peace, but they just went berserk. Our village was in the grip of *goonda raj*.

Most of the members have joined the movement for other reasons though. They joined because, as they say, they were impressed by the party ideology of land reforms, justice, and equity, and were directly influenced by the core leaders of the party. KM, an agricultural labourer of Santal origin, was a teenager at the time of the mayhem, but he remembers other things:

> We poor people were not the concern of the previous regime. Everything was dominated by the rich people. It was all high caste domination then. Wages were a pittance, and sometimes the pittance was not given. If you had a cow, it would get stolen, and if you complained they would slap a court case on you. The party leaders promised us more work and higher wages, and land. Land I have not got, but forget about this; today we are not rich babus either, but the babus like Amitava and Basudev came to our houses, they shared water and food with us and they have given us the feeling that we also, we are human beings.

The family of MD did not suffer from caste oppression, and had sufficient land to live a reasonable life. When she was reading in class VI, i.e. in 1968, the young girl while returning home, was impressed by a land grab procession against a landlord who had seized the land of a poor peasant. The imprint on her girlish mind was so solid that by the time she had passed class VIII, she had converted her family to Leftist politics, and soon also convinced her family into accepting something which was, and still is, very unusual: she fell in love with a party activist and got married in a civil court, without dowry.

MD joined the party when the going was tough. So did MH, who joined the movement in 1962, long before the awards of power became attractive. The son of a religious but poor Muslim family, soon after leaving school he started reading the party leaflets, and before long was himself secretly distributing leaflets and painting the walls with party slogans: 'It came from inside. I belonged to a class which was deprived and being a member of that class, I felt we should join for more justice, and more equity. We knew it could be done, and we had to sacrifice many things.'

MD and MH are no exceptions, but there are also quite a few members who, on the other hand, had a smooth sailing since they did not face any of the hardships which the pre-1977 diehards went through. Some come from poor families, others from better-off families, and since they, especially the latter, stand to benefit from good links with the party, opportunism may be involved. We shall return to this point later when we discuss the extent of rich peasant control over the party and the *panchayats*. One aspect which bears on the later discussion, and also on the point to be taken up next, is the fact that probably close to one-fourth of the *panchayat* members are not enrolled as party members, and are likely to have been nominated for reasons other than reliability and/or pliability. Through these non-party *panchayat* members, the party succeeded in widening its base and in activating civil society.

In Barddhaman, and in Memari, the party base is at its strongest, both in popular support and in organizational maturity. In its selection of members, one would therefore not expect difficulties in finding suitable and enduring candidates. But as many as 57 per cent of the membership of the *panchayats* had been elected for the first time in 1988, and only 22 per cent had been elected in three consecutive elections from 1978 onwards. This fact sufficiently contradicts the claims raised earlier that members tend to hang on to positions of power. The rapid turnover reveals one of the pitfalls associated with government office, the more so when the cadres are freshly recruited. Around a fifth of the ex-*panchayat* members had not been renominated for reasons of bad functioning and corruption charges. Some members were simultaneously dropped from the *panchayat* and suspended from party membership.

The danger, even the reality of corruption, is something that many observers have paid attention to. It is, on all accounts, much less widespread than it used to be, but it lingers on. Together with its less tangible cousin, nepotism, it germinates dissatisfaction with the performance of the *panchayat*. Enterprising young men, not old enough to be identified with the previous regime, can get close to the source of local power and finances. It goes, however, to the credit of the party that it does act against erring members either in the form of official corruption charges or in the form of replacement of the sitting members.

Socio-Economic Background

The many schemes that the three-tier elected bodies are supposed to execute could go awry for many reasons. One reason which has often been noted is that the bodies are dominated by landlords and village elders who want to maintain the exploitative ideological and economic order. In West Bengal, this problem is supposed to have been overcome, but doubts linger on as to whether the rich peasants as a class have really abandoned the field.

In the quotes reproduced in an earlier section, the apprehension has been expressed that the poor peasants and agricultural labourers have not been able to wrest the institutions from the control of the landed and high-caste families. Many rich peasants and landlords are suspected of having trimmed their sails to the wind. It would be reasonable to expect such a development particularly in a district like Barddhaman, with its strong rich peasants' base.

Although the replacement of male Brahmin landlords by female Scheduled Caste (SC) agricultural labourers does not automatically change the class nature of the institutions, a change in the composition of the councils is bound to make a difference, even if only in terms of the weakening of caste hierarchy. This, we assume, will be more so if the new members belong to a party which, ideologically and organizationally, pushes enfranchisement to the forefront. In the next sections we shall first look at the composition of the *panchayats* in terms of caste, gender, and class, and then briefly deal with the tricky question of power. One of the positive effects of an emancipatory policy would be the increasing visibility of those groups who hitherto had not been expected to enter the public arena on equal terms. The public arena in the past has been dominated by the male *bhadrolok* (also spelled as *bhodrolok*: the Bengali gentry). In comparison, in terms of the entry of women, and SC/ST (Scheduled Tribes), the record of the LFG is rather dissatisfactory in respect of the former and highly successful in respect of the latter.

Gender

West Bengal does have a low participation rate of women in public life. Only 6.2 per cent of the women are supposed to be active in the out-house workforce, a percentage which is significantly below the 16 per cent all India average.[4] The low participation rate is reflected in the paltry representation in the *panchayats*: of the 141 members of the *gram panchayat*, in 1988–93, only 7 were female.

The lack of suitable candidates and the unwillingness of women, or their families, may not fully account for this dismal performance seen

[4] Government of West Bengal, *Economic Review 1987–88. Statistical Appendix*: 6.

until legislation intervened. The lack of education and political consciousness is cited by many, also by women members themselves, as a reason for not nominating women. Others argue that women are so much overburdened by the chores at home, that no time remains for public activities. SH, a young Santal agricultural labourer, is appreciative of the work done by the women members, but has serious doubts about his own wife coming to the forefront:

The problem is more acute in the high-caste families, where you find educated women, but they are all tied down to the households and will only rarely be sent to work outside. In our *adivasi* families, the men do contribute to the work in the housework, but certain crucial things like cooking and cleaning is still reserved for the women. I can't see myself doing it. In our panchayat, we have two female members, one Santal and one Bagdi, and it is only because their husbands are helping them, that they have been able to participate in politics.

A 'male-dominated society', that is how most of the members explain the invisibility of women, and quite a few are rather complaisant about it. They have never thought of sharing some of the household work or motivating their spouse to take part in public activities. This attitude, in its extreme form, is expressed by CS. A Santal like SH, but not a party man, he would not like to change the division of labour: 'The males are doing hard labour, and when I return home, I feel too tired to help her. Moreover, her contribution in the *panchayat* would be much less than that of a man.'

An even stricter conviction is expressed by the pious AA, who apart from being a *Madrasa* teacher is the owner of two tractors, and seems a strange choice as the candidate on a CPI(M)-controlled list: 'They have asked me to have a seat in the council, but I hardly attend the meetings and cannot tell you how the women in the panchayat perform. I am a pious Muslim, and I must accept *pordah* for our women folk. It would be against our religion if they would go and attend meetings.'

Such talk, however, is anathema to most of the party members, particularly the more seasoned ones. MH, also a Muslim, in his third term as a *panchayat* member, comments:

This has nothing to do with religion. It is all done by people, from all religions. Women have been treated as slaves by Muslims, by Brahmins, by Santal, by Chamars, by Sadgopes, and until recently they did not have a voice and were backward, and obviously when they enter into an organization they usually are not yet as good as the male members. But once the social bar of treating them only as a housewife is overcome, then they can turn out to work better than males. This work is going on. Don't forget that until recently we didn't have any of them.

The party secretary of the block does not discount the religious factor, but singles out the continuing paternalistic mentality as the basic cause. He is aware of the need to involve more women. In his own *panchayat* three women have been selected, and in the next elections, he hopes to bring in a few more women. Such a step should not be difficult. Many women have come forward as skilful organizers in the mass literacy programme, and the sitting female members in any case have shown that women can stand their ground. If given a chance to prove themselves, they do stand up. In one case, the female member, SB, initially gave the impression of being unassertive and shy. She, however, turned assertive after I had suggested that a timid person like herself could not really look after the interests of the village and the demands of the women: 'Of course', she said, 'in the panchayats and elsewhere I do stand up. If I do not speak up, who will?' SB indeed, I later learned, was one of the more zealous and committed council members.

The women generally regret that the party has not been able to break the strictures of the male dominated society. There have been some campaigns, like the movement against drinking, with some success, and the family planning drive, with more success. Agricultural wage rates for men and women have been equalized. The movement against dowry, however, did not have much of an impact. The female members themselves agree that particularly women, for various reasons are opposed to its eradication but that the *panchayat* should be more concerned and should organize a concerted drive. One of these female members is MD. Married to a party wholetimer, she has to look after the 1.5 acres of land, attend the meetings of the *panchayats*, take literacy classes, cure the small illnesses and injuries in the village, settle family quarrels, and organize the women in the Mohila Somiti:

I don't deny that the work is strenuous. The women generally are still backward [*pitche*], and there are so many family constraints. There are the children and the cattle to look after, and the danger of scandal mongering when women move around, but my experience is that women are very much interested. They have been working very hard from behind, and when given a task, they feel very concerned. In the literacy campaign, they took on the major brunt of the work, and the attendance of women also was much better compared to the men. Much has changed in the minds of the more conscious people. I don't think that there is really much opposition from the male members, but rather from the *protha* [custom], and that is something which will take time. But really, much more concentrated attention is necessary: *kikikaj kora utchit* [so much remains to be done].

Caste

The problem with gender resembles the problem with caste. Earlier, since the formation of the *panchayat* system in the late 1950s, the lower castes and tribals had a symbolic representation only. The contention then was between the *zamindars* and the rich Sadgope peasants. The Bagdis, Bauris, Domes, and Santals were cajoled into supporting one of the factions, but, as one of them told A. Danda and D. Danda (1971: 52), the portent of *panchayati raj* was obvious: 'At least we can put our grievances before the public. Until the introduction of the panchayati raj system no one cared to know whether we had anything to say.'

From 1978 onwards, they could say it in the *panchayat* body itself on more than a token basis. They, however, were still very much under-represented. Of the ten elected Congress members, nine were still of *bhadrolok* origin, and also the CPI(M) still had more than three times as many high-caste as low-caste and tribal members.[5] In the consecutive elections the ratio changed dramatically. Of the members who were elected on the CPI(M) ticket in 1988, 12 were Brahmin, 22 Kayastha, and 41 SC/ST. The presence of the latter members in the new bodies is more or less a reflection of their share in the total population.

The progress in comparison with the earlier bodies is remarkable, as Figure 2.1 clearly illustrates. It is, as summarized by some of the elder members, an *zameen-aasmaan* (earth and heaven) difference. Since Congress had only a few members elected in the three elections in the *panchayats* in Memari II, it is difficult to assess the differences between both parties. On the basis of data from another study, in Birbhum district, we, however, can make such an assessment. The increasing share of SC/ST members in the consecutive elections in Birbhum to a great

---

[5] The Hindu castes have been divided into two groups: on the one hand the Brahmins and the original Satsudras, and on the other hand the other jolchol (water worthy) castes, known as the *navashaka* castes (the nine trading and artisan castes), represented mainly by Mondal, Pal, Ghosh and Karmakar. The 'unclean' castes are mainly Saha, and the 'untouchable' castes mainly Bagdi and Chamar. The Scheduled Tribes are almost exclusively Santal. See N.K. Dutt 1965: 114.

CASTE, GENDER AND CLASS IN *PANCHAYATS* 47

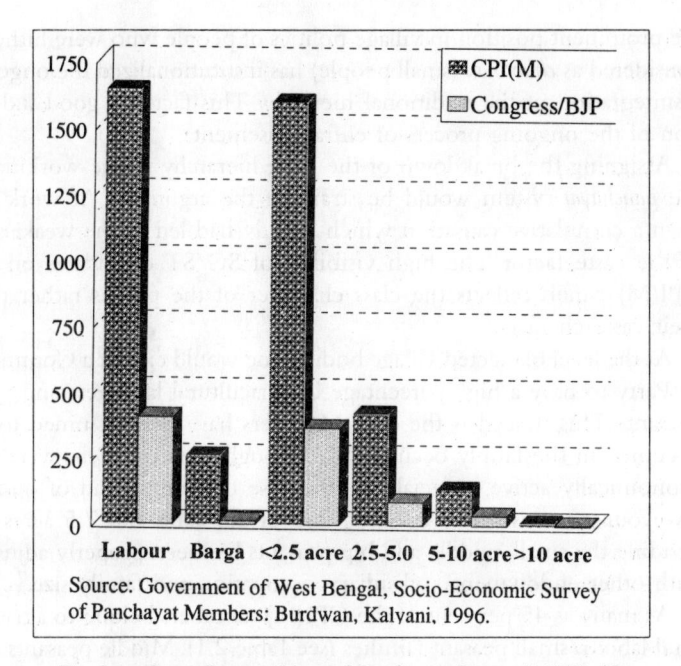

[Bar chart showing CPI(M) vs Congress/BJP panchayat members by category: Labour, Barga, <2.5 acre, 2.5-5.0, 5-10 acre, >10 acre. Y-axis ranges 0 to 1750.

Source: Government of West Bengal, Socio-Economic Survey of Panchayat Members: Burdwan, Kalyani, 1996.]

Fig. 2.1: Caste Composition of *Panchayats*, Memari, 1978–93

extent was due to the higher number of such CPI(M) candidates as opposed to INC candidates being elected. It also turned out that the INC in the later election rounds was engaged in an interesting catching-up process by introducing more non-*bhadrolok* candidates. It, however, still appears to be a party dominated by the upper and middle castes.[6] In contrast, the CPI(M) appears to be non-discriminatory in terms of caste.

Class and Power

In a revolutionary shift, caste has been significantly bereft of its stigmatic and discriminatory meaning. Although it may not be the only factor,

[6] From the 1978 election in Muhammad Bazar in Birbhum, the INC emerged with only 2 successful SC/ST candidates but with 9 Brahmin/Kayastha and 13 other hindu *navashaka* caste candidates, mainly Sadgope (Mondals), the dominant peasant caste. During the next election, there was a remarkable increase in the nomination of SC/ST candidates, increasing further to 31 out of 107 in 1988. The CPI(M) fielded approximately half of its candidates from the SC/ST group (Lieten 1992a).

the prominent position in village politics of people who were hitherto considered as *chhotolok* (small people) has institutionalized the ongoing disintegration of the traditional hierarchy. This fact is a good indication of the ongoing process of enfranchisement.

Assigning the breakdown of the caste hierarchy to the working of the *panchayat* system would be straining the argument. At work has been a cumulative causation which already had led to the weakening of the caste factor. The high visibility of SC/ST candidates on the CPI(M) panels reflects the class character of the parties rather than their caste character.

At the level of elected village bodies, one would expect a Communist Party to have a high percentage of agricultural labourers and poor peasants. This indeed is the case. Members have been assumed to be occupied in the family occupation, although some of them were not economically active, especially in the case of women and of quite a few young activists. The dividing line of 2.5 acres and 7.5 acres for dividing the small, middle and big peasants has been properly adjusted with other endowments, subsidiary occupation and family size.[7]

As many as 45 per cent of the CPI(M) members belong to agricultural labour/small peasant families (see Table 2.1). Middle peasants and people running a small business represent a further 25 per cent. Together with salaried employees (e.g. in a cooperative society) from among similarly placed families, the percentage adds up to approximately 75 per cent. The results from the Memari survey are comparable with the results obtained earlier in Birbhum. In the latter case, a comparison could be made with many Congress and Forward Bloc candidates contending for a seat. Most of the big traders and rich peasants who ventured into the election process in that area still preferred Congress. They accounted for 44 per cent of the INC candidates, including the biggest landowners of the area. The representation of agricultural labourers, *bargadars*, and small peasants among INC candidates was considerably lower, but even then with a share of 32 per cent, in contrast with the CPI(M)'s 57 per cent, not too bad either. A significant number of landless and near-landless villagers thus appear to have been given tickets by Congress as well, possibly in a catching-up process as has been noticed in the case of caste (see Figure 2.2).

[7] A member of a nuclear family with 2 acres of land, a pump set, and half a dozen cows has been appropriately classified as middle peasant. On the other hand, a member of a large joint family with 3 acres without irrigation facilities has been classified as poor peasant. Such a qualification has also been made for agricultural labourers with some marginal land as owners or tenants.

Table 2.1: Occupational Distribution of *Panchayat* Members in Memari

Occupation	CPI(M)	Others
Agricultural Labour	30	1
Sharecropper, Small Peasant and Artisan	30	
Middle Peasant (2.5–7.5 acres) and Small Business	33	1
Big Peasant and Big Business	13	3
Teachers and Professionals	20	1
Service	9	
Total	135	6

Source: *Panchayat* member survey, Memari II in 1992.

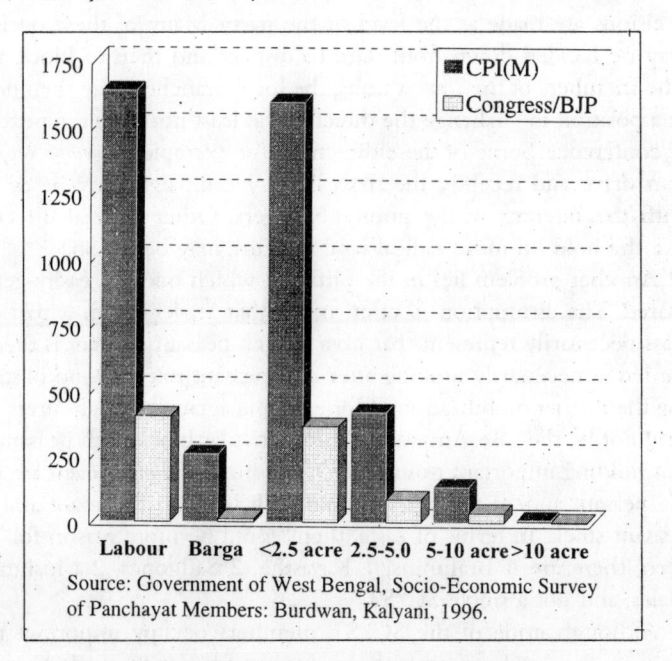

Fig. 2.2: Landownership of *Gram Panchayat* Members in Barddhaman District, 1993–8

Representation and Control

More and more representatives from among the poorer sections have made it into the *panchayats*. Even then Westergaard may be correct in her assessment, quoted earlier, that 'by and large this representation has not resulted in any significant increase in their control over these institutions'. The provision of full enfranchisement to the poor villagers has been one of the major verbal commitments of the CPI(M) leadership, if not the main one. In a speech in 1969, the Minister of Revenue and Land Reform, Harekrishna Konar told the West Bengal Legislative Assembly: 'We cannot give anything to millions of the toiling people of the villages, nor can we give them money for food, loan, etc., but one thing we can give them and that is their sense of humanity and consciousness for struggle' (Konar 1977: 113).

In exploring this relationship of power, we realize that we are skating on thin ice: the actual decision making processes are tied up with a number of variables which require an intimate and protracted acquaintance with official and non-official proceedings. It is clear that although not all CPI(M) candidates are party members, the major decisions are made at the level of the party. Many of these decisions may be handed down from state to district and then to block level. The members of the lowest units, the local branches, may then not be in a position to challenge the directives, at least not until the next party conference. Some of these directives, for example the *barga* registration drive and recently the mass literacy campaign, may be in tune with the interests of the poorest villagers. Other general directives, like the hold on more radical land reforms, may be less so.

Another problem lies in the pitfall in which one can easily get ensnared. The assumption is often made that leaders from a particular class necessarily represent that class. A rich peasant *prodhan* is then regarded as necessarily looking after rich peasant interests and obstructing the further mobilization of for example agricultural labourers. That may not be the case. Anyway, in this particular block, rich peasants are not holding important positions. Of the nine *prodhans*, seven are middle peasant and/or teacher, and one each is of small peasant and rich peasant stock. In terms of caste, there could be more reason for concern: there are 4 Brahmins, 1 Kayastha, 2 Sadgopes, 2 Muslims, all males, and not a single SC/ST.

Although none of the SC/ST members occupy important positions in the *panchayat*, they themselves prefer not to attribute this to high-caste or rich peasant control. BD, a poor ironsmith, in his second term as member and active in the school committee, the health committee, the cultural club, and the Kisan Sabha, knows the difficulties involved: 'Leadership and running an administration are difficult matters. To hold an important position and give leadership, one needs some basic education'. This position is echoed by MT, a small sharecropper, who recently, together with many other Santals, has learned to read and write:

Most of our own people lack in education and many also in political consciousness. For this reason, we had to depend very much on the leadership of persons coming from the more educated families. Moreover, generally, they have more time to spare. For the poor people, it is impossible to spend so much time on party activities and panchayat work. I have got only my evenings left. And then I am tired, that is a fact. But then, the middle peasants do not dominate us. There is democracy here, people know their rights, and if necessary, the rich peasants will be thrown out of the party. Yes, the *prodhan* is one of them, but it does not mean that they are in control. If they would not look after the poor people, they would soon lose their position.

Dissatisfaction with the low-level position of the agricultural labourers and small peasants is actually more frequently aired by middle and rich peasants themselves. A number of them are not satisfied with the organizational effort on behalf of the party to raise the consciousness and administrative capabilities of the poorer sections. SG, a Brahmin, owns 12 acres of land which he has given on *barga* cultivation. He has been politically active since the early 1950s and now, as the *prodhan*, he devotes all his time to public life. He is busy in the sporting club, rural library, and school committees and sees in the excessive time devoted to these various functions a reason as to why not more cadres have been trained:

I have seen the tremendous progress, but I am not blind. We still suffer from a lack of mature village leadership. The leadership is still too often in the hands of the middle classes, and if we really want to turn society upside down, then the proletariat has to take over the reigns. The party, despite all its achievements, has been rather weak in spreading education and consciousness. This also has to be done if we want to serve the people.

A dilemma obviously exists between the requirements of the work in the *panchayats*, the empowerment of the village poor, and just distribution of resources. The *panchayats* are state institutions, supervised in terms of resources to a certain degree by the Department of Rural Development in New Delhi. Many of the procedures are afflicted by red tapism, and are open to lobbying and arbitrary decisions. Some degree of arbitrariness may persist in all societies, and the question is therefore whether an endeavour is made to contain it so that the deserving people may benefit from the *panchayats*, even if the *panchayats* are run by the better-off families of the village.[8] An important corrective instrument is the compulsory bi-annual meeting of the *gram sabha*, i.e. the village assembly at the level of each village constituency.

As per the amended Panchayat Act 1973 (sections 16A and 17A added in 1984), the budget and the working plan for the next year as well the works accomplished, the report on the audit of the accounts and the list of beneficiaries are to be presented at the *gram sabha* meetings. All the people in the constituency are invited to these meetings 'by beat of drums as widely as possible', and it would be possible for political adversaries, as well as for the disgruntled sympathizers of the party in power, to raise specific issues of corruption and nepotism. The opposition can use this public arena for a direct confrontation, for firing the flames of discontent and for redirecting the priorities. The CPI(M) members have to remain attentive to this democratic countercheck, but in view of their seemingly unassailable dominance need not necessarily do so.

The *gram sabha* meetings have an important democratic function, but they do not make policy. They form a forum for eliciting opinions about proposals for major works to be undertaken by the *panchayats*, but the decisions are prepared by the local party committee and the *gram committee*. The *gram committee* again is an innovation with a tremendous democratic potentiality. In each *gram*, 15 people are selected to sit on the committee and to monitor the local problems and the allocation of loans and subsidized inputs. Congress members complain that the committees are stuffed with party people, and that their suggestions do not count. NJ, a teacher in his early forties, agrees that arbitrariness does occur, but he rejects the accusation that it is a unilateral party affair. He himself is the son of an important Congress leader. He joined the Marxist student organization while studying at the university in the late 1960s and only recently was admitted as a candidate member of the party:

[8] The few Congress members argue that their proposals do not count and that only people with close links with the CPI(M) leadership get nominated for subsidised loans and special benefits. The Marxist members, on the other hand, hold that decisions are generally taken democratically and that corruption has been stopped. Allegations about corruption and nepotism are bound to crop up in political altercations, particularly under conditions of paucity of funds. This is usually the reply by the CPI(M)-supported members. Generally, on the basis of a limited number of observations, the reply is not convincing enough but sounds valid.

Here party affiliation is not the major factor. At the gram sabha meetings, names for the beneficiaries committee can be proposed and usually they will be accepted on one condition: they should think for the welfare of the village and they should be clean in their dealings. It includes a cross-section of the villagers. I only regret that even some *goondas* of the Congress regime have been given a place. Of course, we have a majority, but when we distribute subsidized inputs, we look in the first place at who are the needy people.

At the *gram sabha* meetings, the members are informed of the demands of the villagers. These demands are rather conservative, and usually relate to roads, electricity, irrigation and loans. Alternative, innovative initiatives like the establishment of cooperatives, tree planting drives and the launching of rural industries are usually not forthcoming. Opposition members, and occasionally also CPI(M) cadres, express dissatisfaction about omissions and wrong priorities, but they see the importance of the *panchayat* administration in yet another field, namely in the increasing access of the poorest section of society to the public space.

In their dealing with the administration, the poor people have acquired respect and self-respect. The reference to 'human dignity' is often heard, especially among the SC/ST members. Given the limited resources, applicants for loans and jobs are more often than not left empty-handed. At the same time, however, they throng the *panchayat* building and the Block Development Office, which in earlier days were usually out of bounds for them, as one of the Santal members, KM, recalls:

When we were young, we were restricted to our adivasi *para* (hamlet) and the *bhadrolok* were our intermediaries with anything outside the village. The field on which we worked was theirs, the *prodhan* was theirs and the *chowkidar* (village watchman) was theirs. We would not dare to venture to the *babus'* offices or to send our children to school. But this has changed. Now the *morols* do not even dare to shout at us. Even the lowest section of society knows where the member lives and where the *panchayat* is located and when we go there we are received and given proper attention.

KB, a Bagdi, also appreciates the distance which has been covered, but he knows that the going is still rough. His story is an account of ambivalence, and as such an appropriate reminder of the slowness of changes in society:

The changes have been overwhelming, but also, how can I be satisfied? So many things remain to be done. Society hasn't changed very much. I only have to look at my parents who are still quietly behind Congress, and still stick to many superstitions. But also among many of own supporters, the mentality is still to change. Yes, they come to our meetings and rallies, but as soon as they reach home, they often again start thinking in their old ways.

Conclusion

The assumption that rich peasants still dominate rural politics and institutions has been dealt with on the basis of detailed information from one block in Barddhaman district. The district, more than any other district in West Bengal, in the past has been known for the dominant position of rich peasants and for the distinct class cleavage.

The survey indicates that the character of the public space has changed, and as such confirms the picture which resulted from an earlier survey in Birbhum (Lieten 1992a). Poor peasants and agricultural labourers, and therefore also the SC/ST, have very much come to the forefront in the public arena. It is a shift which continues to operate, and there is therefore much basis to conclude that the CPI(M) is actively and consciously furthering the process. A similar shift in gender visibility had been less explicit until the 1993 elections. Underlying the shift has been the concentrated effort at the political level to include the hitherto marginalized groups, and a distinct growth in productivity in a modified agrarian context, which allowed these groups more freedom to operate in the public space. Enfranchisement involves a continuing economic, political, and social process in favour of hitherto marginalized and/or suppressed groups. The antiquated hold of landlords and rich peasants on rural politics and economics has been breached and a reasonably democratic institutions has been put in place.

The institution of the *panchayat* is possibly not a modern edition of the Greek *demos* (which anyway excluded the majority of the people). The *gram sabha* comes somewhat closer to the exalted example of the *demos* since it ideally involves all the adult people in the village. The extent to which the ideal is being realized has to be further investigated, but it seems that the attempt to involve all and sundry is on. The attempt is undertaken by village leaders who, in the new post-land reform context, appear to have shifted 'from radical activism to consensual politics', but they have steered clear of a 'narrow management notion'. The conclusion of Webster and others that this has been accompanied with a shift from 'class' to 'non-antagonistic institutional management' does not follow from the observations we have made.

CHAPTER 3

Panchayats in Western Uttar Pradesh: Namesake Members

The programmes of *Comprehensive Rural Development* and *Panchayati Raj* have been associated with the rural economy and polity of Uttar Pradesh since the early 1950s. On the basis of a case study in the Green Revolution area in the north-western zone of the state, answers are sought in this article to a number of related questions on the effectiveness of these programmes. After an examination of the composition and the internal functioning of the *panchayats*, some aspects of the ideological predispositions of the members are looked at. Although the discursive ground is shifting, the bottom line is that the rich peasants do not tolerate a democratic and enlightened departure. At the same time, they have been at the helm of a fairly radical peasants' movement that in the 1980s, for the government in New Delhi, was a force to reckon with.

Peasant activism in western Uttar Pradesh, which has been identified with Muzaffarnagar district, has been superimposed on the existing *panchayat* structure, and a study of the *panchayats* in this particular area may give some idea of the impact of the peasant movement on the social and political structures. Muzaffarnagar is known to be a Jat area. Brahmins and Agarwal Vaishyas have some importance in professions and trade respectively, and in some areas Rajputs dominate, but otherwise it is the Jats (and Gujars) who rule the roost. They have major divisions according to the area (*khap*) of residence. The Baliyan *khap*, which consists of 82 villages under the command of Chaudhury Mahendra Tikait, is situated in the area around Sisauli.

In the early decades of the twentieth century, the Baniyas were the dominant landowners in the area. At the time of the Final Settlement around 1930, they still owned 24 per cent of the land, as compared to 17 per cent owned by Jat families. The Jat, unlike the Baniya, would cultivate his *khudkasht* land himself and would take *zamindari* land on occupancy or non-occupancy rent. Tenants were considered to be paying reasonable rent so that they were be left with 'a sufficient margin to reach a much higher standard of living than is usual in the province' (FS Report 1931: 10).[1] Particularly the Jats, who then already cultivated one-third of the land in Muzaffarnagar, were expected to expand: 'He is industrious, thrifty, skilful, a shrewd man of business and a true lover of the land. He has secured for himself the tracts most favoured by nature and elbowed other castes into the poorer localities. His women work with him, and it is a common saying that in the field a Jat woman is the equal of a man of another caste' (FS Report 1931: 7).

Among the Other Backward Castes (OBC), the Dhimars, a subdivision of Kahars, form the dominant group. They used to work as water-carriers, and are usually employed as (male) agricultural labourer or as (female) domestic servants. The Scheduled Castes (SC) account for 15 per cent of the population in the district. Most of them belong to a cobbler *biradari* (Chamars, Yatavs, or Jhusias) or a sweeper *biradari* (Bhangi or Khukrab, renamed as Valmiki).[2]

Politically the area is famous for two helmsmen: Chaudhury Mahendra Singh Tikait and Chaudhury Charan Singh.[3] Both have taken on themselves the mantle of the peasant stock, the first as a peasant union activist, and the second as a party politician. Chaudhury Charan Singh, until his death in 1986, had put his stamp on political and rural economic developments in Uttar Pradesh. After his defection from the Congress party in 1967, he set the ball rolling for the '*aya Ram gaya Ram*'

---

[1] In the *zamindari* settlements, constituting around 50 per cent of the district, surplus appropriation may have been harsher, and may have left the actual cultivator deeply indebted and dependent (for the late nineteenth century see Whitcombe 1972: 46–8). Whitcombe (1972: 199) further argues that the 'scientific revenue assessment' helped the wealthy *zamindar* and greatly depressed the villages.

[2] The *biradari* is the actual unit to which the members of a jati relate. In the past, these different *biradaris* did not have any social cohesion or common mythology. The only meeting ground was their common occupation (Blunt 1931: 225). Under the impact of the Arya Samaj movement and the Hinduization of the Bhangi, a common Valmiki mythology was sought to be introduced. According to the mythology, Valmiki is supposed to have been a robber in Karnal district who later turned into a saint, and who then wrote the *Ramayana* epic. The Valmiki caste movement, associating the Bhangi sweeper caste with Valmiki, has claimed a rightful ranking in the ritual vicinity of the Brahmins (Kolenda 1983: 238–49).

[3] See Gupta 1988; Singh 1992: 87–122 (on Tikait) and for example Brass 1985a, 1985b with many positive contributions on the Chaudhury as the defender of rural peasant, and backward caste interests.

pattern in UP (and Indian) politics (Baxter 1975: 119). In terms of party politics, the region indeed at best can be characterized as maverick. Party fortunes and electoral support have fluctuated wildly. The earlier unchallenged Congress superiority in 1967 gave way to election victories of the Communist Party of India (CPI) in the Lok Sabha and Legislative Assembly Elections. After the Emergency, the Janata party, Congress, and BJP had interchanging positions. The explanation for the dramatic changes in party fortunes has probably less to do with the population at large being maverick in its political fancies, and more to do with the fact that electoral fraud has allowed a small coterie of rich peasants to decide on the booth results. Particularly after the victory of the Congress-supported CPI candidate in the 1971 Lok Sabha elections, the Congress was kept at bay by strong arm tactics. The voting procedure may be captured with the local expression *fatafat* (fast, at one go, i.e. stuffing the ballot boxes).[4]

In terms of democratization therefore, no tangible improvement seems to have taken place in the area, despite the expansion of the post-Green Revolution economy and despite the organized peasant movement. A study of the area in the mid-1970s, which was commissioned by the Dag Hammarskjöld Foundation in its search for alternatives in rural development, concluded that substantial visible changes in the economy and infrastructure had taken place, but that on the other hand:

The economic power of the Jats has greatly increased and has been translated into de jure local political power through institutions like cooperatives and *panchayats*.... Under these circumstances, the working of the democratic process and even of a just law and order is difficult. Manipulation of the dependents accentuate political and caste factionalism and systematically

[4] The voting procedure helps to explain why the victorious party usually walked away with close to 50 per cent of the votes. Janata in 1985 secured 48.6 per cent of the votes, and in 1989 even 82.0 per cent. Two years later 48.2 per cent went in favour of the Bharatiya Janata Party (BJP), and only 10.9 per cent of the electorate voted for Janata. By that time, the Indian National Congress party (INC) polling had been reduced to single digit numbers. The *Economic Times* (18.06.1991) commented on the notorious booth capturing practices in the area: 'Fear is the key. No blood and gore. The daunting *lathi* suffices. Calmly and unhurriedly, ballot boxes are stuffed with the votes of the people who have long since realized that discretion is the better part of valour—and franchise—and decided to stay at home.' In its journalistic rendering, the stark reality (or myth) of a democratic deficit in the region is conceived as an evasive battle between the muscular and sturdy and the faint and feeble.

discourages—even suppresses—possibilities of united collective action, which is perceived as a threat to the status quo even by those factions of the elite who want some change in their favour. (Mehta et al. 1977: 83)

The study, moreover, came to the conclusion that 'both the fear-ridden self-esteem and disunity' were related to the commanding position of the Jat rich peasants, a number of them with a feudal outlook. External assistance for rural development, for example in the form of project loans, would probably exacerbate the vulnerability and powerlessness of the people at the bottom. It would increase the dependency: 'In a political sense, too great a reliance on external sources would mean dependence on the new entrepreneurial class with increasing external linkages. . . . Becoming a junior partner to the new class would only perpetuate the subjugation of the oppressed' (Mehta et al. 1977: 87).

In Chapter 9, attention will be paid to some of the issues related to self-esteem and self-reliance, within and without the *panchayat* system, and to the various attitudes and ideational stands *vis-à-vis* traditional social structures and changes therein. The perception of categories like caste and gender and the opinion on some crucial developments, the appearance of communalism to start with, will help to draw the outlines of the world view, single or multiple. In this chapter, we shall consider the functioning of the *panchayats* and the views of the *panchayat* members on what could be done and on what went wrong.

In order to get an idea of the composition of the *panchayats* and the involvement of the members, a survey was undertaken in the 7 *panchayat* bodies in a *nyaya panchayat* around Sisauli in Shahpur block. In addition to an analysis of the quantitative composition in terms of a number of social variables (like age, education, gender, caste, and class), some forays are also made into some qualitative and ideological aspects. These forays may help us in judging the potential of *panchayat* members as social reformers and in any case as representatives of the people in the villages.

Members and Meetings

'The *panchayat* system is in full force in the district, and the parties to a jury of this kind usually take an oath on a *lota* filled with salt to abide by any decision that may be arrived at.' Procedures have changed since Atkinson (1876: 76) described the caste *panchayats* as a tribunal dispensing justice and as the upkeepers of the moral order, particularly of the caste rules imposed by the Brahmins (Blunt 1931: 104–31).[5] Their purpose has also been changed from a law-making and law-enforcing body[6] to a development agency, and its legitimization has been based in the democratic election process, open to all.

Despite a whole range of mandatory and discretionary tasks and functions, the formal *panchayat* structure in Uttar Pradesh appears to have remained a languid body. It appears to have not grown beyond its perceived primary task, namely the dispensation of the financial resources coming in from the higher echelons. In order to be allowed to do this, *panchayats* have to be constituted democratically through an election process. The general conclusion is that indeed they have been so constituted: candidates have been nominated (2.5 million candidates for 0.8 million seats in the 1995 *panchayat* elections), elections have been organized (though very irregularly in the past), people generally have been allowed to vote, and swearing in signatories have been obtained so that the *panchayats* are enabled to start functioning as the lowest elected organs of the state.

The first issue to be taken up is the socio-economic composition of the councils. General statistics on one block in Muzaffarnagar indicate that the *panchayat* membership is a fair reflection of the socio-economic composition of the population.

An interesting development has taken place in the occupational background of the members. In the earlier *panchayats* (until 1995), middle peasants made up around 40 per cent of the council; agricultural labourers and a dozen small peasants together also accounted

---

[5] They existed mainly among the higher castes. Even among the Jats, permanent panchayats existed only in a few areas as *thok* (lineage) *panchayats* (Pradhan 1966). The offences that could be put on trial by the caste panchayat varied, but usually included the following: (inter)caste adultery, breaches of customary rules, drunkenness, insulting Brahmins, cow-killing, etc. The sentences included pilgrimages, compulsory begging, public humiliation, and, as a rule, fines to be used to feed the brotherhood and an extra fine to feed the Brahmins (Blunt 1931: 115–17).

[6] This function of the caste *panchayats* has not altogether vanished from the area. It is occasionally still made use of when the village patriarchs wish to impose their rule and lifestyles on deviant family members, caste members, or villagers. One gruesome example in the district relates to the beheading by the *panchayat* of a young harijan couple who had eloped to Delhi, and which, after having been enticed back to their village with sweet promises, was conferred the ultimate verdict, executed with an axe by one of the fathers (*Times of India* 10 August 1993; *Economic Times* 14 August 1993).

for around 40 per cent of the total. In the new councils, agricultural labourers have become the biggest group (44 per cent), and together with small peasants (15 per cent), they numerically dominate the *panchayats*. Rich peasants, although only one-fifth of the membership, provided and continue to provide five to seven *pradhans*. While in the previous councils, there was only one professional, a teacher, who acted as an *upopradhan* (vice-chairperson), or *chhotapradhan* (small *pradhan*), in the new councils, there is no professional. In the previous council, more then 10 per cent of the members were out-migrant workers. Their participation in the meetings was out of the question, and it may be assumed that they did not attend a single meeting. There absent status did not disqualify them as *panchayat* members since, as we shall elaborate, the involvement of the resident members also was practically nonexistent.

The situation in *panchayat* A for example was typical of the other *panchayats* as well: two members resided near Muzaffarnagar town as brick kiln workers, one member resided with his family in Shamli town, and one member was absconding after having committed a murder. The other nine members did reside in the village, but since two of them were women, the effective maximum strength was seven members only. Indeed, in none of the cases have women ever been involved in anything related to *panchayat* work or public work in general. Some of the women did not know even that they were members. Once or twice the *pradhan* had dispatched a document to them for signing, but they did not know what it was for. Without being derogatory to women in general, the impression is that women stand better chances of becoming a member of the *panchayat* if they are illiterate, frail of body and of mind and rather old. Even the women who at least knew that they were *panchayat* members, very rarely went to the meetings. If they did, then they only did so in order to put their thumb impression or to sign and then came back. The usual procedure, however, is for the *pradhan* to send the document to be signed to the house.

This procedure, as a matter of fact applies not only to the women, but to most of the male members as well. In the *panchayat* which we have been describing (*panchayat* A), after the necessary deductions, we were left with seven male members residing in the village. They were potential candidates for participation in the functioning of the *panchayat*. Four of them declared never to have attended and never to have been invited for a meeting. Two other members declared that they had attended whenever the *pradhan* wanted, i.e. one or two times a year. Even the *upopradhan* could not recall having attended more than one or two meetings. The *pradhan* himself, on the other hand, claims that meetings were held once a month, as per the guidelines, and that 'everybody turns up, the women also'.

A similar situation prevailed in *panchayat* B. The *pradhan* asserted that he had meetings every month, the *upopradhan* and one orphaned member who works for the *pradhan* contended that they met every second month, one female member stated that she was occasionally called to the *pradhan's* house to sign a document which she did not understand, two members reside outside the village, and seven members had never attended a meeting.

Marginal Differences

Are the other villages different? One village apparently is so. In *panchayat* C, the procedures appear to be more in conformity with the legal specifications: not only did the *pradhan* assert that he had meetings once a month, but also the *upopradhan* and two other members could recall that during one year or so, some five meetings had taken place. In addition, five members recalled that they possibly had attended two meetings. In this *panchayat* too, the meetings were spaced irregularly, and took place only 'whenever the *pradhan* wants us'.

According to the *pradhan* of *panchayat* C, the decision making process is very elaborate: voting takes place after all the arguments are heard. He appears not to be standing alone in stating this. Three members asserted that some discussion takes place on the proposals and then a vote of approval is taken. But most of the members insisted that they only went to the *pradhan's* house in order to sign the papers and then returned home: 'The meeting is a formality. Often the work we have to decide upon has already been executed. Whatever still has to be done has already been decided by the *pradhan* and we just put our signature.' In *panchayat* B, and in other *panchayats*, disagreements on proposals usually do not take place because of the simple reason that the *pradhan*, as noticed above, calls only his own people to the meetings, if he calls any at all. In two of the seven villages, even the *upopradhan* had never been called for a meeting.

Disagreement with the *pradhan* leads to ostracizing. Disenfranchisement indeed appears to be the logical reward for insistence on democratic rights. It is definitely the case that the members who have fought the elections on the list of the defeated candidate for pradhanship, will not be invited by the victorious *pradhan* to the meetings of the *panchayat*, assuming that such meetings occasionally do take place. Some of these members bitterly complained that even their signatures must have been forged since they have never signed any document. They are probably correct. The following case may be taken as an instance. Bishambhar Singh is in his early forties and claims some political commitment as a member of Mulayam Singh's Samajwadi Party. He is a bachelor who looks after the land (2 acres) and the family of his deceased brother. Since he was planning to get into politics, and aspired to become the *pradhan* after the next election, in 1988 he decided to stand for membership: 'People voted for me but now I realize I am here for namesake [*nam ke lije*] only. The *pradhan* never asks for our views and when we tell him our suggestions and our complaints about some developments, he just does not listen to us. I take this as an insult. We are members for namesake only. People make a joke of us.'

One of the *pradhans* was a relatively young man who in 1983, at the age of 35 years, became the *pradhan* as the heir to his father. He owns 25 acres of good agricultural land and a brick kiln and has important political connections. Despite his enormous wealth and his dynastic ascent, he spoke like a man imbued with democratic principles. He preferred to solve problems in an amicable way, and wanted the *panchayat* members at the monthly meetings to come forward with their own proposals and to put them on the agenda of the meeting. However, he did not like them to vote on the proposals: 'Voting will only create *tanatani* [tension], and I prefer to shelve controversial proposals for the time being. In this way, I can maintain an amicable atmosphere. As a matter of fact, we are one big *biradari*.'

The excellent words did not fail to impress, but doubts began cropping up when he had some difficulty in telling the names of the *panchayat* members whom he was supposed to have met at least once every month over the last so many years. These doubts turned into incredulity when it was revealed that names of the members provided by the *pradhan* actually were not of the members of the present *panchayat*, but of the old *panchayat* which had been superseded four years earlier.

Fear Psychosis

It is not surprising why many of the new members deplore their membership. It is only for some of them that the dissatisfaction is because they had expected to be in a position, as they claim, to do something for the development of the village. For most of the dissatisfied members, however, this factor does not carry much weight: they were asked to stand for the elections, and in obeisance to the *pradhan*, they agreed to the proposal. Some of them even claim that their nomination had been filed by the *pradhan* without their consent. Santosh Singh, an illiterate labourer, was exactly thirty years old when the *pradhan* approached him for membership:

I am a member for namesake only [*nam ke lije*]. The *pradhan* wrote my name, filled my nomination form himself, and informed me that I am a member. I thought that he was cracking jokes, but when I put my thumb impression, I was convinced that I had become a member. But it is absolutely *begar* [useless]. A member is a *bakwash*. [stupid fool]

'The *pradhan* forced it on me', is a complaint often uttered by members. They consider themselves as *zabardasti* (coerced) members. In a number of cases, the coercion is a pure physical threat. Forever wary of potential conflicts, they have learned not to talk openly about village affairs to strangers, and quite a few members were reluctant to respond to our queries. In a few cases, they even insisted that the *pradhan* be present at the interview. The justification was of two kinds. They either pleaded that as poor people they did not know anything. They characterized themselves as *garib anparh admi* (the blind poor people) and the *pradhan* as the *malik* (master) of the village. They said that he was the only person who would be able to say what was supposed to be done and what had been done. Many devious ways of making them speak up failed.

Compliance with the wishes of the *pradhan* is in a number of cases related to economic reciprocity: as agricultural labourers on the land of the *pradhan*, or as recipients of Integrated Rural Development Programme (IRDP) loans or of houses built under the government programme, they are obliged to the *pradhan*. Mahindar Singh is a brick kiln worker of the Bhangi caste. Just before the *pradhan* proposed his name for membership, he was given a loan for house construction: 'I myself was interested in membership, but it is really an insult. I have never been called for a meeting. I suppose that the *pradhan* wanted to buy me over. He filled my paper and informed me that I am a member. I think because I have some influence over my community people.'

On the other hand, some people complied with the offer of membership by the *pradhan* as they expected thus to get involved in working for the betterment of the village. This orientation is quite common among the younger members. Some of the women also appeared to be genuinely interested in taking up some initiatives. Indira is still in her late twenties and now wonders why the *pradhan* had asked her to become a member. She had to fight a battle with her relatives but because of the support of her husband, she could accept the offer: 'At home I don't have much work and so I wanted to do some social work, but becoming a member was a great disappointment. Women should become self-sufficient and self-reliant but although I am a so-called member, even I am kept absolutely useless.'

Muzaffar, a poor trader and casual worker, is in his thirties and already in his second term as a member. He was fancied by the *pradhan* because 'he thinks that I am his man'. Behind the back of the *pradhan*, the discourse changes from gracious compliance to a litany of accusations. They are accusations of what has happened, among others the proverbial corruption, to which we shall return later, and of what has not happened. Muzaffar has a whole list of works which should be taken up by the *panchayat* but since 'the *pradhan* is corrupt and careless about the poor people', not much has been done. He lists four of them as the most important: village roads (better) educational facilities, drinking water supply, and health facilities.

These are the priorities that are high on the agenda of most of the members who apparently had given a thought to what could be done. Illustrative of the non-involvement of the *panchayat* members is the fact that more than one-fourth of the members, excluding the absent members could not come forward with suggestions for any improvement which they considered necessary, despite our insistence and cajoling. The reason why around one-fourth of the *panchayat* members could not offer any suggestions should probably be imputed to the fear psychosis rather than to mere ignorance and callousness.[7]

Public Works and Private Corruption

The works that are listed by the members as requiring priority attention, as Muzaffar did in the previous section, involve those basic and rudimentary provisions which one had expected to already have been put in place after many decades of rural development planning in one

---

[7] A non-response is often wrongly translated by the interviewer as a lack of knowledge and perception. Respondents often indeed prefer to talk up to the interviewer, agreeing with the assumed world view of the interviewer, the superior outsider, or to keep silent and refer the interviewer to the people who should

of the richest regions of India. It is not that the facilities are altogether absent. Primary schools (up to class V) have been constructed but the maintenance leaves much to be desired and the teachers often do not turn up. Most villages have only a primary school which makes it imperative for the young children to go to a junior high school in the next village for further education. Especially for girls, this is seen as going a step too far. Government primary health centres are absent or have not been functioning since their inception. In *panchayat* D, for example, neither a doctor nor a nurse have ever turned up, and the building by now has become decrepit. The inter-village roads are quite good, but the intra-village lanes are in a decrepit state. Public water pumps have been installed, but there are only two or three such pumps per village. Some houses for SC families have been constructed and some IRDP loans for the purchase of carts (buggy) have been provided.

As to the reasons why the works have not been undertaken or completed, the *pradhan* and the members differ fundamentally. The *pradhans* are quite explicit while enumerating all the good deeds they have done: all roads have been constructed and repaired, loans have been distributed to the poor people, houses have been built for them, handpumps have been installed, etc. One of them, generally regarded as the most corrupt *pradhan* in the neighbourhood, blames insufficiency of funds and wrong allocation by the government as the reason for slack performance:

We want to work even harder for the improvement of the village, but the funds are insufficient. And also, the government has earmarked the money for certain purposes. So we are constrained by this wrong allocation. The pradhan should have more power to use the money where it is needed. Also, people in the village do not cooperate. And then there are the *dalals* (middlemen) and *goondas*. They are protected by the block officials and by the politicians. All this prevents the money from being used for village development.

The *pradhans* are unanimous that they should have more discretionary powers in allocating the money that has been earmarked for village development. They prefer to go back to the pre-1975 days when decisions could be taken at the village level. Nowadays, they complain, all the rights have been given to the block level and higher

---

know, i.e. the *malik* (the husband, the employer, or the dominant village elite). Many of the interviewees actually told us to go and see the *pradhan* and to find out. If we were to insist, we could interview them, but only in the presence of the *pradhan*.

officials. It is alleged that they take their cuts before handing over the money. One *pradhan* knows for sure that people who want to get a loan will give money to the block officials, and that since the *pradhan* himself is excluded from the transactions and from the decision making process 'unfortunately, harijans and poor peasants never get the loans'. Shekar, a Brahmin who has been a member of the *panchayat* since the mid-1970s, agrees with the quote (he himself got a loan for a cart), but disagrees with the shifting of the responsibility, and actually alleges that the *pradhan* himself is part and parcel of the operation: 'The pradhan himself is very shrewd. He does everything on his own, and the block officials will deal with him only and with nobody else in the village. The pradhan and chhotapradhan and the block officers can tell you who is getting the loans and how much money is being spent on the works. We do not know anything.'

All the members, whether they are Brahmin, Jat, or Harijan/Dalit,[8] literate or illiterate, have one common handicap: except for the *pradhan*, and in most cases the *upopradhan* as well, nobody knows how much money is available to the *panchayat*. The key to the safe is with the *pradhan*, the block officials, and the bank managers. Most of the members put all the blame for the non-execution of works on the *pradhan*. Some consider him to be lazy and incompetent. In any case, practically all members rebuke his secretive manners which leaves them in the dark about the money that is supposed to come to the village. Most other members are of one opinion, which is expressed in many variations: 'The pradhan has eaten up all the money. He is a *chor* [thief] and a *sharabi* [drunkard]. He is lazy and stupid. He should be kept behind bars. He should be punished. He is friendly with the goondas and only helps his *chamchas* [sycophants]. He has destroyed the village.'

The village *pradhan*, with the exception of the *pradhan* in *panchayat* C, is accused of not only pocketing the money provided by the government programmes, but to have also collected money from the villagers for *shramdan* programmes which did not materialize. Of course, the villagers say, he has also taken up some works, but each time he has seen to it that he was paid properly, either as a bribe or just by using false signatures. *Panchayati raj* could be made to function as a good system for the village in the sense that it already has contributed a

---

[8] Earlier, I have used the word *harijan* to refer to the group of 'ex-untouchables', who are officially referred to as SC (Scheduled Castes) and as *dalit* in the language of the political movement for SC emancipation.

small measure to the development works in the village, and in the sense that it could dispense with justice and maintain peace. But in the way it is organized now, the members feel, it all falls flat on account of the *pradhan*. The solution proposed by some members who apparently have pinned their hopes on more power and resources coming their way, is that the *pradhan* should be more efficient and should be more of a *zimmedar* (trustworthy person). The members should get more power to intervene and to be involved. There should be honesty and efficiency. If only the sitting *pradhan* could be replaced by a good and efficient person, and if they themselves could do the job, 'it would have changed the face of the village', as one of them contended. Expectations of an improvement in the system are indeed maintained by a number of members. One of them, a young Jat who has attended college and now looks after 8 acres of land, expressed his public concern as follows:

In the first place, the pradhan should convene the meetings regularly. Secondly, the pradhan should not do any work without consulting the members. Thirdly, the money which comes for the poor should go to the poor and should not be consumed by the pradhan and the block officials. The government policies should be executed and the poor people should be listened to.

These hopes remain mere pipedreams, for the economic base supporting the political structure remains unaltered. As long as there is money coming into the village, the *pradhan* and his intermediaries will have an incentive to corrupt and more money will help in spreading more dishonesty. Politics is more and more being conceived in terms of *goonda-gardi* and corruption. It is an old story, as on old women exclaimed in despair: 'In India, this problem will go until the Universe will be recreated by God. I have lost all faith in the democratic institutions of India. Police, the politicians, the big people, they all have their goondas. So, since the protectors have become the destroyers, who can protect the normal people? There are no checks on the system.'

Such pronouncements are common. They belong to the village discourse, and do suggest an adverse predisposition towards politics. However, this is not necessarily the case. Attacks on the *goonda-gardi* are more often than not used to heap suspicion and misgivings on leaders of other factions. They are hence also forthcoming from the most corrupt *pradhan* in the area, and from some other important members who because of their closeness to the *pradhans*, may not be above board.

Social Void

Panchayat membership is seen to be related to age. More than four-fifth of all the members are in their forties and fifties, while the *pradhans* are in their fifties and sixties. More often, they have a long career of village politics behind them, and have been functioning as *pradhan* for at least two terms. Very few members are in their twenties: a nominated housewife, a brick kiln worker residing around New Delhi, a member of an influential political family, and a rich peasant's son. For younger people, *panchayats* obviously do not serve as a vehicle for starting a political career. Nor are they an arena in which young people can get involved and start social activities. Most of the members (around 80 per cent) do not have any social involvement outside the *panchayat* membership.

Surprisingly, only twelve members, mostly the bigger landowners, were stated to be involved with the BKU (Bharatiya Kisan Union), most of them rather passively. Only six members were associated with educational institutions. One of them, a seasonally migrating factory worker, is himself an illiterate person. Otherwise, the *pradhans* are the only people to have educational connections as members of the various colleges in the area. Two of them were also members of a religious organization (the Arya Samaj). Two members were somewhat actively involved in party politics. Membership of social organizations is limited. The explanation for this could well be that except for the BKU, there is not much organizational activity which one can get involved in. Active involvement on issues or in movements around social issues is even more limited, and in fact nonexistent. Most of the members have never been called upon to intervene even in small social matters. Only seven members were prepared to state that they were involved in social issues, which in each case meant that they commanded so much authority or respect that they would be called upon to solve smaller conflicts in their neighbourhood. if *panchayat* bodies are to play a role not only in economic development, but also in changing the mores and values of the people, *panchayat* members themselves should be expected to contribute to social renewal. Such a renewal could be active, for example, in respect of the undermining of the caste system and in respect of the emancipation of women. We shall see below whether this was the case indeed.

The women members themselves usually pretend not to know much about the *panchayat* system, but when it comes to their own position, they usually are clear about their priorities. Sona, the middle-aged, poor peasant Valmiki, was nominated by the *pradhan* to become a member. Although she has ideas about latrines, maternity centre, etc., she has never been asked to do anything or to attend a meeting. It is her *kismat* (pre-ordained luck), but she also considers herself lucky with a good husband:

> I know many women who are suffering at the hands of their husband. There should be more independence for them. Some financial freedom is required so that one can go and buy things in Sisauli without having to go and ask the husband. Education is important, but it also depends on how the husbands change and how society changes.

Indira is fifteen years younger and has received some education in the village school, but otherwise her situation is comparable to that of Sona. Her family too is a poor peasant family, but with a modern line-up of husband, wife, and two children:

> I want equality among men and among women, and between men and women also. Women should become self-sufficient and self-reliant, and they should get educated; only then things can change. Jobs are necessary for women. I want to go and work, in the hospital, stitching work, or so, but the men in the in-laws' house do not allow it. I wish I could do something through the panchayat, but that also is not allowed.

Some of the better educated males of well situated families have adjusted. Ravikant Pal insists that he treats the women in his joint family as human beings. His daughters have studied up to class XII, and one of them contracted a love marriage. A few other Jats and harijans agree that the male should not continue to be the absolute *malik*, but argue that it is difficult to bring women into public life. The problem can be seen at an early stage itself, as early as when the girls have finished class V, and should then go and visit the high school in adjoining villages. This is considered difficult, however, due to the prevalence of eve teasing, and a not very conducive atmosphere.

Most male members, however, do not see this as a problem. According to them, girls should go to school, but only to learn to read and write, and there is no need for them to go for higher education, for in that case they might 'go and sit on the head' of the males. Their freedom should be limited, and they should not indulge too much in public activities. They are regarded as not knowing anything, and of not being of much use in the *panchayats*. 'She should take proper care of the house only' is an often heard proposition.

The composition of the *panchayats* reflects that of the village population. More than half of the members are Jats, and one-fifth are SC. The remaining members are Brahmins, OBC and Muslims. The Brahmins do not have much of a moral or ritual order to defend in the area. Hegemony does not derive from them reconfirming the ideological order, but instead from the economic, social, and political dominance of the Jats. The Brahmin members, even if they have broken with the scriptural understanding of social order, do not feel the urge to fight the caste-based domination by the Jats either. A typical case is that of Yogendra Sharma, a 40 year old poor and illiterate *kisan* (farmer). To start with, he has got a grudge against the local Jats because they do not allow him to vote. But even otherwise, he considers the caste system in the present era as absolute nonsense: 'These days, nobody belongs to his own caste. Hardly anybody is doing the work which was associated with the varna.' In the villages, unlike in the towns, unfortunately, people are still adjusting their lives in terms of caste. The system, he argues, is fostered by the politicians, but he himself, although a member of the *panchayat*, has never thought of starting any activity which may lessen the impact of caste suppression.

A large number of Jat members argue that the caste system is bad, that only humanity counts, and that therefore the politicians should stop this game of setting up one caste against another. The allusion is to the politicians who have been successful in directly appealing to the lower castes, and the negative reference to caste by Jats may directly stem from a threat to their previously unquestioned caste/class dominance. It is true that an unambiguous defence of the caste system by the Jats is hard to come by. With a handful of exceptions, however, they continue to locate themselves in caste terms, even if only restricted to marriage. In the discourse, Jat members are on the defensive in the sense that rather than defending the caste system, they argue that like any social arrangement, it has some advantages, and that anyway, it cannot be abolished with one stroke. In the meantime, not only Bhangis and Chamars, but Brahmins as well complain that village life, and the *panchayat* structure, are clearly dominated by the Jat families. All *pradhans* are Jat. The dominance and muscle power of the Jats is so imposing that at election time, others are not even allowed to vote. SCs and OBCs, unlike the Brahmins, feel the caste oppression in their daily life also. Earlier, the Jats would not come near the houses of the harijan, and the harijan would not be allowed to sit on the *charpoy* (string bed) or take food other than being served straight into the hand.[9] The SC members feel that they are still considered as *acchut* (untouchable), although they also agree that social behaviour is not as bad as what it used to be. Many of the earlier restrictions have waned. But as long as the money and the jobs are with the upper castes, respect for the lower castes will remain minimal. They hope that some change will be brought in from the outside; they themselves are unwilling to start any social movement which may break the rules set by the Jats.

Opinion of Villagers

Reactions to village politics and to the role of *panchayats* in development have been canvassed among a random sample of 149 households in two villages in Shahpur block. First we shall look at the way in which the people perceive the *panchayat*, its leaders, and its works. The *panchayati* system had been erected in order to bring democracy closer to the people, i.e. to have a direct rapport between the elected members of the lowest development institution and their constituency. It has been operational for almost half a century, and one can therefore reasonably assume that it has established itself as institution that people are aware of.

In a small community—one member represents around fifty adults—one would expect most of the people to know at least one of the members of the *panchayat*. But, as it turned out, almost 42 per cent of the respondents could not mention any name and a further 8 per cent mentioned the name of a person who verily resided in the village but was not (any more) involved in the *panchayat* work. Although women were equally (un)informed as men, the names of women members were not mentioned, except by two respondents who actually happened to be family members. At least the *pradhan* is known by all the villagers in the two villages which were taken up for a more intensive study.

Some activity has been taking place. Most of the people knew about the *karangi* (brick stone) roads that had been constructed by the *pradhan*. Around three-fourth of them were also aware of a couple of hand-pumps that have been installed, and a handful mentioned that the construction of houses for SC families have been facilitated. References

[9] In the mid-1950s, it was reported to Kolenda (1983: 136) about the Rajputs in the same area that 'the Rajputs are ever ready to have contact with our women, but with us men, they don't even let us touch their clothes'.

to the works are often accompanied by sneering remarks about the money which has gone down the drain. The bricks used for the lanes were recovered from the old lanes which had been constructed in the 1960s. Earlier, the bricks had been put horizontally; now they have been put vertically and some extra bricks have been purchased in order to cover the difference. There are numerous complaints that although the expenses have been duly entered into the books, most of the money in fact has gone to line the pocket of the *pradhan* and of some of his friends as well as the pockets of the block officials. The village roads usually taper off towards the harijan end of the village. This is an extra cause of dissatisfaction, since the Dalits complain that it is they who have put in most of the work under the *shramdan* (free labour) scheme. Insufficient maintenance and non-coverage of the areas where the poor people live are among the recurrent complaints. The need for roads and handpumps in these areas is high on the priority list of the poor villagers.

Probably half of the respondents did not have an opinion on what else the *panchayat* could do. The other half had a mixed bag of requests, with sanitation as the only clear common denominator. Landless Chamars and Bhangis have more fundamental wishes which the *panchayat* could help to solve. They want land for housing purposes, and, if possible, agricultural land as well. '*Land to the landless*' is definitely still a slogan which activates the minds of the landless. In the opinion of around 15 per cent of the respondents, the allocation of land to landless people is spontaneously mentioned as the first priority in removing poverty. The demand is not new: 'The desire is to become self-sufficient farmers and essentially to delink themselves . . . from the Jat-controlled economic system' (Mehta et al. 1977: 80).

The landless remember the early 1970s, when Indira Gandhi's spectre was in dominance and the district had elected a Communist member of parliament. Many harijan families had then received one acre of agricultural land, but none of them could take full possession of that land, although some landless families could take possession of some of it. The rest was 'snatched away' by the rich Jat peasants. Fullo, in her complaints about decreasing employment opportunities and wages that do not keep level with rising prices, recollects the days of Indira Gandhi when land distribution was still possible:

I worship the idols kept in my house, but I know that they will never provide me with bread. It is only through work that we can make a living. For that we need employment. We need factories in the villages or we need land. There is still 250 bigha of land lying vacant in this village, and so many rich people have too much land. Indira at least helped us. Without her, I don't know what the panchayat can do. The panchayat is not for us. It is for the rich people. Some land is still available for distribution, but most of the land they have already snatched away.

Are there other ways to eradicate poverty? Most of the people, despite all the complaints about the deterioration in economic and social life, still appear to be confident that somewhere or somehow, circumstances could improve, and they also realize that there have been many gains. They have witnessed the giant progress which has pushed the area into one of the top-notch rural districts in the country, and they are generally hopeful of more development and progress coming their way. The acceptance of poverty as the natural state of affairs is an attitude that is rare to come by. A number of respondents are nevertheless quite convinced that the economic and political system prevents the further reduction in poverty. If poverty persists, it is because of the exploitation by the 'capitalists', i.e. the rural rich, and their friends in the government, as some of the statements suggest.

Despite the antagonistic attitudes, as expressed in the statements, and despite the added cynicism about political parties, positive expectations prevail in the assessment of most people. Foremost as a poverty eradication instrument is employment. A few people do see some solution in loans for self-employment, but at least one-third of the suggestions argue for regular employment in factories and rural industries so that landless families particularly will be able to get one job per family. The other solution, apart from land reforms and employment, which scored relatively high is the eradication of corruption so that the benefits of the government schemes may reach the target group. This in fact suggests that the need is for more government intervention rather than less. Government is generally not despised for what it does, but for what it does not do, namely its inactivity in eradicating corruption: 'When dishonesty will disappear, poverty will end.' Several statements, particularly by the poorer people, indicate that the government is doing its best, but that the middlemen have occupied the space at the delivery point, and that the all-pervasive corruption prevents the benefits from reaching the people. The local *panchayats* thus are seen as obstructing development and government plans rather than helping them.

Economic Benefits and the State

The prosperity in the district is abundantly visible in the form of brick houses and mansions to live in and tractors to work on, but even then close to one-third of the sample does not even possess a cycle. Relative poverty in their case, however, usually does not amount to destitution. Agricultural wages are reasonably high (an equivalent of 10 kg of wheat), and the occasional seasonal migration to brick kilns helps many families to overcome the lean periods. The brick kilns in the area, rather than helping the migrant labourer into servitude appear to have served as the wedge to break open the low wage structure. The kilns appear to be a far cry from the kilns as mechanisms of labour bonding which Chopra (1985) has described,[10] and from the 'deproletarization through labour bondage' which Brass (1990) has documented for some locations in Haryana.[11] The economic condition of these families, contrary to what has been predicted as a consequence of the Green Revolution, has not worsened, not only as a consequence of what happened within agriculture, but rather as a consequence of alternative external sources of livelihood as well.

State intervention through the *panchayats* does not appear to have made a contribution to the fortunes of the poor villagers. The upward mobility of the landless class is occasionally related to increasing wages in combination with a lower dependency ratio, but more often occurs as a consequence of one or more of the family members having secured a *pakka* (real, concrete, tangible) job. Such a pakka job—a sweeper with the railways, a bus driver, enrolment by the UP police, or an employee in one of the municipal or government departments in Muzaffarnagar or Delhi—has helped many of the poor peasants to experience a qualitative leap in their well-being. The joint family system, which even many landless families keep in place, helps in adding

---

[10] On the basis of a study of approximately 350 brick kiln workers, Chopra (1985: 174) concluded: 'the Muzaffarnagar evidence would make bondage appear as the traditional method of appropriating the labour of women and children as they become attached to dependent males in their life cycle'.

[11] A combination on the one hand of increasing commercialization in agriculture and on the other hand the relative shortage of labour may lead to an enhanced bargaining power of agricultural labour. In order to circumvent this eventuality, landowners are recorded as having taken recourse to the extension and intensification of permanent forms of unfree labour controlled by the debt bondage system. Rich peasants, in their confrontation with agricultural labour power, thereby succeeded in 'preventing or curtailing both its commodification and the growth of a specifically proletarian consciousness' (Brass 1990: 37).

modern comforts to life through a joint use of the diversified sources of income.

On the other hand, the material conditions of a number of agricultural labour families have deteriorated. They are the families for whom no alternative employment avenues are open and who are condemned to three to four months of unemployment in the lean agricultural period. Although the decline has not been dramatic, downward mobility of the agricultural labour class was experienced as frequently as upward mobility. Indicative of the polarization as a consequence of the commercialization of agriculture in the region is the fact that whereas one-third of the families do not even possess a bicycle, more than 40 per cent of the total sample have a television and 12 per cent possess a motorbike. A television set in the house of a landless labourer or small peasant is still an exception. In the house of middle peasants, it has become a normal sight. For rich peasants, not only a television, but a motorbike and a tractor have become standard assets.[12]

Direct state support benefits, which are routed through the *panchayats* in the form of subsidized loans, house construction allowance, or *gobar* gas installations, have been received by one-fifth of the respondents. Their windfall, however, has not always been enjoyed by them. The non-payment of a bribe while attracting a loan is the exception rather than the rule. Whereas at least twenty persons had paid a bribe, the three persons who reported not to have paid anything agreed that the VLW (village-level worker) is a good man, but they also confided: 'The VLW is my close friend, and so he helped me out'. One of them received money for a horse and horse cart, but since the money was insufficient, he used the cash for other purposes. This turned out to be a common practice, and an advantageous one, even after paying a hefty price in terms of graft money. The alternative avenue for loans is the local moneylender who charges anything between 2 and 5 per cent interest rate per month. Getting a government loan, even if the subsidy element is cut by the intermediary, brings a double benefit, as numerous examples illustrate: a much lower interest rate and less stringency in repayment conditions.[13]

---

[12] One of the motorbikes was actually owned by a near landless Chamar. Two of his brothers are employed with the Government in New Delhi, and with his other brother he looks after one acre of land. His mother, the four wives, eighteen children, one daughter-in-law and one grandchild enjoy the joint income.

[13] One Chamar in 1988 got a loan of Rs 5,000 for a buggy (cart). After deduction of graft money, he was left with Rs 3,000. With a subsidy element of 50 per cent of the loan, he was left with Rs 500 subsidy and an outstanding debt, at

The people who have not received any direct government benefit, can be classified into three groups: those who are not eligible (and may hush up the receipt of subsidized loans), those who have tried to get a loan but who were not willing to pay the price, and those who have made up their mind that it is safer not to risk falling into the debt trap since the officials walk away with the loan subsidy anyway. There is also a fourth group, however: those who did not want to take a loan, and who were presented with a buffalo, ostensibly as a reward for the sterilization under the government programme, but it later turned out they had not only signed for the buffalo but for a loan deed as well.

Concluding Remarks

The survey of close to a hundred members of seven *panchayats* around Sisauli has revealed an interesting and rather simplistic typology. By and large, *panchayats* exist in name only, and most members appreciate their own membership as such: it is a formality only.

The dominance of the *pradhan* has been allowed to grow to such an extent that he is the only hinge on which depends the deployment of state resources and initiatives. The system is allowed to continue as long as it keeps joint business with officials from the higher echelons. Such an important, personalized position, has in none of the cases been shown to lead to more than mere token interventions for the common good. It is the *pradhan* who decides the type and the modalities of the works to be undertaken, with, in the best of cases, a passive involvement of some of the members.

---

11 per cent interest, of Rs 2,500. The pay-off amount to the intermediary is not always as high as in this case. Sometimes, it is only a few hundred rupees, and sometimes it appears not to be exacted. Only apparently though, for the usual procedure is either to extract a high bribe, or to lower the bribe amount and to allow for only one-third subsidy element so that the remainder of the loan subsidy can be siphoned off by the officials. In a few cases, the total subsidy amount has been withheld at the source itself. One Jat, with six acres of land not to be included in the target group, got a loan for a buggy in 1986, but without the one-third subsidy to which he was entitled. His stoic attitude is: 'No subsidy, no repayment'. In one case, a TV-owning Valmiki, upwardly mobile on account of two sons in government jobs, received Rs 4,400 which was meant to be used for the purchase of a buffalo. He should have received double that amount, but apparently the bank was short of money, and he has been promised that the subsidy element would be paid at a later stage. It may not be paid, but even then he stands to gain since he will be repaying the principal at a lower rate of interest, that is if he ever repays at all.

The inactivity of the *panchayat* members is a reflection of the general absence of social involvement. Since politics and activism are the domain of the dominant personalities in the Jat *biradari*, no autonomously-initiated movements can take place. Although on many social issues, the continuation of the caste system and the position of women for example, the ground is shifting, a further shift is blocked by the position of the dominant *thok* leaders. They maintain the traditional social order to the extent that it further maintains caste/class and gender suppression.

The high hopes of some members, including female members, of furthering their human, social, and economic development through the *panchayats* have proven to be out of touch with reality.

CHAPTER 4

Panchayats and Natural Disasters: Floods in Jalpaiguri, West Bengal

Although natural disasters are probably fairly evenly spread over the globe, countries in the Third World seem to be disproportionately disaster-prone. The explanation for the disproportionate suffering from natural disasters by populations in the Third World has to be located in the economic and political environment. Developing countries are usually bereft of abundant technological means, logistic resources and financial reserves, which are important factors in dealing with emergency scenario's. In addition, however, the social texture and its political organization play a pivotal role in preparing against disasters and reducing the ill-effects of disasters. Manor (1993) has made the point that one such political institution, the *panchayats*, 'if they are strong', can be effective instruments. He argues: 'Panchayati raj institutions are not only a foolproof source of early warnings about potential calamities, but also an effective means of ensuring that such warnings do not go unheeded' (Manor 1993: 1019). The judgement is based on a broad assessment of the *panchayats* in Karnataka between 1987 and 1991 when a reasonably effective panchayati system was in place.

Whereas Manor has used the example of Karnataka, we shall test the argument on the basis of evidence from West Bengal. In West Bengal, the inexperienced yet strong and enthusiastic *panchayats* in 1978 were credited by friend and foe for their role in responding to the severe floods which inundated many areas in the delta. In the ensuing years, the foes and some of the friends indicted the *panchayats* for having slid into bureaucratic inertia. This chapter is a study of the *panchayats* in the north-eastern Jalpaiguri district that were struck by massive floods in 1993.

Floods have fairly regularly played havoc with the land and its people in Jalpaiguri. In the 1993 rainy season, the river water went on a rampage once again. The onslaught of the monsoon, the excessive silting of the river beds at the foothills of the Himalayas, and the water rushing from the catchment areas downward led to flash floods and devastation. In the three days following 18 July 1993, against a yearly normal rainfall of around 3,353 mm, the downpour as measured at Hasimara, north of Falakata, was 1,378 mm (District Magistrate 1993: 2). The impact of the floods was devastating, particularly in the Alipurduar subdivision on the border with Assam (Alipurduar, Kalchini, Madarihat, and Falakata blocks).

Reporting on the Floods

Falakata, with its two lakh population taking the brunt of the raging Torsa and Muznai rivers, was one of the most affected blocks. The first flooding started late on 18 July. The next night disaster struck. In the pitch-dark night, as the torrential rain battered the land, a huge wall of water breached the banks at the confluence of two rivers (Teeti and Bagri) in Madarihat block just north of Deogram. Many low-lying areas were under 12 feet of water and the entire block was cut off due to numerous breaches in the road system.

The flash floods on the night of 19 July resulted in the widespread loss of life, crops, and property. Around 200 people were reported dead or missing, and more than 1,00,000 cows and buffaloes were drowned. The road and railway system was breached at several points; bridges and culverts were washed away, and access to the area was initially cut off altogether, hampering the relief operations. According to the official report 80,000 houses were destroyed, and a further 95,000 were damaged. Around 8,00,000 people were marooned for one or more days.

The task was formidable. With torrential rains and raging water swirling over roads and fields, the rescue operations would have been difficult even if the houses were in nucleated villages. Given the scattered clusters of *taris* (usually a couple of houses only), the task of reaching the marooned people was even more daunting. In the absence of any support from the divisional headquarters during the first couple of days (all road connections were cut), all resources and initiatives had to be developed at the local level.

Newspapers reports excelled in drawing the extent of the agony suffered by the people. The reports suggested and confirmed that the political structures failed to respond. Uday Basu (*Statesman* 31 July 1993) was one of the reporters who had gripping stories to tell: 'Village after village in the districts look like the killing fields, devastated by bombardment and savage plunder by some enemy unknown.' Basu had earlier set the tone for most of the reports. Referring to Madhyaranjlibagna in Madarihat, he reported: 'while state government relief is virtually non-existent here, the villagers may be forced to loot whatever they can lay their hands on' (*Statesman* 26 July 1993). Reporters were greatly concerned about the fact that the administration, particularly the *panchayats*, failed to raise to the occasion: 'Indeed, at the critical moment, State Government employees were more busy saving themselves than going to the rescue of the people. While the administration remained inert for five consecutive days, townspeople and clubs and voluntary agencies in the neighbouring Cooch Behar district reached the ravaged areas long before the State Government made its token presence there' (Uday Basu in the *Statesman* 27 July 1993). This report referred to one of the worst affected areas in Alipurduar block, but the situation in other blocks was stated to be similar. As a consequence, 'the starving, homeless people here directed their wrath against the Left Front Government', so much so that one Amalendra Roy in Sishubari village in Madarihat told the reporter about his sense of betrayal: 'Four bridges in this block were blown away and we were marooned for four days. We looked for our Left Front *panchayat* members, but they were nowhere to be seen.' A local Revolutionary Socialist Party (RSP) leader in Sishubari was quoted as saying that 'the politicians failed to activate the Government to raise to the occasion' (*Statesman* 29 July 1993).

The reports and suggestions carried by the *Statesman* are a specimen of what appeared in the *Telegraph*, *Uttar Banga Sambad*, and *Ananda Bazar Patrika*.[1] They all conveyed the message that the administration, particularly the *panchayat* leaders, had become bureaucratized, apathetic, and impervious to the misery of the people. They tended to confirm the assessment by D. Bandyopadhyay (D. Bandyopadhyay 1993; Mukarji and Bandyopadhyay 1993), who earlier was the top civil servant in charge of *panchayats* and land reforms. The gist of his argument is that the *panchayats* have become 'lifeless and sterile' bodies, and that the CPI(M) cadre are the 'new rich' who drive around in 'cars with sirens and red lights'. It would thus seem to be a far cry from the early beginnings of the *panchayats* when, in 1978, massive floods swept over much of Bengal, and the fledgling *panchayats* were galvanized into action.

The official account dismisses the allegation, as reported above, that

[1] I am greatly indebted to Prabhat Datta for having helped me out with the collection and translation of the newspaper reports on the floods, and for having facilitated my visit to the area.

the administration and the *panchayat* system failed to respond to the calamity. Discussions with the Block Development Officer (BDO), the *Sabhapati* and their subordinates suggest that they were informed of the first floods on the night of 18 July, and rushed to a locality in Deogram village where some people had been marooned. Since they 'were smelling the floods', on 19 July at 5.30 a.m., a crisis meeting was called. The administrative staff and the political leaders of the three major parties there and then took the first decisions to cope with the impending disaster. The crisis team took the central decisions and then decentralized the execution to the local teams around the *panchayat* offices.

The official account suggests that the crisis management was organized logically and efficiently: the block leaders co-ordinated and took the major decisions, the local leaders acted as a link with the local committees set up in the villages, and the support of non-governmental organizations (NGO), which started coming in after a couple of days, was directed by the block committee to one of the 64 points where relief work was organized. Even the traders cooperated in the sense that they provided around 2,000 quintal of rice and wheat 'on credit' to the relief efforts. The local transport association offered their lorries and vans for the distribution of the relief materials. Polythene sheets and dry food started coming in from the district headquarters after two days, and were distributed immediately. Private doctors and government doctors co-ordinated their work in three shifts.

Two weeks later, when we first visited the area, the water had receded from the fields, and life seemingly had returned to normal. Boulders and layers of silt in the field were the only apparent signs of the recent floods. Bridges on the *panchayat* roads had been repaired, houses had been (partially) reconstructed, and the first new handlooms had been brought in and had started working. The ongoing relief efforts had been taken over by NGOs, such as the Ramakrishna Mission, and the worst suffering seemed to be over.

Local Assessment

In the official account of the flood relief operations, it was claimed that the relief effort was a cross-party affair, with the marked absence of the BJP. It was also claimed that the rescue and relief operations were performed zealously and efficiently. The official report was obviously at variance with the newspaper reporting which had hit the headlines, and which had suggested that the administration had broken down, and that the *panchayat* leaders had not lived up to their task. In order to decide on the validity of both representations, we decided to sample, during three months starting in October 1993, 251 households in three villages each in two of the most affected *panchayats* (Deogram and Guabarnagar) in Falakata, and a further 50 households in two severely affected villages in Madarihat block just to the north of Falakata (Sishubari and Madhyaranjlibagna). Both villages figured prominently in two newspaper reports referred to earlier.

The random sample of 10 per cent of the households in the selected villages, concentrating on the low-lying areas, included a representative segment of the local population, except for gender. Women accounted for only one-third of the respondents. In terms of other characteristics, the sample more or less reflected the population. In terms of education, more than half of the sample was illiterate.[2] In terms of caste, Brahmins are conspicuous by their virtual absence; slightly more than half of the sample (51.5 per cent) are SC, mainly Rajbansi.[3] The economic position of the respondents reflects the structure of a small peasant society. As many as 52 per cent of the respondents had no land or less than 0.5 acres of land, and 26 per cent had between 0.5 and 2.5 acres; on the other hand, only 4 per cent had more than 7 acres. The households are generally poor, probably just beyond the threshold of starvation but with no means to bargain in the face of disaster. As many as 48 per cent of the households did not have any durables (like cycle, watch, radio, etc.). Most families thus obviously belong to that group of people to which the prediction of Robert Chambers is expected to apply. Chambers (1983: 108 ff.), while describing the 'deprivation trap', isolates five interlocking clusters of disadvantage (poverty, physical weakness, isolation, powerlessness, and vulnerability). Vulnerability (in the face of

[2] On the basis of the Census Reports, a slightly higher percentage could be expected, especially since among women, illiteracy is still depressingly high. Male literacy in Falakata in 1991 had gone up to 49.7 per cent (up from 26.4 per cent in 1971), and female literacy to 27.0 per cent (up from 9.25 per cent). In the eight villages, as per the 1991 Census data, male and female illiteracy stood at 45.9 per cent and 72.1 per cent respectively.

[3] This is a fair reflection of the caste structure in an area where the mainstream caste system has only been introduced in the fairly recent history (Census Jalpaiguri 1951: CXL–CXLV; Das Gupta 1992: 11–26) and where the Rajbansi, although formally SC, have had multi-caste functions and aspirations. Falakata's population in 1991 included 41 per cent SC and 20 per cent ST. In the eight selected villages, the proportion of SC and ST in the population is respectively as high as 59.5 per cent and as low as 3.9 per cent. Of the latter group, which resides mainly on the higher lying tea estates, only a few persons were covered by the sample.

natural disasters, for example) hits the poorer people disproportionately hard: for them it is 'a poverty ratchet' which swallows their last buffers against contingencies and leaves them exposed to usury and the sale of the very last assets in the struggle for survival. Floods of the magnitude as experienced in Falakata should have a devastating effect on these poverty ratchet-prone families.

Another variable which may influence the assessment of relief efforts is the party affiliation. Here again, the sample fairly proportionately reflects the electoral position. In the then just concluded *panchayat* elections, the division of the vote had been as follows. CPI(M): 47.8 per cent, RSP: 14.7 per cent, Congress: 19.1 per cent, BJP: 10.0 per cent and no party preference: 8.4 per cent. Political loyalties had hardly been shifting. Apart from the gains of the BJP (5.9 per cent from Congress and 3.1 per cent from CPI(M), there had hardly been any vote switching as compared to the previous elections.[4]

We have established that the survey was representative of the population. We have not established that the *panchayats* under study were not exceptionally good as compared to many other also-ran *panchayats*. The *panchayats* in Jalpaiguri have been subject to political processes similar to those observed in the rest of West Bengal, namely a combination of growing consciousness and intense party political competition for the coveted seats of local power. The revitalized *panchayat* system endangers the loss of crucial electoral support whenever the sitting *panchayat* leadership forsakes its duties or engages in corrupt practices. The public alertness to the inactivity of *panchayat* leaders explains for the fluctuations in popular support which in the four consecutive elections from 1978 onwards, in Jalpaiguri as well as elsewhere.

The fluctuations in the combined overall support of the Left Front in the block indicate a certain degree of dissatisfaction with the performance of the *panchayats*. The extent of dissatisfaction can be quantified. We have confronted the respondents with a number of statements and have asked them to express their stand, ranging from strong approval

[4] Whereas Madarihat has a slender RSP majority in the *panchayats*, in Falakata eight out of the ten *panchayats* are controlled by the CPI(M). In Deogram, it secured 53.2 per cent of the votes, up from 44.7 per cent in the 1988 elections, mainly because of the collapse of the RSP support. In Guabarnagar, because of the same reason, the electoral support of the CPI(M) expanded from 46.0 in 1983 to 51.5 in 1988, and then dwindled to 48.0 per cent in 1993. As a consequence of the emergence of the BJP, the opposition votes got split, and the *panchayat* remained safely in the hands of the CPI(M).

to strong disapproval. The answers were entered on a scale ranging from 1 to 5, i.e. from strong disapproval to strong approval whereby the middle point 3 indicates no commitment either way. The aggregate picture, in Table 4.1, indicates that people in the *panchayats* under review are reasonably satisfied with the functioning of the *panchayats*.

They are generally satisfied with the changes in the power relations as a consequence of which the poor people are listened to and in the sense that they can approach the administration for help. With only one exception, all respondents backed the statement that poor people these days have a greater say in village affairs, and they generally also agreed that the *panchayat* members can be approached for help. They reject the proposition that the *panchayat* members are corrupt. Congress supporters are less convinced: their overall score (2.29) contrasts with the aggregate score of CPI(M) supporters (1.82), which indicates that practically all supporters of the latter party are convinced that *panchayat* members by and large are not corrupt.

On the other hand, there is some unease that *panchayat* members have become bureaucrats in the sense that they spend more time in running the administration rather than in contacting and organizing the people. The view is slightly more pronounced among BJP and Congress supporters, often actually in areas where the councillor belongs to their own party, than among the supporters of the Left Front parties. The overall score (2.46) is slanted by a relatively large number of respondents who have wished to express categorically their dissatisfaction with this tendency of some councillors. They insist that the *panchayat* leadership

Table 4.1: Opinions on the *Panchayat* Councillors in Jalpaiguri Villages

Panchayat members	A	B	C	D	E	Score
They are corrupt	73	104	58	15	1	2.08
They have become bureaucrats	36	130	50	3	32	2.46
They help only their own people	159	73	–	13	6	1.54
They don't oblige poor people	184	66	–	1	–	1.27

Note: The 251 respondents had five options: A = vehemently disagree; B = disagree; C = no opinion; D = agree; E = definitely agree. The scores were then totalled, and divided by the number of respondents in order to get the average score.

is not corrupt, and is available for help and advice, but that it should take a more active part in mobilizing the villagers. This relates to the mode of functioning, not to the substance. Indeed, when it was suggested to the 251 respondents that the councillors do not help the poor people, only one of them approved, and a vast majority disagreed vehemently. Also with only a view exceptions (a 1.54 score), the villagers disagreed with the statement that *panchayat* leaders only help their own people (see Table 4.1).

The data on relative satisfaction and dissatisfaction with the *panchayat* members suggest that the *panchayat* leadership in the villages hit by the floods have performed reasonably well. This may explain for a coherent response to the disaster, but it may also be the case that they were average performers and that throughout West Bengal, the local reaction to a disaster-like situation by and large may not have been different.

Coming to the more substantive issues, it appears that the *panchayati raj* structure in the aftermath of the floods was equal to the daunting challenge. From the respondents in the sample, the position which emerges is clear: the *pradhan* and the members of the *panchayats*, assisted by scores of other volunteers, hectically moved around their wards to assess the situation and to render aid. If they had not yet done so by themselves, the affected people were taken to the *panchayat* office, to the school buildings or to other buildings where they could stay safe from the water. During the first couple of days, food was provided with consignments 'borrowed' from the traders, and later with supplies coming in from Jalpaiguri. When it had become possible to return to their homes, the uprooted families were sent home each with a small supply of rice, floor, and *chira*. The amounts were small—5 to 20 kg—and were no match to the loss of foodgrains that had actually been suffered. Large families got more supplies, small families got less.

No compensation was paid for cattle, fowl, agricultural tools, and utensils. The damage to houses, on the other hand, in all the cases was looked after. Most of the houses are simple constructions of bamboo mats between bamboo poles supporting a corrugated iron roof. A number of these houses had been torn apart or had been swept away. In each case, within a couple of days, tarpaulin sheets were provided, and two months later Rs 1,000 was paid as compensation. Furthermore, after three months, the three families in the sample which had suffered one death case, were paid Rs 60,000. Two families which had suffered more than one casualty had not yet received the grief money, but were expecting soon.

The information provided by the respondents is twofold. In the first place, the local government personnel (elected leaders, staff, and volunteers organized by them) emerged on the scene of the disaster right at the beginning and organized rescue and relief work throughout. In the second place, relief materials appear to have been distributed evenly, without cuts or discretionary benefits for close supporters.

This actually is the conclusion that has been drawn by the villagers themselves. We have asked the 251 respondents to assess the involvement of their own *panchayat* member in the aftermath of the floods. The aggregate verdict runs as follows: 8.8 per cent was very satisfied; 76.1 per cent were reasonably satisfied; 13.5 per cent were not satisfied; only 1.6 per cent assessed the involvement of the member as worthless. One must remember that close to one half of the sample in each ward supports an opposition party, and is therefore possibly that villagers are not too eager to shower praise on the *panchayat* member. This was particularly the case with people with a (recent) BJP allegiance: they signed for almost half of the dissatisfied people. Since they were not discriminated in the relief efforts, their grudge may stem from political vendetta rather than from dereliction of duty by the *panchayat* member. Disproportionately more dissatisfied respondents were found in Bhutnirgat North which happens to have elected a BJP member.

The population was generally appreciative of the involvement of the local administration and its leaders. They were also appreciative of NGOs (*besarkari*). Where the government finances fell short, the supply and distribution of food by the NGO 'saved us from starvation', as many flood victims stated. The Rotary Club, the Ramakrishna Mission, Ananda Marg, Bharat Sevashram, various youth clubs, traders' associations, etc., came forward at the relief stage and helped, apparently without partiality or propaganda. The block administration directed them so that all wards remained attended.

The newspaper reports had suggested that the impact of the devastating floods could have been allayed if the government had taken timely action when it was informed by the Bhutan Government that it had opened the sluice gates of the Chukha Hydel Reservoir. As one report suggested: 'Entire North Bengal has been rife with the rumour that the devastation was the result of an extremely callous and negligent administration that did not pay heed to the warning of the Bhutan Government' (*Statesman* 31 July 1993). How did the local population explain the floods? The story about the floodgates in Bhutan hardly has any takers. A few persons do blame the government for having neglected the area, and for not having applied enough resources on flood control measures. Relatively more people assign the cause of the floods to a different institution: God. The floods are seen by around 10 per cent of the sample as a punishment by God, a punishment for the sins committed. The floods are seen as the unpredictable wish of God (*bhagwaner itsa, ishwaner itsa*). Most of them are elderly people, particularly Muslims. The vast majority, also among the elderly and also among the Muslims, however, takes a germane attitude. They argue that, given the climatological specificity and given the geographical relief of the area, floods can possibly not be avoided. What can be minimalized, though, is the disastrous and unsettling after-effect of the floods.

After-effects

In order to determine the extent of disastrous and unsettling effects of the calamity, we have looked at two variables: the self-perception regarding economic fortunes and the degree of indebtedness.

Indebtedness usually follows in the wake of natural disasters. The vulnerability of poor households is put to a severe test when utensils and food supplies have been destroyed and the supply constraints force the prices upwards. The survival strategy then necessitates a recourse to the infamous moneylender. A couple of months after the floods, as one element in the survey, in order to assess whether this process had been at work, the financial position of the population was tested. While interpreting the results, a reference should be made to the high number of landless and near-landless (52 per cent of the sample), and to the fact that most of the respondents had been affected by the floods, some of them severely. Nevertheless, it turned out that 43 per cent of the families were free of any debt obligation, and that 36 per cent had borrowed money for productive purposes (from bank, cooperative, or moneylender). In 5 per cent of the cases the families had been supported by friends and relatives, and 16 per cent had to contract non-productive loans from a moneylender. These cases were not necessarily related to the aftermath of the floods: the progress in agricultural productivity and employment in Jalpaiguri is trailing behind that in the southern districts of the state, and poverty, on a limited scale, still forces some households to take recourse to survival loans. Around 9 per cent of the respondents had to approach the moneylender for food consumption loans. These loans relate to families which already under normal conditions find it difficult to scrape through, and occasionally have to borrow money for the bare necessities of life. A safe conclusion is that the natural disaster that struck an already poor population did not have dramatic economic consequences, thanks to the prompt intervention of the *panchayats* and the administration.

In the second exercise testing the after-effects, the respondents were asked to assess their own economic condition in terms ranging from considerable progress to considerable deterioration. This is a subjective statement which may be coloured by various extraneous considerations (for example in order to express satisfaction or dissatisfaction about the political party in power). The aggregate results, however, indicate that such extraneous factors did not seem to interfere much. For example, CPI(M) and Congress supporters produced similar results. As Table 4.2 indicates, only 14.8 per cent of the respondents complained about a worsening in their economic position. A significant majority of the small and middle peasants in the sample claims to have experienced an improvement in the material conditions.

Among the landless and near-landless respondents, the picture is more ambiguous: only 41.2 per cent indicate an improvement in their fortunes, and 19.1 per cent have experienced a worsening scenario. The findings are incongruous with the findings in Birbhum, Barddhaman, and Medinipur (Lieten 1992a, 1993, 1994c), but, given the devastation which had struck the area, they are hardly surprising. In fact, one would have expected a much higher percentage of households under deteriorating circumstances. The study was conducted a couple of months after the floods, which had hit the landless families disproportionately hard: not only do they have less reserves to fall back upon, but by and large, and more importantly, they often have their settlements in the marginal

Table 4.2: Assessment of the Economic Position in the Flood-affected Villages in Jalpaiguri

	Frequency	Big increase	Small increase	No change	Small decline	Big decline
(Near) Landless	131	4	50	52	19	6
Small peasant	66	2	39	18	4	3
Middle peasant	45	6	27	7	5	–
Rich peasant	9	2	6	1	–	–
Total %	100	5.5	48.6	31.1	11.2	3.6

and low-lying areas. It is these areas which took the brunt of the flood waters.

Indeed, among the six cases that experienced a stark decline in their economic position, we find one family which lost two lives, and one family which lost five lives. They included two children, the parents, and the mother-in-law of one of the respondents, who, despite her immense grief, nevertheless declared herself to be satisfied with the way she was looked after by the *panchayat*.

Conclusion

We can conclude as follows. From the representative survey, the conclusion to be drawn is clearly that the *panchayats* in Falakata and Madarihat did not fail the flood-stricken people. Our findings tell much about newspaper reporting. For me, the specific instances has made me utterly weary of newspaper reporting. The reports on the aftermath of the floods were a direct invitation to go and find how bad it was and to find out what had gone wrong. Locally, however, I found a world that was totally at variance with the reports that had appeared in the newspaper and that were supposed to be deontological pieces of what a journalist stands for: to inform the public about disasters and about the wrongdoings of politicians and civil servants.

The newspaper reports at the time of the floods can hardly be considered as reliable. As a consequence of the crisis management by the *panchayat*-centred institutions, the entitlements of the people were not impaired and the natural disaster was not followed by a social disaster. The 'poverty ratchet' did not gobble the poor families. On the contrary, people were reasonably satisfied with the rescue and relief efforts in which the *panchayats*, both the political leadership and the officials, played an important role. In the end, the argument that the *panchayats* have become bureaucratic institutions and therefore have lost much of the zeal, which helped them to deal with the floods in 1978, an argument advanced by many of the detractors, does not hold.

The *panchayats* in West Bengal are an institution of local democracy, which is answerable to the people. In times of calamities, as is shown by the example of Jalpaiguri in 1993, it continues to stand up to the occasion. Given the close electoral contest, political parties are continuously pressed to deliver the goods. This environment helps in times of normalcy as well as in times of calamity.

The findings tell much about the crucial place that the *panchayats* in

West Bengal have occupied as a social institution in the interface between state and the people. As such, it can draw on the enormous state resources, and its technical manpower, and on the voluntary involvement of the people in the area. In times of disaster, it is these people, more than anybody else who are interested in finding solutions as quickly and as efficiently as possible and who are directly knowledgeable about the conditions to be tackled. It is the cooperation of the state (*sarkar*) and civil society (*besarkar*) at its best.

CHAPTER 5

Land Reforms at Centre Stage: The Evidence on West Bengal

In the recent past, policies and debates in the world arena of development thinking have undergone marked changes, and the advocates of land reforms appear outdated and outnumbered. In the not so recent past, however, the scene was different. Montek Ahluwalia and Hollis Chenery, in the early 1970s, in a study promoted by the World Bank and arguing along the lines drawn by its president, Robert McNamara, advocated an alternative economic development policy based on direct government intervention. It included an increased direct investment in the physical and human assets of the poverty groups, with a possible short-run cost to the upper-income groups to be followed by the benefits of the 'trickle-up' effects of greater productivity. They proposed that 'in areas such as land ownership and security of tenure, some degree of asset redistribution is an essential part of any program to make the poor more productive' (Chenery et al. 1974: 49). In the same study, Clive Bell and John Duloy concluded: 'A land reform which breaks the power of large farmers and the rural elite will . . . provide a framework within which public goods and services can be directed to the target groups with minimum leakage' (Chenery et al. 1974: 135).

The above quoted authors very soon and with surprising ease, in a dramatic leap in development theory, turned to the defence of liberalization and the rolling back of the developmentalist state.[1] The call for land reforms was classified as an obsolete Marxist mode of thinking and accordingly disappeared from the dominant agenda.[2] The counter-revolution proceeded in disregard of the historical experience

[1] John Toye (1987) has aptly described this transition towards an emphasis on the benefits of the markets and the danger of controls and structural intervention as the counter-revolution in economic thinking.
[2] Chenery, a vice-president with the World Bank, retracted within a year from his earlier position, and argued that the recognition of the importance of asset distribution 'does not necessarily lead to the Marxist conclusion that the redistribution

in Japan, South Korea, Taiwan, China, and North Korea, the five Asian countries which appear to have accomplished a structural break. It also proceeded in disregard of many non-Marxist approaches that, in the margins, continue to plead for asset redistribution.

In this chapter reference shall be made to some of these contributions. The main purpose is to examine the usefulness of land reforms in the development process. The argument will draw on the developments in the Indian state of West Bengal where the process of land reforms initiated in 1977 has been accompanied by a significant growth in agrarian production and an apparent decline in polarization and poverty.

West Bengal

The necessity of land reforms has been a consistent strand in Indian agricultural studies and in the policy approach. One dominant theme in the approach was the conjecture of an obstructive impact of the socio-political and economic power bloc of landlords-cum-moneylenders on the growth potential, apart from the back-breaking intensity of exploitation.

Land reforms have been on the agenda for many decades. After independence, the various states went ahead with the abolition of *zamindari* and *taluqdari* estates. Reforms that would benefit the landless population and the lowest rank of tenants (sharecroppers) were not undertaken until the late 1950s in the state of Kerala.[3] In West Bengal, India now appears to have a second state which follows the example of Kerala in a number of respects, particularly in its priority to land reforms.

The Bengal region has a long tradition of radical movements and progressive thinkers. From its soil emerged revolutionary nationalist organizations and left-leaning peasant unions. The latter were instrumental in the spread of the *tebhaga* movement after the mid-1940s, a movement of the sharecroppers (see Sen 1972; Cooper 1988). Although the Indian Congress party continued to have a majority in the regional state government, the call for land distribution and tenancy reforms secured a growing political support for the Communist Party

---

of existing assets is the only alternative. Measures to redistribute increments in income and new asset formation are more likely to be acceptable to the majority of the population and less disruptive of development in most countries' (Chenery 1975: 313).

[3] The Kerala experience has been described and analysed in Franke and Chasin (1992), Herring (1983), Nossiter (1982), Tharamangalam (1981), and Lieten (1982).

of India, and later for the breakaway CPI(M), the Communist Party of India (Marxist). The United Front (UF) governments, alliances of Left and centre parties which were formed in the late 1960s, interspersed with Presidents' Rule imposed by New Delhi. In the UF period, land reforms were high on the agenda, but at the same time this exacerbated the political chaos. The economic fortunes of West Bengal reached a nadir. It was a period of growing unemployment, declining real wages, and lagging food production. The combination of economic distress, the appeal of the leftist economic programme, and the high-handed and corrupt Congress government which took over after the UF in the first half of the 1970s, in 1977 led to a political watershed. The Left Front Government (LFG), dominated by the CPI(M), was voted into office, and thereafter swiftly moved to intervene in the agrarian structure.

Early on after it took over the running of the state administration, the LFG implemented the land ceiling legislation and distributed excess land to the landless, it applied the newly introduced tenancy legislation, intended to provide security of tenure and a higher share for the sharecropper, and revitalized the *panchayats* as elected village councils. Since then, antagonists and protagonists have been at loggerheads in the debate on the impact of the land reforms programme on development-cum-justice. In their critique, some of the authors argue that 'nothing substantial has been achieved' (Osmani 1991: 348), and that it was impossible 'to find at least one significant reform program that was successful' (Mallick 1993: 5; see also D. Bandyopadhyay 1993; and Mukarji and Bandyopadhyay 1993). In an interesting article, John Harriss (1993) has posed the question of what has happened in rural West Bengal, and basically made two points. On the one hand, unlike the authors just mentioned, he agrees (with Kohli 1987; Lieten 1992a; Webster 1992) that higher productivity and a more equitable distribution have reversed the process of immiserization. On the other hand, he locates the positive departure in higher wages and in the efficient use of groundwater resources by means of minor irrigation rather than in the policy and implementation of land reforms as such. In this chapter, we shall confront this line of argument. We shall first consider the claim that the West Bengal countryside has witnessed a number of positive departures, before looking at the possible explanations for the same.

Polarization and Depeasantization Reversed

The West Bengal experiment with land reforms is in need of detractors, for a number of things have gone wrong and institutions have been functioning at suboptimal level. Nevertheless, the experiment with land reforms also does show that rural development has taken place. Many indices may be used as reference.

The first observation relates to the trend in agrarian production and in rural employment. Whereas in most Indian states, the percentage of male rural non-workers between 1981 and 1991 has risen (with a national average of 1.5 per cent), in West Bengal the percentage of non-working rural males has dropped significantly from 51.5 per cent in 1971 to 47.9 per cent in 1991. The additional labour force to a great extent has been absorbed by the secondary and tertiary sector, averting a process of agricultural involution.

The meticulous study of Boyce (1987) has marshalled sufficient data to conclude that during the long pre-LFG period, foodgrains production was adrift being almost one percentage point behind population growth, and that roughly 70 per cent of the population was short of the officially defined minimum calorie intake. After the early 1960s through the mid-1970s, growth rates remained abysmally low, despite the introduction of high yielding varieties (HYV). After the accession of the LFG to office, output augmentation of rice and potato is marked (with the exception of two troughs respectively due to exceptional floods and drought). The sharp production (and productivity) increase[4] is indeed a far cry from the situation prevailing between the 1950s and the 1970s when the state shared in the dismal performance of Indian agriculture. The official government statistics suggest that, during the 1980s, foodgrain production has grown at an annual rate of growth of around 6.5 per cent, vastly superior to the 2.7 per cent aggregate growth rate of foodgrains for India. The output figures suggest that during the Seventh Plan (1985–90), West Bengal has come to occupy the first position among all the states in terms of per capita foodgrains consumption and in terms of growth of foodgrains production. Government statistics, using National Sample Survey (NSS) data, indicate that in the 1980s, per capita cereals consumption rose from 473 gm per day to 513 gm when the same declined from 493 gm to 466 gm for the

---

[4] Saha and Swaminathan (1994: A–6) provide separate figures for yield and area growth. Production increase of *aman* rice (the traditional wet season rice) was mainly on account of yield increase: 4.37 per cent annually as compared to only 0.57 per cent between 1965 and 1980. *Boro* rice (the dry season rice, a novelty which came with the HYV technology) shows the opposite trend: a further growth in area (10.3 per cent per year) and a lower yield increase (2.1 per cent).

country as a whole (Chandrasekhar 1993; Saha and Swaminathan 1994).[5]

As a second indicator of the changes in agriculture, a qualitative change, it appears that the process of polarization and depeasantization has been stopped.[6] It is even possible that a process of repeasantization has or had occurred: between 1981 and 1991, West Bengal was the only state where the percentage of (male) agricultural labour in the workforce declined (India: +2.35 per cent; West Bengal: −1.75 per cent). There are possibly other ways of explaining two concurrent developments: a relative increase in the working population and a relative decrease in the agricultural labour force. The interfering factor of course is that the percentage of cultivators has declined (with approximately 2 per cent). The net result, however, was a decline in agricultural labour/cultivator ratio from 0.74 to 0.72.[7]

In respect of two major districts, we have looked more closely into the data as provided by the Census Report. Barddhaman, the Green Revolution district par excellence, and Medinipur, the biggest district in India (exceeding a population of eight million), display similar trends, but repeasantization took place in Medinipur only. During the 1960s, both districts, and rural West Bengal as a whole, were cudgelled by immiserization, polarization, and proletarianization. The percentage of male non-workers increased at an alarming rate (around 6 per cent relative increase over the decade). The number of cultivators in both districts actually decreased even in absolute terms. This does suggest

---

[5] The quality and veracity of agricultural statistics depend on the rigour and honesty of the statistical agency, which is the government itself. S. Datta Ray (1994), an ex-director of BAES (Bureau of Applied Economics and Statistics, the bureau involved in crop-cutting and aggregation of statistics) has raised serious queries on the (defective) methodology involved. Rejoinders to the use of official statistics fall back on the argument of fudging and methodological inaccuracies.

[6] Depeasantization may be said to occur when the ratio of agricultural labour to cultivating peasants (with land ownership or with land in possession) increases. The ratio epitomizes growing landlessness, usually in a stagnant economy since otherwise the growing group of landless families would be absorbed in secondary or tertiary sector and would be replaced by labour-replacing technology.

[7] Only the rural male population has been studied, for two reasons: it makes the 1961 data a bit more compatible and the entry of female agricultural labour is not usually a consequence of depeasantization but rather of an increase in the public participation rate. Ratan Khasnabis (in a communication *A Note on Land Reforms in West Bengal* has calculated that repeasantization, if valid, applies to five districts only).

that in the period before the United Front and definitely before the Left Front came into office, a spurt in depeasantization had occurred. The dramatic increase in the agricultural labour force during the same period has to be qualified in the sense that the 1961 Census uses incompatible definitions.

Inter-census comparison between 1971 and the consecutive census operations do not pose major problems. By the 1981 census, the process got reverted. The data in Table 5.1 strengthen the case for a theory of repeasantization (see Lieten 1990). Such a case would appear to be very strong in respect of Medinipur. The case for Medinipur is obvious: from 1981 to 1991, rural male population grew by 22.2 per cent and the number of cultivators grew by more than 30 per cent. The agricultural labour force on the other hand grew at 6 per cent only. In Barddhaman both cultivators and labourers in the same period increased at levels just above the population growth level but also, unlike Medinipur, with a higher increase of agricultural labour.

From Table 5.2, to which we shall refer later, one can glance from the first column that Medinipur occupies the sixth position in terms of land redistribution, while Barddhaman occupies the eleventh position. The respective position is reflected in the data contained in Table 5.1, and is also reflected in the changing ratio of (male) agricultural labourers to (male) peasants. In Barddhaman, it soared from 0.53 in 1961 to 1.04 in 1971 (which is, in view of Census definitions, an unreliable figure), and then remained at that level (1.04 in 1981 and 1.07 in 1991). In Medinipur on the other hand, after the increase from 0.30 in 1961 to 0.60 in 1971, it dropped to 0.58 in 1981 and 0.47 in 1991.

Table 5.1: Indices of Repeasantization: Barddhaman and Medinipur

	Non-workers Barddhaman	Non-workers Medinipur	Cultivators Barddhaman	Cultivators Medinipur	Agricultural labour Barddhaman	Agricultural labour Medinipur
1961–71*	+34.7	+42.5	−6.3	−4.5	+83.9	+97.5
1971–81	+8.0	+18.1	+19.0	+11.8	+19.0	+5.3
1981–91	+9.7	+13.5	+20.6	+30.7	+24.3	+6.4

Source: Census of India Reports.
Note: *Inter-census comparison with the 1961 data poses serious problems in the sense that the then category of marginal workers is likely to have included a sizeable number of agricultural labourers.

As a third indicator of the notable changes in the West Bengal countryside, the reversal of the process of polarization and pauperization gains significance: poverty remains, but destitution is less apparent. The population below the poverty line, according to the *Economic Survey 1992–93*, based on the NSS data, has shrunk rapidly (from 52.5 per cent in 1978 to 27.6 per cent in 1988), but remains high in the neighbouring states of Orissa and Bihar (44.7 per cent and 40.8 per cent respectively).

The statistical data, provided by contestable survey methods, can be complemented by micro information. Fieldwork in villages in four districts (see Lieten 1992a for Birbhum, 1993 for Medinipur, 1994c for Barddhaman, the previous chapter on Jalpaiguri) indicate that, particularly among the agricultural labourers and small peasants, the opinion, with the exception of the coastal Medinipur villages, is practically unanimous: the economic position has definitely improved (*onek bhalo, mothi bhalo, khub bhalo*, i.e. much better). These micro-level data are in sharp contrast with the data obtained from villages in various regions of Uttar Pradesh (Lieten 1994a; 1994b). Other village studies confirm that agricultural labourers and poor peasants have fully profited from the improvement in agrarian production, although it should be added that this may vary between regions. Neil Webster, on the basis of his elaborate fieldwork, and despite his misgivings about what he perceives as the substitution of consensual politics and management for further structural reforms, has come to similar conclusions. He argues that the poor households have benefited from the agrarian progress, and concludes that 'development without increased polarization is clearly more desirable than the polarization, proletarianization and increased impoverishment that has been experienced elsewhere with the green revolution' (Webster 1990: 207).

Comprehensive Intervention

In the previous section, at a broad level, we have indicated concordance with the assessment by Harriss (1993). In respect of the causal explanations for the described developments, however, discordance props up. Visits to a couple of villages by Harriss led him to conclude that economic progress has been significant, but that there is no evidence to support the view that 'any really significant change' in the agrarian structure has occurred (Harriss 1993: 1246).[8]

---

[8] Whereas macro data may reflect gross generalizations, concealing disparate inter-regional trends, micro level studies may catch the exceptions rather than the rule. Such studies are useful as a means of analysing processes, and not as evidence for or illustrations of aggregate developments. The view expressed by Harriss is not

We shall first argue that the magnitude of land reforms has not been as unimportant as is assumed by Harriss. Really significant changes, the radical transformation and elimination of all bigger landowners which is projected in many maximalist expectations, are constitutionally out of bounds. The LFG has been working within the constraints of what Kohli (1987) has called the feasibility frontier. Summing up an earlier research in the same area, Harriss (1983: 38) had concluded that agrarian reforms had left 'the structure of local power intact'. His figures then and his figures now, however, do suggest that the agrarian structure has undergone changes. The Lorenz curve of land ownership has come appreciably closer to the diagonal, indicating a more egalitarian distribution of land, and *bargadars* have by and large made full use of the legal rights. The data on landlessness (Harriss 1993: 1242) indicate that a process of repeasantization has been operative. The land reforms programme in fact has been a major and in a sense decisively contributing factor. Further the redistribution and barga registration have not been trivial affairs. I shall explain both positions.

The prospect for recovering excess land in West Bengal, under the existing legislation, was considerably smaller than in the rest of India. In the early 1970s, West Bengal took the twelfth position among all Indian states in terms of the quantity of estimated redistributable land, or less than 1.8 per cent of the national figure. Ten years later, it occupied the first place in terms of land declared surplus, with 19.1 per cent of the national achievement. At that time, the state accounted for 1.4 million of a total of 3.2 million land distribution beneficiaries in the country. The state of West Bengal exhibits the unique feature of having seized more land than was originally estimated to be surplus (Lieten 1992a: 133–9). Sunil Sengupta (1981: A-69) has calculated that around 1980, vested land amounted to slightly less than 8 per cent of the operated area of the state, and that the number of actual beneficiaries represented close to one-third of the total number of landless rural households.

In respect of tenancy reforms too, a major breakthrough has been recorded. By 1991, almost 1.1 million acres of land had been assigned to over 1.4 million *bargadars*, a majority of whom belonged to the SC/ST sections. In addition, around 2.5 lakh families have been provided with homestead land. Obviously insufficient to make a living, homestead land is of enormous importance, both to check migration and to provide a secure living space.

---

supported by his own micro level data, which show a perceptible lowering of the Gini coefficient of land ownership.

Mere land ceiling and distribution would almost certainly not have delivered the goods, as the historical record in many countries bears out. The impact depends on numerous factors such as the existing agrarian structure, the objectives to be achieved, the legislation and the methods to be used, the prevailing political structure and the presence of a groundswell of support.[9] At stake, however, also seems to be a definitional problem. Is the reform programme conceived as the enactment of land ceiling and distribution and tenancy arrangements, or does it include an attack on the institutional and organizational constraints on (small) peasant farming? The introduction of the former may actually backfire on the beneficiaries, and on production levels in agriculture in general, if there is not a scaffold public structure of credit, input supplies, infrastructural facilities, and marketing.

In many approaches on land reforms, the concept has therefore been widened to include the ambient factors as well. In essence, land reforms/agrarian reforms include the whole gamut of interventions in the agrarian structure, both in the relations of production and in the forces of production.[10] Doreen Warriner, in her seminal work on land reforms across the globe, refers to this 'integral reform' as 'the American conception of reform' which includes supervised credit and extension, and organized marketing and which amounts to 'the redistribution of income from land' (Warriner 1969: 59, 374). She herself prefers to stick to another definition ('land reform in the strict sense', thus ceiling and tenancy reforms) because the 'American' integral definition is 'a definition of what land reform *ought* to be, rather than of what it generally is' (Warriner 1969: 15). She also uses the more limited definition because the definition in the wide sense blurs the real issue, namely the complicated and politically arduous task of expropriation.[11]

[9] Positive and negative examples are given in Warriner (1969), Radwan (1977); Riad El Ghonemy (1990); Rehman Sobhan (1993).

[10] This dual meaning of land reforms can be found in Todaro's textbook *Economics for a Developing World*: '(the) deliberate attempt to reorganise and transform existing agrarian systems with the intention of improving the distribution of agricultural incomes and thus fostering rural development. Among its many forms, land reform may entail provision of secured tenure rights to the individual farmer; transfer of land ownership away from small classes of powerful landowners to tenants who actually till the land; appropriation of land estates for establishing small new settlement farms; instituting land improvements and irrigation schemes, etc.' (Todaro 1992: 496).

[11] Johnston and Kilby (1975, Chap. 4), do exactly what Warriner had warned against, namely to concentrate on the extension work and to gloss over the tricky business of assets redistribution. They circumvent the issue by subsuming land

The integral definition, framed as 'new-style reform', is advocated by Lipton (1993). After arguing in favour of 'genuine old-style reforms' (redistribution of land to small family farmers) and rejecting the validity of a number of arguments against land transfers (inclusive of the fashionable argument that the inverse relationship of land size and land productivity is no longer applicable), Lipton (1993: 643, 653) elaborates on the additional requirements:

> New-style reform involves burden sharing, credible compensation; combination of small-scale farms with large-scale services to reduce unit transaction costs; and decentralised political and market incentives to small scale farming . . . and region-steered 'rural development' that steers inputs, infrastructure, health and education, agricultural research, and rural non-farm opportunities towards the poor.

Land reforms, as a third factor, usually not focused on by economists, moreover include changes in the superstructural elements. The latter elements are not only 'thrown up' by the basis, but also function as the scaffolding structure, either legitimizing and/or coercing the social agents to accept the exploitative system or to empower all types of peasants to enter the input and output market on broadly equal terms.

The regulation of the labour market is an important aspect, which ideally should correspond with assets redistribution. The changes which have been introduced in the land structure, however small, may have been the necessary, additional, or ultimate trickle which helped to turn the political balance in favour of the landless and near-landless families. The expectation was that in the process agricultural wages would rise. This relationship actually has always been stressed by the CPI(M) as an essential element in solving the agrarian problem. The distribution of land, even of unviable mini-plots, was seen as crucial to strengthening the bargaining power and breaking the feudal bind. Since the scope for recovering excess land was limited and the land hunger remained immense, the policy of land distribution, therefore, was to distribute the land among as many families as possible so as to enable them to walk on two legs: the minimum security of land, and food income from it, would enable them to press for higher agricultural wages. After the Left Front came to power, the average size of the plots allocated to the beneficiaries fell dramatically to hardly one *bigha* (one-third of an acre), down from around three *bigha* in the early years of the LFG.

---

reforms under the 'unimodal strategy of agrarian change', as opposed to the bimodal strategy of crash commercial modernization based on a dualistic size structure.

Causal Factors

Having argued that land reforms were a significant intervention, and that agriculture in West Bengal has witnessed a remarkable upsurge in productivity and multi-cropping, the question to be now addressed is the causality between the two. In other words: has the knock-on effect been caused by old-style land reforms, or by the introduction of infrastructural facilities, particularly of irrigation, as Harriss argues.

Since 1977, initiatives have been under way in the three realms of land reforms: the land distribution and tenancy reforms, the increasing financial allocation to agrarian inputs, and the new local power structure through the *panchayats*. It would be safe, but too simplistic, to suggest that changes in the three realms have contributed their share to the positive departure in agriculture.[12]

When I started my research on West Bengal in 1987, I had a long interview with the peasant leader and Minister of Land Reforms, Benoy Chowdhury. His words did not betray any illusion about a unicausal relationship between land redistribution and increase in productivity, but rather stressed the necessity of the three basic elements in land reforms, namely the improvement of the forces of production, the changing power relations (the hearts and minds of the people), and the change in the relations of production:

We do not have any illusion that a comprehensive agrarian revolution, something which is essentially different from land reforms, can be executed under the present constitution of the country. Those limitations on real agrarian reforms are there, and by imposing ceilings, the system can only be kept within bounds, it cannot be abolished.

What we then try to achieve under the present circumstances is to organise on a mass scale those forces which want to change and go forward. The improvement in the technical forces of production is important, but we are also concerned about the hearts and minds of the people. Most of our peasants are males and females with small pieces of land. If they can be made enthusiastic, if they can feel safe and secure, they will start producing more, but that can only be done if they can produce for themselves and not for others. That is what in this stage, redistribution and barga registration is about.

The crux of the matter, as grasped by Benoy Chowdhury, is that the multiple changes are intrinsic elements of land reforms, at least if land

---

[12] The contribution is not to be assumed as a linear one. As Susan George (1992: xix) has noticed in a different context, a one-to-one causal link between events is very rare in social life: 'Thus we stress feedbacks more than linear connections.'

reforms is understood comprehensively, as I have indicated earlier with reference to Warriner and Lipton. Unfortunately, the maximalist definition of land reforms usually has been collapsed into its exclusive and minimalist meaning: land ceiling and tenancy legislation only.[13] Also the LFG in its official writings often does attribute the increasing productivity to 'land reforms', whereby it is not always clear whether land reforms is used in its inclusive or in its exclusive meaning. However, the *Economic Review 1992–93*, the yearly review by the Government of West Bengal, uses the inclusive meaning of land reforms to explain for the 'structural change' in the agricultural production:

This significant change is a result of the overall development strategy of the Government in the rural areas of the state. The strategy begins with land reforms which involves the distribution of ceiling surplus land to the land-less and the registration of sharecroppers so as to provide them with security of tenure. The beneficiaries of land reforms measures as well as other poor farmers are provided with crucial non-land inputs like credit, seeds, fertilisers, irrigation facilities so as to allow them to participate in productive activity. The strategy is, therefore, not only to redress the inequitable distribution of land holding but also to rely on small and marginal farmers as well as beneficiaries of land reforms measures, to provide the growth impetus to agricultural production. . . . It is this strategy that has brought the poor in the rural areas into the production fold while neutralizing the pernicious hold of the feudal elements over the rural economy. (*Economic Review 1992–93*: 13–14)

The *Economic Review* thus attributes the productivity effects to 'the overall development strategy', starting with land distribution and tenancy reforms and then providing non-land inputs. It then continues by stressing the importance of minor irrigation. Asim Dasgupta, the state Finance Minister, in his *Budget Statement* (1993–4: 13), explicates the same sequence: land reforms and non-land inputs 'based on land reforms'.

Harriss (1993: 1247) turns this sequence around, and actually goes much further in a uni-causal explanation which, probably inadvertently, is akin to the dominant World Bank thinking on the subject: price

[13] In the writings and addresses of Surjeet, for many years the General Secretary of the Kisan Sabha and presently the General Secretary of the CPI(M), the fundamental question of the inclusive meaning of land reforms ('the agrarian revolution') is usually not asked. The following extract is exceptional: 'In the absence of radical changes in the socio-economic structure in the rural area due to the semi-feudal relations, prevalence of caste system, illiteracy, low level of culture and religious obscurantism, it is unthinkable to change the face of our degraded rural life and unleash the productive forces in the agrarian sector' (Surjeet 1992: 159).

incentives and improved technology as the instruments of successful agrarian trickle-down strategy. He is led to the conclusion 'that the Left Front government's classical preoccupation with agrarian reform laid to a misplaced emphasis in its agrarian policies, and that the expansion of production by means of improved technology and price incentives has been more important than it, or its apologists, are yet prepared to concede'. Since the importance of land reforms in itself is dismissed, the crux of his argument is thus clearly that the reforms cannot have been instrumental in increasing agricultural production. The commendable production performance of West Bengal at the macro level as well as at the micro level is therefore largely on account of its policy on minor irrigation facilities. The causality leading to higher productivity is stated by Harriss (1993: 1243) in the following words:

> The point that I think does emerge is that the successful change which is observed [in the village] cannot be shown to have followed at all directly from the agrarian reform programme of the Left Front government. . . . Almost certainly the upward pressure on agricultural wages which has been maintained . . . has been more important. More important too, has been the expansion of the productive potential through the development of groundwater irrigation.

The LFG in 1977 had a go at the rural political structure, relations of production, and forces of production. At one stage, it was faulted for not paying enough attention to technology (e.g. Westergaard 1987). Now, it is suggested that West Bengal has concentrated on technological inputs, particularly on minor irrigation, and that land distribution and tenancy reforms as such did not have a significant impact. The next section attempts to give some indication as to why the emphasis on minor irrigation is probably misplaced. The argument is not that irrigation is not important; it surely is. The argument is rather that the importance of irrigation depends on the nature of the agrarian system which has been put in place.

Disaggregating the Argument

On the basis of aggregate figures for West Bengal as a whole, it is manifestly difficult to prove or disprove anything. What we have done, therefore, is to disaggregate the figures to the district level. Since the districts themselves are mega-entities, such an exercise leaves much to be desired. As a stopgap operation, it does provide some answers though. One district, 24 Parganas, which has now been split up into two separate districts, has been excluded from the exercise.

For each of the districts, crucial variables have been collected. The variables relate to the redistributed land, the registered barga land, the use of fertilizer, the annual groundwater draft, all of them as a percentage of the cultivated area, as well as the cultivable area as a percentage of the total area. A second set of variables relates to the increase of production and productivity of cereals in the period 1989–92 over 1971 and 1981 respectively. All states have then been ranked in descending order. One of the weaknesses of the multivariate comparison is that whereas the second set of rankings refers to the dynamism in comparison with a benchmark, the first set registers the ranking at a particular point of time only. The results have been summarized in Table 5.2.

The ranking in Table 5.2 shows that a correlation is difficult to establish. Any protagonist of the exclusive minor irrigation argument

Table 5.2: Ranking of West Bengal Districts in Terms of Land Redistribution, Technological Inputs, and Productivity Changes

	A	B	C	D	E	F	G	H	I
Barddhaman	10	9	11	3	8	6	10	4	3
Birbhum	9	2	6	7	3	13	8	9	5
Bankura	8	13	12	8	4	9	3	10	10
Medinipur	6	14	10	6	5	7	4	6	9
Howrah	14	10	9	9	6	3	1	11	1
Hugli	13	6	7	11	14	10	13	2	2
Nadia	12	11	2	1	2	1	2	1	4
Murshidabad	11	12	3	4	9	4	11	3	7
W. Dinajpur	4	7	1	5	1	8	6	7	11
Malda	3	3	4	2	10	2	7	5	6
Jalpaiguri	1	1	14	14	13	14	14	12	13
Darjeeling	2	8	8	10	7	5	5	14	14
Cooch Behar	7	4	5	13	11	12	12	8	8
Puruliya	5	5	13	12	12	11	9	13	12

Notes: A. Percentage redistribution of land as per cent of cultivable land;
B. Percentage registration of barga land as per cent of cultivable land;
C. Percentage of cultivable land to total land mass;
D. Productivity cereals, increase over 1971;
E. Productivity cereals, increase over 1981;
F. Production cereals, increase over 1971;
G. Production cereals, increase over 1981;
H. Annual irrigation groundwater draft per hectare;
I. Fertilizer application per hectare.

would tend to jump on the figures of Nadia, a district which has not experienced the effects of land distribution and barga registration. It nevertheless had the best performance in terms of production and productivity growth in the period 1971–91. It also had the highest groundwater draft. Hugli, the district with the second highest groundwater draft, on the other hand, in comparison with districts with a much lower irrigation cover-age, had a quite dismal productivity and production increase. As a caveat, it should be remembered that we are comparing the production index with the irrigation intensity, and not with the irrigation index. A benchmark comparison of productivity and irrigation increase could possibly reveal more correlation, in the sense that irrigation in Hugli has possibly grown slower in comparison with other districts.

West Dinajpur, Darjeeling and Malda, on the other hand, with a good performance in land redistribution, have done much better than the fertiliser and groundwater use would suggest. The case of Jalpaiguri, however, puts the land ceiling and distribution argument in disarray: despite its highest ranking order in terms of land redistribution and barga registration, in terms of its production and productivity performance, it has landed at the bottom of the list, neatly correlating it with its position on the irrigation and fertiliser ranking.

The level of irrigation is surely expected to have an impact on both productivity and the expansion of multi-cropping. By and large, the districts which traditionally have had the highest irrigation intensity appear to be doing better than districts with a lower irrigation intensity. Nadia and Jalpaiguri, the districts at the top and at the bottom of the production increase statistics, already in the early 1970s were situated at the two extremes of irrigation coverage: 'irrigation intensity was highest in Nadia, which had the greatest reliance on tubewells, and lowest in Jalpaiguri, which had the greatest reliance upon canals' (Boyce 1987: 175). Inter-district comparison, however, also shows a wide variation in the impact of irrigation. Districts like Hugli and Murshidabad, although they have at least three times more groundwater draft per hectare than West Dinajpur, Medinipur, Barddhaman, and Cooch Bihar, have not outdistanced these districts in terms of agricultural production.

If a correlation is to be found, the best fit could possibly show up between the increase in production/productivity and the availability of (good) cultivable land (column 3). If Nadia has done so well in comparison with the other districts, the simple explanation may well be that (small peasant) agriculture has flourished in the extremely fertile *nadia*, the river bed. This in fact would establish that the state policy has helped the intrinsic productivity of the land to develop. Tillage of the less fertile soil in many areas of Jalpaiguri or Puruliya, for example, is an altogether different cup of tea.

The quality of land and the broad agro-climatic conditions may thus turn out to act as major determinants of agrarian growth. Growth differentials then relate to micro-climatic and micro-geological variations, within the new elan engineered by the inclusive land reforms approach. The inference that productivity increase is promoted by the availability of irrigation facilities follows from the integral definition of land reforms: assets redistribution without a corresponding supply of agro-inputs is as ineffectual as the public expenditure on irrigation facilities without a corresponding shift in the land and power relations. The latter statement will be followed up in the next section.

Irrigation

The inter-district differences do not establish a case for any uni-causal relationship between irrigation and productivity increase. The inter-state comparisons fail to do so as well. If minor irrigation is the panacea, then the sky would have been the limit for the states surrounding West Bengal, where on the basis of the public outlay on irrigation, a relatively higher agricultural growth rate should have occurred. In the last decade, however, West Bengal has recorded appreciably higher growth rates.

Table 5.3, brings together the expenditure on irrigation during the Sixth Five Year Plan (1980–5), the Seventh Five Year Plan (1985–90) and the budgeted allocations for the Eighth Five Year Plan. West Bengal stands out by its low share in irrigation expenditure during the Sixth Plan and during the Seventh Plan (2.2 per cent of all Indian states) as well as in allocations for the Eighth Plan.

The share of West Bengal in the national budget for irrigation, somewhat with the exception of minor irrigation, is well below its share in population, agricultural land, and agricultural production. The share is also well below West Bengal's share in fertilizer consumption, which has sharply grown from about 3 per cent around 1970 to about 6 per cent of the national consumption in the 1980s. Finances for irrigation facilities through private sources could have made up for the deficient public resources. However, the possibility is more virtual than real. If the term loans of one of the major financing bodies, the National Bank for Agriculture and Rural Development (NABARD) is used as an

Table 5.3: Irrigation Expenditure during Seventh and Eighth Plan

	Major irrigation			Command area			Minor irrigation			Total
	VI	VII	VIII	VI	VII	VIII	VI	VII	VIII	VI–VIII
Bihar	709	1,333	1,927	19	28	71	208	284	1,021	5,600
Orissa	330	591	2,614	9	12	33	96	183	389	4,257
UP	920	1,245	2,599	73	91	90	293	589	400	6,300
Bengal	166	234	380	5	5	18	81	86	370	1,345
India	7,449	10,979	22,310	559	929	1,679	1,729	2,959	5,662	54,255

Note: Actual Expenditure during the Seventh Plan and allocations for the Eighth Five Year Plan in Rs Crore.
Source: Government of India, Planning Commission, Seventh Five Year Plan 1985–90, Vol. II: 85–93, and Eighth Five Year Plan 1992–7, Vol. II: 73–91.

indicator, the conclusion is that West Bengal gets only half of what it would get proportionately on the basis of its rural population and land mass (Reserve Bank of India, various years). Because of these lean financial flows, it is not surprising that in terms of operating electrical pumpsets, the state's record is unimpressive: close to 40,000 sets in 1985, less then 1 per cent of the national stock (*The Seventh Five Year Plan 1985–90*, Vol. II: 164). Also in terms of electricity consumption for agrarian purposes, West Bengal in 1989 accounted for only 0.66 per cent of the national aggregate (GOI 1992: 122).

Since Uttar Pradesh, Bihar and Orissa have spent much larger amounts of money on large-scale as well as minor irrigation, without the desired results in terms of production increase (except for western UP of course), the explanation must go beyond the terms of the irrigation policy.

The explanation may be seen in terms of the political economy of corruption. In UP, Bihar, and Orissa, much of the money, apart from lining the pockets of contractors, administrators, and politicians, may have been spent on irrigation projects which were badly planned, shoddily constructed, and indifferently maintained. In that case, it is arguable that the land reforms programme in West Bengal (i.e. the integral land reforms, inclusive of the new power constellation) has been instrumental in turning the scales from a political economy of corruption to a political economy of rural development. In this political economy, the pivotal role in overseeing the irrigation works and in planning additional irrigation through a planning-from-below model is played by the democratically elected village *panchayats*. In these village councils, the representatives from among small peasants and land reforms' beneficiaries, by and large have an important input.

Early on it was decided to induce shallow tubewells into government ownership 'and to ensure a socially controlled utilization of the irrigation water' (*Economic Review* 1980–1: 15). Local beneficiary committees were constituted with representatives from the *panchayat* in order to make the water available to the small peasants and sharecroppers. In this way, it has increased the irrigation facilities manifold, and has secured poor peasants' access to irrigation. In other words, in the terminology of Amartya Sen, it has created collective endowments and has institutionalized the individual entitlements.

The explanation for input/output difference with the neighbouring states may also be seen in terms of appropriate irrigation technology. The higher expenditure on irrigation in the surrounding states may have created irrigation facilities which, for financial or political reasons, in practice have remained accessible to a small layer of peasants only. Most minor irrigation facilities remain in private hands, borrowed under the refinance facilities of NABARD, and by and large are likely to be accessible to richer peasants only. The LFG appears not to have put all its eggs in the groundwater draft technology (shallow tubewells), but has rather concentrated on the more cost-effective and labour-intensive tank excavation.

The difference in approach and the difference in outcome with Bangladesh testify to the importance of having a comprehensive intervention in the factors of production as well as in the relations of production. Despite the considerable financial outlay and despite all kinds of international expertise, *aman* and *aus* production (the rainy season rice) in the twin country has hardly grown; the increase has come from additional cropping in the dry season (*boro* rice and wheat). Overall, food production has barely grown faster than the rate of growth of the population (Palmer-Jones 1992; Chowdhury 1993).

The recent Bangladesh findings confirm the analysis of a somewhat earlier period by James Boyce. On the basis of some of his statistical exercises, Boyce (1987: 162–200), concluded that water, rather than fertilizers or HYV, was the 'leading input', but also that the correlation was positive with yield but only moderate with cropping pattern intensity. Boyce, unlike Palmer-Jones, after having argued that irrigation is the leading input, then went on to look at the institutional barriers which, he concluded, had acted as a break upon irrigation and water control. Apart from problems of the indivisibility and the disarticulation of the technology, the inequality in the agrarian structure has posed significant constraints:'Evidence from a number of sources, relating to a number of irrigation techniques suggested that the pace and direction of water control development in the region have been distorted by these features of the agrarian structure' (Boyce 1987: 246). Since the cropping pattern, also because of the continuing tenancy arrangements, has not intensified as much as in West Bengal, the irrigation infrastructure has not produced optimal affects. The inefficiencies in irrigation and water control were established to be associated with the larger farm size and sharecropping, and are therefore expected to persist with the unchanging agrarian structure.

The institutional mechanisms which would allow for a full utilization of existing and future irrigation assets, Boyce (1987: 248) concluded, require a reduction in inequality in the agrarian structure (as) a precondition for the successful development of such institutions. A small farm structure, however, is clearly not, in and of itself, sufficient to resolve inefficiencies of this type. The above analysis thus points to the central importance of institutional changes to achieve collective action in water control. It is here, rather than in land distribution per se, that the greater potential for productive gains from agrarian reform on the region may lie.

Concluding Remarks

The debate on the primacy of land redistribution versus technological inputs cannot possibly be clinched. Examples of successful agrarian developments without land reforms and examples of floundering post-land reform farming have given plenty of ammunition to the counter-revolution in (rural) development thinking. In the process, the plea for land reforms has largely been silenced.

Nevertheless, broad choices do necessitate judgements: the choice between a trickle-down and an up-ending strategy, or between a bi-modal and an uni-modal strategy. The maldistribution of assets tends to hamper rapid development and provides a hurdle to democracy and human development. In countries with a high Gini coefficient, the 1993 *UNDP Human Development Report* (p. 28) has argued, 'there can never be true participation in the rural areas without far-reaching land reforms'. This is also the position of Samir Radwan of the International Labour Organization (ILO). Reformulating his earlier plea for land reforms as a powerful means for ensuring equitable growth (Radwan 1977), distribution of assets is considered as necessary but not sufficient: skill endowment, the provision of inputs and optimal pricing policies are the required complementary measures (Radwan 1993).

The World Bank has abandoned this line of thinking. An almost collective paradigmatic adjustment has followed in development sociology and development economics. John Harriss, by no stretch of imagination an advocate of 'the counter-revolution', suggests that the issue in rural development, in the case of West Bengal, is irrigation rather than redistribution of assets. We have argued against such a position, not in order to question the importance of irrigation, but in order to indicate the close relationship between the (changes in the) agrarian structure and the efficiency of the inputs.

Land reforms, in the inclusive, comprehensive sense, has been at the basis of the West Bengal scenario. It has included a minimal restructuring of the agrarian assets and the relations of production, a technologically appropriate upgrading of the forces of production, including irrigation, and a political realignment which has given small peasants more freedom of operation and a direct access to the technological inputs. There is sufficient evidence to conclude that the approach has worked, with 'water as the leading input' in the way Boyce (1987) had formulated it.

CHAPTER 6

West Bengal after a Quarter Century of Land Reforms

Politically, the Indian state of West Bengal in many respects during the last quarter of a century has witnessed something that in political terms is quite close to a miracle of sorts. After the turbulence, violence, repression, chaos, and deepening of poverty in the 1960s and 1970s, from 1977 onwards, the state in eastern India with around 65 million inhabitants, has been administered by one government alliance (the Left Front Government, LFG hereafter) and by one chief minister, Jyoti Basu.[1] In the 2001 assembly elections, the LFG was returned with a comfortable majority for the sixth consecutive time. The other Indian states, and the federal government, during the same period have witnessed a perennial indulgence in the politics of coveting chairs, with governments being overthrown or being radically reconstituted. The stability in West Bengal is a pointer to an underlying process of economic change that may not have been fully understood. The stability in the institutions, with more than a dozen successfully conducted local, state and national elections, is in itself a reflection of stability and gratification in the social texture below.

Contrasting Arguments

The stability, and the apparent placidity that can be observed in the villages, demand an explanation that goes beyond past discourses. Much of the discussion on West Bengal in the past has been partisan. Scholars have had either a positive or a negative disposition, and unattached scholarship has been rare. Studies on West Bengal were confronted with major paradigmatic choices. Since the major partner in the government called itself the Communist Party, and indeed also had a Marxist way of

---

[1] Prior to the 2001 elections, 84-years' old Jyoti Basu was replaced by Buddhadev Battacharya, for a long time the second man in the cabinet.

defining its political programme, the stand of scholars *vis-à-vis* 'communism' was one of them. Some scholars lambasted the Left Front Government (LFG) from the right (e.g. Mallick 1993), but more scholars have done so from within a leftist and even Marxist point of view. They have questioned the tactical line and the success of implementation and have reprimanded particularly the leaders as the new government *babus* of the CPI(M) as corrupt, revisionist, managerialist, and the class-collaborationist leaders.[2]

These studies are dated, and fail to explain the long-standing stability of a government that constantly draws the ire of the media and of the federal government. One major publication that has come out recently unfortunately does not provide such an explanation; it rather appears to be on the old polemic track of attempting to show how inefficient and how power-hungry the LFG has been (see Rogaly et al. 1999). The book is an interesting collection of papers resulting from a workshop that was meant to compare the agrarian developments in West Bengal and Bangladesh.[3] Another understanding is that the golden years of growth in West Bengal in the 1980s are over and that the phenomenon is now one of 'the plateauing of the rice production after 1991–92' (Rogaly et al.: 13).

The book on *Sonar Bangla?* (which means Golden Bengal?) is critical of the West Bengal policy regime of land reforms and decentralization.[4] This is very much the case with the four contributions that deal with local politics in West Bengal. There are four ways in which the LFG, actually the CPI(M), is characterized. The more moderate view

---

[2] Particularly the pages of *Economic and Political Weekly* had poignant contributions by Rudra (1981), Khasnabis (1981), and others. See also Baruah (1990) and Webster (1992).

[3] The comparison proceeded from the understanding that Bangladesh was growing as much as West Bengal, and that the land reform policies of the LFG in West Bengal thus appeared not to be significant as a causal factor Agriculture in Bangladesh, however, grew with 2.79 per cent, 2.32 per cent and 0.37 per cent in the 1970s, 1980s and early 1990s respectively, which is just above the population growth rate. Gazdar and Sunil Sengupta in their article on West Bengal take 1983–4 as the base year and calculate a 4.3 per cent growth, which is double the Bangladesh figures. The book also has a long article by Shapan Adnan. He pointedly reverts to the question of the semi-feudal hold on agriculture in Bangladesh, and explains why technological modernization has failed to bring about a solid structural change.

[4] A notable exception is Sugata Bose in the same volume who, after an historical overview of Bengal agriculture, praises the achievements in production increase and even more so in the decrease in poverty.

(Webster) is to attribute to the party positive initiatives and considerable progress but to associate this with the earlier stage of agrarian intervention. The longer the party is in power, the more ossified, bureaucratic and insensitive it becomes, and the more is there a need for a third force. Another argument is that some real changes have occurred in class relations, but that traditional village politics, which is the politics of 'dol' (groups, factions), are still dominant (Glyn Williams). Engelsen Ruud argues that all poor people have experienced enhancement in their social position, economic well-being and political representation, but that the beneficiaries are usually selected on the divisive basis of caste. Even more critical, in a sense an effort to characterize the CPI(M) as a party which does not have any concern for poor people, is the contribution by Dwaipayan Bhattacharyya. The CPI(M) is projected as defending the interests of the rich peasants. It is the party of 'middleness', and it has not only deradicalized itself but it is also actively fostering deradicalization in the countryside. It is, as Rogaly et al. (1999: 24, 29) summarizes, a party that in comparison with other states in India has done more 'to change the structure of property relations in favour of less well-off people (though not necessarily leading to exceptional achievements in terms of well-being . . .)'. But at the same time, it has created the following situation: 'At least as far as the villages were concerned the new 'big men' in rural West Bengal—as elsewhere in rural India—were the middle and rich peasantry. This trend is quite in line with the rise of rural 'backwards' in Bihar, UP, Tamil Nadu and elsewhere in India.'

Moreover, according to the same author (Rogaly 1998: 2731), class struggle by agricultural labour against the entrenched interests of the rich peasants, has been contained by a strategic alliance that the CPI(M) leadership has carried out. It is an alliance based on local patron-client ties, which in vertical terms is controlled by a party leadership that 'is mainly Hindu *bhadralok* urban middle class. The party itself has power which is disassociated from its class character—it is a powerful network, almost a club, and a provided of jobs for the boys.'

The point of debate is not that West Bengal politics cannot possibly be analysed in negative terms. On the contrary, the aspects which Webster, Williams, Ruud, and Rogaly have drawn attention to are important for an understanding of village politics and for a correction in the degeneration of pro-poor policies. There are, however, some factuals that should also be included in an assessment of the LFG period. The political stability in West Bengal is likely to be related to a positive record of the government, particularly in respect of the well-being and the well-feeling of the poor. If a 'hindu bhadralok middle class' was in power with some populist measures for the poor in a patron-client relationship, the political stability, with numerous local, state and national elections over a period of 25 years, would be difficult to explain. It is more likely that the outstanding stability that is characteristic of the state is associated with the progress that has been made in many fields of economic and human development, particularly in the 1990s. This chapter intends to elaborate on these developments.

A somewhat more unattached treatment of the case of West Bengal can now be envisaged. In my analysis, I shall keep in mind the 'feasibility frontier' (see also Kohli 1987). The LFG is not an autonomous government, unimpeded by the Indian Constitution and by the relative strength of class forces and forces of production. The terms dictated by the constitution, and monitored by the federal government, by the President and by the Supreme Court, are obvious. Even in terms of the Concurrent List, which includes items like land reforms and labour relations, on which both the central and provincial governments can legislate, the central laws get precedence over the state legislation.

The idea of feasibility performance, and the assessment of the LFG for what it has done, and not for what it ideally could have done and ethically should have done, underlies the treatment in, for example, Bergman (1984) and particularly in Kohli (1987). Kohli (p. 96) disregards the class nature of states and the limits on government action following from this. He analyses governance in terms of political willingness, in terms of a regime weakness or strength to implement its programme. West Bengal, he argues, had all the elements underlying the capability of a government to introduce redistributive changes:

A coherent leadership; an ideological and organizational commitment to exclude the propertied interests from direct participation in the process of governance; a pragmatic attitude toward facilitating a non-threatening as well as predictable political atmosphere for the propertied, entrepreneurial classes; and an organizational arrangement that is simultaneously centralized and decentralized. The communist government of West Bengal, more social-democratic than communist in practice, possesses most of these attributes. (Kohli 1987: 10)

It is, states Kohli (1987: 111), because all these characteristics were present that, despite the weaknesses, omissions, and failings, and 'whereas many others in India have paid lip-service to these redistributive goals, the CPM alone has made systematic and impressive beginnings towards accomplishing them'. In the mid- and late 1980s, the progress looked impressive, for a number of reasons.

In the first place, there had been an impressive spurt in agrarian production and productivity. The departure was in stark contrast with the period of feudal stagnation preceding it,[5] but on the other hand was also explainable in terms of the low benchmark that crop production could be compared with. In the second place, there was the restoration of democracy which, if one recalls the dark period of semi-fascist rule that the state went through in the decade before 1977, has been a great performance. Illegality, the naked use of force, corruption, and lack of transparency, were the rule in all institutions of the state, and one of the major promises of the LFG was to undo the crumbling of the state institutions. In terms of restoring law and order, and in terms of recommissioning the civic amenities and substantially reducing corruption, the state has done fairly well.[6] In the third place, it has done a superb job by recharging the *panchayats* as democratic institutions at the village level. Although much more can be done in terms of a real devolution of power from the state level downwards, a unique achievement is on record.[7] The village councils are not instruments of local empowerment and of 'village democracy', and under the umbrella of the modern state will never be, but as institutions, they have become the lowest hinge between the rural people and the state infrastructure. By their democratic and disciplined functioning, they have helped to make the state institutions and the benefits of the state programmes transparent and accessible to the people. The active involvement of women, who since the early 1990s have occupied one-third of the seats and one-third of

[5] Semi-feudalism as the inhibiting factor in agriculture in West Bengal has been studied extensively, for example in Rudra (1992) and Boyce (1987).

[6] As one who has lived in Calcutta and has moved through the countryside in the 1970s, I must agree with the picture drawn by Basu (1997: xi): 'Poverty and destitution stalked the countryside. Civic amenities were under tremendous stress. Power failure was a daily occurrence. Educational institutions were on the verge of ruin. Anarchy was let loose in the academic sphere.'

[7] In Chapter 1, I have compared West Bengal with Uttar Pradesh (see also Lieten 1996a and Lieten and Srivastava 1999). A comparison with the neighbouring states (Bihar, Orissa, Madhya Pradesh, Assam) would present an equally sharp contrast. Kohli (1987: 113) had the following astute observation to make: the *panchayat* membership 'has never been so free of landlord and rich-peasant domination as in contemporary West Bengal. The CPM has thus achieved what no other Indian political force has been able to achieve as yet, namely, comprehensive penetration of the countryside without depending on large landowners.'

the village mayorships, has brought women onto the public stage. In the fourth place, agrarian progress had combined with a decreasing degree of polarization both in terms of land ownership and in terms of the level of income. Agrarian reforms had not had a radical effect on the redistribution of land (only around 8 per cent of the operated area of the state), but it nevertheless had benefited close to one-third of the previously landless households. Unlike in the rest of India[8] where a process of depeasantization was on, many areas in West Bengal have witnessed a process of repeasantization (Lieten 1990). The distributed plots were small, but they helped to increase the bargaining power of agricultural labour households. As a consequence, agrarian wages began to rise in real terms, and in the period from around 1980 to the early 1990s, the rise actually may have been higher than in all other states (Rawal and Swaminathan 1998: 2599). Together with an increasing labour participation rate, and with more income remaining in the hands of the *bargadar* (sharecroppers), rural poverty declined. Declining poverty, as the fifth feature, combined with improving human development indices as the sixth feature of the West Bengal rural scenario, but, at least up to the early 1990s, progress in the latter respect did not seem to be spectacular.

Higher production, an accountable and responsive administration, village democracy, less polarization, less poverty, and better health and access to education constitute a copious basket of positive departures. Other features of social, economic, cultural and political life in rural West Bengal could be added, but at the same time three questions arise.

The first question has been put forcefully by the editors of *Sonar Bangla?* (Rogaly et al. 1999). Has the progress sustained or has there been a significant slowdown in the food production increase and in the poverty decline? The second question relates to West Bengal's performance in comparison with the other Indian states. The third question relates to the performance in terms of the Human Development Index (HDI).

Agrarian Growth

With respect to agrarian growth, and of economic diversification in general, West Bengal has done exceptionally well. The position of West Bengal as a matter of fact has risen dramatically from somewhere at the

---

[8] N. Bandyopadhyaya (1988: 25) notes that whereas West Bengal has only 2.88 per cent of the cultivable area of the country, it accounts for a fifth of the land declared surplus, in spite of the fact that the average size of the plots was considerably smaller. See also Ghose (1983: 91–137).

bottom of the rank order of the Indian states to a position close to the top. In terms of per capita growth of Net State Domestic Product (NSDP), it topped the list of states with 6.88 per cent in the period 1991–8, ahead of Maharashtra (5.14 per cent) and Gujarat (4.81 per cent). It is interesting to note that the surrounding states (Orissa: 0.08 per cent, Bihar: –1.70 per cent, Assam: 1.21 per cent) did distinctly worse.[9]

In the 1980s, West Bengal, with a per capita growth rate of 2.64 per cent only, had not been able to keep up with the national average. As a matter of fact, since Independence, the ranking of West Bengal had been slipping: from fifth position in 1960 and seventh in 1970 to the twelfth position in 1980 and the sixteenth position in 1990 in terms of the NSDP (Ghosh and De 1998: 3040). By 1995, it had returned to the eleventh position, and it does seem that the state is slowly recovering the ground that it lost during a protracted period of secular decline. This breakthrough gains in importance when we add that the regional disparities in India have accentuated during the 1990s, and that the backward states, such as Bihar, Orissa, Uttar Pradesh, and Madhya Pradesh, have witnessed a worsening of their position. Of the backward states, only West Bengal appears to have narrowed the gap with the national average. N.J. Kurian (2000: 542) notes that this has occurred in a situation in which the share of manufacturing in the state has come down from 24.4 per cent of NSDP in 1980–1 and 19.9 per cent in 1990–1 to only 14.1 per cent in 1996–7. The major contribution to the growth in NSDP thus appears to have come from agriculture, which has a share of around 30 per cent in the NSDP.

Let us therefore look closer at agriculture. Agrarian growth in West Bengal has been consistent since the late 1970s, after a very long period of stagnation in the preceding period, a stagnation that has been well documented. Boyce (1987: 141) in a superb marshalling of evidence has calculated that from Independence up to 1980, the rate of growth of per capita output was—0.69 per cent, mainly because of a very sharp decline until the mid-1960s. In a review of some of the recent studies

---

[9] Personal communication by Ravi K. Srivastava. Ahluwalia (2000: 1638) has calculated the growth in per capita Gross Domestic Product over the same period differently: Gujarat (7.57 per cent), followed by Maharashtra (6.13 per cent) and Bengal (5.02 per cent). The World Bank (2000: 35) has calculated the real per capita income growth for the period 1990–7 (in descending order): Gujarat 8.6 per cent; Maharashtra 7.4 per cent; Tamil Nadu 5.2 per cent; West Bengal and Kerala 4.9 per cent; Madhya Pradesh 4.1 per cent; Rajasthan 3.9 per cent; Andhra 3.8 per cent; Punjab 2.8 per cent; etc.

on agrarian growth, Amiya Kumar Bagchi (1998: 2975) has concluded that the 'agricultural *impasse* has ended, at least for a decade or more, in the 1980s, and that positive changes in the ratio of growth were associated with an amelioration of the living conditions of the poor in the state'.

Growth rates in the 1980s indeed were calculated to be impressive. West Bengal, once the metaphor of stagnation, made it into the top league among Indian states.[10] Statistical fudging, for example the choice of a low base-line year for comparison, may make the progress look more impressive than it actually has been. Sengupta and Gazdar (1997: 165) have calculated a growth rate of 4.3 per cent over the period 1983–91. The high estimates of a 6.4 per cent annual growth between 1981 (an exceptionally bad crop) and 1991 by Saha and Swaminathan (1994) have got a cynical reception. Some of the observers accordingly have tried to explain the apparent high growth rates in West Bengal in terms of such fudging. They have also argued that after the sharp increase in the 1980s, there has been a 'plateauing' at the levels reached at that time (see for example Rogaly et al. 1999). By the time the latter book got published, however, statistics up to the late 1990s had become available. They suggest that indeed for the time being, one can ignore the phenomenon of a 'plateauing', and the major hypothesis of the editors may lack a solid foundation.

Indications are, on the contrary, that the rapid pace of agrarian expansion has continued unabated. Whereas foodgrains production in the entire country increased by 2.6 per cent between 1980 and 1997, the corresponding rate in West Bengal was 4.5 per cent. On the basis of the index at 100 in 1970, West Bengal in 1994–5 had reached 299, ahead of Punjab (254) and also clearly ahead of the neighbouring states with similar climatic and soil conditions (Bihar: 162, Orissa: 214, Assam: 132) and Uttar Pradesh (196), although the latter state also benefited from the Green Revolution (Table 14 in Fan et al. 1999).

Figure 6.1 on production increase of rice and potato crops shows how the upward trend that started after the crop failures in the early 1980s has continued unabated. Bumper crops, like the potato crop in 1997, also tend to have a negative reflex resulting from a glut in the

---

[10] Since 1970, a remarkable increase in agrarian production has taken place in Punjab and in the western area of Uttar Pradesh. These areas, because of appropriate land size, soil, and climatic conditions, in the wake of the invention of HYVs have become the cradle of the so-called Green Revolution. It is remarkable therefore that West Bengal, over a quarter of a century, has achieved the biggest spurt in agrarian growth, even superior to that in Punjab.

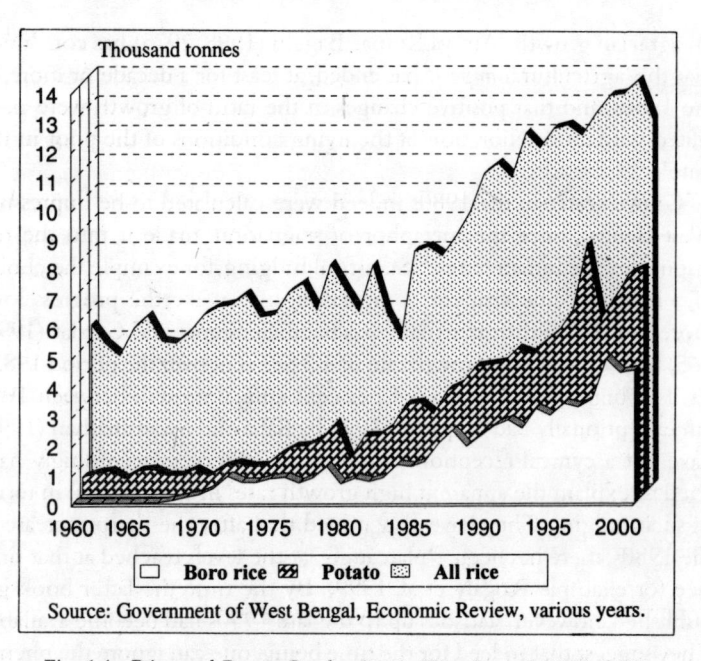

Fig. 6.1: Rice and Potato Production in West Bengal, 1960–2000

market and declining prices. A decline in the area under cultivation together with adverse weather conditions, may impact temporal troughs in an otherwise upward trend. It would be inappropriate on the basis of these temporal declines to conclude that the dynamic upswing has started dissipating.

Much of this growth was on account of factor productivity growth. West Bengal, with an index that had reached 252 in 1994–5, was in a league on its own. Even Punjab was trailing at 207, and the national index of productivity growth (with 1970 as the basis) stood at only 152 (Table 15 in Fan et al. 1999). Productivity growth has combined with the expansion of multicropping, extending the agricultural season over the entire year.

In a major study of the output growth, M.K. Sanyal et al. (1998; see also Rawal and Swaminathan 1998) have calculated that the productivity growth of foodgrains over the period 1977–94 has been 5.12 per cent. Expansion in cropped area was restricted, for obvious reasons, and the overall production growth was 3.62 per cent, a growth that clearly 'surpasses the rate of growth of population and marks the end of impasse in West Bengal agriculture'. Productivity growth in the so-called non-foodgrains (potato, sugar cane, pulses, cotton) was less impressive

(3.60 per cent annually), but, as a consequence of a considerable increase in acreage brought under production, total production increase reached 4.70 per cent over a period of almost two decades. Multicropping has not only generated higher agrarian output, beneficial to the consumers and to the producers, but has also induced a higher and more sustained worker participation throughout the year.[11]

It has been established that agricultural production has been fairly impressive. Sengupta and Gazdar (1997: 165) agree that a break with the sluggish trend before the mid-1980s can be noticed, but that this break 'has mainly taken the form of reversing and compensating for the relative decline of the seventies'. They further suggest that since a trend break also seemed to occur in some neighbouring states, explanations for the break in trend need not be specific to West Bengal, and to the possible effect of agrarian reforms. West Bengal indeed has not been the only state in India where consistent growth has occurred. In many other areas as well (Andhra Pradesh, Karnataka, Tamil Nadu, Gujarat, Punjab, Orissa, etc.), peasants have made use of the new seeds and the new technologies in order to increase their production. Overall, however, in terms of foodgrains output, the share of West Bengal in the Indian total output has increased by with around half a percentage point. In the 1990s, the state consistently accounted for between 7.0 per cent and 7.5 per cent of the Indian foodgrains production.[12]

Economic development is a basic element in the process of development. As important, however, is how the access to food, and the access to the basic necessities of life have increased. Especially in recent years, the essence of development has become more and more associated with the evolution of the Human Development Index (education, longevity, and levels of income), and with the quality of life in general. We shall look at the HDI after first dealing with two variables as approximations for improving economic standards of living: the inequality and the poverty levels.

Poverty and Inequality

The increasing agrarian production has proceeded parallel with a decreasing Gini coefficient, an indication of the less uneven distribution of rural incomes. The rural Gini coefficient, which stood at 29.8 in

---

[11] I had earlier calculated (Lieten 1996c: 114) that whereas in most Indian states, the percentage of male non-workers of all ages rose between 1981 and 1991, the percentage in West Bengal dropped significantly from 51.5 per cent to 47.9 per cent.

[12] West Bengal has 7.7 per cent of the rural population in India and 2.7 per cent of the cultivated land.

1978, thereafter decreased and reached 22.4 in 1997. Income inequality in West Bengal by the end of the century was lower than in any other state of India (Jha 2000), while many states, particularly the neighbouring states, witnessed an increasing inequality in the rural areas.[13]

One can expect the less uneven distribution of income to have a positive impact in terms of poverty reduction. The discussion on poverty levels has been conducted with different approaches and different methodologies to calculate the number of people below the poverty line and the distance from the poverty line. Whatever methodology one chooses,[14] West Bengal stands out for its sharp reduction in poverty levels, and, moreover, for a reduction that continued into the 1990s. An interesting discussion on the various approaches and the implications for West Bengal is conducted in Chatterjee (1998). He infers that the number of poor has sharply declined between 1983 and the late 1980s, and that, on the whole, the situation of the ultra poor in rural west Bengal seems to have improved more than that of the poor. The poor, he continues, have profited more than the non-poor from the combination of technology-induced productivity upsurge and institutional reforms like Operation Barga, land distribution, and decentralized planning. Chatterjee (1998: 3007) continues: 'As a result, West Bengal which was first among Indian states in terms of rural poverty in 1961–2, ranked only 18th in 1986–7, . . . [and] the relative success in poverty alleviation in rural areas of West Bengal is clearly a lesson for India as a whole.'

The factors associated with a reduction in poverty are factors that have been operative in the rest of India as well: wage increases, increasing on-farm and off-farm employment, government target group programs, etc. Stronger mobilization in West Bengal may have put extra pressure on the effective wage rate. Extra income from assigned land that accrued to around one-third of the landless families may have made a significant contribution to well-being and security.[15] Increasing employment in the farm sector as well as in the non-farm sector are likely

[13] In rural Uttar Pradesh, the Gini coefficient increased from 30.3 to 31.3 over the respective period. In rural Assam and Bihar, it increased from 18.8 and 26.2 to respectively 24.2 and 38.8. Only in Orissa, it decreased marginally from 26.8 to 25.4 (see Jha 2000).

[14] I consider myself too much of a layman to even consider commenting on the different methodologies used by the Planning Commission Index and the expert Group Index or on the relative advantage of using the Squared Poverty Index or the Sen Poverty Measure rather than the simple Headcount Index.

[15] Empirical data collected by Sengupta and Gazdar (1997: 180) suggest the importance of these incremental earnings for the considerable improvement seen.

to have augmented the total pay received by the rural poor. West Bengal, according to Gill and Ghuman (2001: 821–2) is the only state where the share of hired labour in total human labour is increasing and the share of agricultural labourers in the total workforce is decreasing. The share of hired labour increased despite the fact that the proportion of agricultural labourers in the rural workforce decreased. In this respect also, West Bengal deviated from the general trend in India.[16]

The World Bank country study of India concludes that 'notably Kerala and West Bengal had the fastest rates of poverty reduction over 1978–94' (World Bank 2000: 35), faster than several more rapidly growing states, and attributes this to land reforms:

> In the case of West Bengal, land reforms and high agricultural growth over the period may have been important causal factors. Further analytical work on such issues [and the linkages between growth, poverty reduction and governance] would help our understanding of the determinants of growth at state levels. (World Bank 2000: 36)

In Table 6.1, we have arranged the major Indian states in terms of the poverty head count ratio, comparing the position in 1997 with the position in the mid-1970s. From the table, it appears confirming the argument made previously, that West Bengal has witnessed a dramatic reduction in poverty levels. Whereas in 1974, almost as many as two-thirds of the rural population in the state still had to eke out an existence below the poverty line, by 1997 the share of the population below the poverty line was just about one-fourth.

In the 1990s, the process of *garibi hatao* (removal of poverty, in the 1970s the slogan of Indira Gandhi) appears to have continued. An important additional point is that in many other states, rural poverty and inequality appear to have started increasing again after the introduction of the more liberal IMF-induced economic policy regime around 1990. In India as a whole, and in practically all the states, poverty levels have started to increase. In Uttar Pradesh, the poverty ratio had come down from 55 per cent in 1974 and 45 per cent in 1978 to 36 per cent in 1987,

---

They, however, also state explicitly that union action and the role of the *panchayat* in wage settling has not resulted in an additional wage increase in comparison with other states. Their calculations are based on official agricultural wage data which for other states may be considerably above the actual wage rate in the field.

[16] In West Bengal it decreased from 35.0 per cent in 1971 and 33.6 per cent in 1981 to 32.2 per cent in 1991. The only other state with a declining proportion was Kerala. Madhya Pradesh and Maharashtra witnessed a decline in comparison with 1971, but not in comparison with 1981 (Gill and Ghuman 2001: 822).

Table 6.1: Changes in Rural Poverty in Major Indian States
(head count ratio: per cent below the poverty line)

Ascending order 1997	1997	1974	Rank in 1974
1. Punjab	16.1	32.3	1
2. West Bengal	26.9	63.2	11
3. Tamil Nadu	30.2	59.3	7
4. Kerala	32.1	62.1	10
5. Andhra Pradesh	32.2	56.8	4
6. Gujarat	33.1	58.1	5
7. Karnataka	34.1	61.0	9
8. Orissa	37.4	58.7	6
9. Uttar Pradesh	39.1	55.6	2
10. Maharashtra	45.4	64.6	12
11. Rajasthan	46.1	59.3	7
12. Assam	48.1	56.0	3
13. Madhya Pradesh	55.1	66.1	13
14. Bihar	62.1	69.5	14

Source: Based on Jha (2000).

and then again increased to 39 per cent in 1997. The two extreme cases were West Bengal and the neighbouring state of Bihar. Whereas in the latter the Headcount index (based on the Planning Commission's methodology) declined from 67.5 per cent in 1969 to 58.7 in 1987, and then climbed to 62.1 per cent in 1997, in West Bengal the decline during the same period was uninterrupted from 69.6 per cent to 43.1 per cent and then down to 26.9 per cent.[17] At that level, West Bengal was rapidly closing the gap with the Punjab.

Human Development

The variables of what in the 1990s, after the United Nations Development Programme (UNDP) introduced the concept, has been referred to as Human Development, have always been considered as important indicators of development. In West Bengal, it seems, the political battle has been around direct class issues related to economic development, as illustrated in the previous sections. Less attention has been paid to direct and wholesale interventions in the field of human development. The commendable growth in economic output, particularly in agriculture,

---

[17] The figures have been taken from Jha (2000). Orissa, it should be added, also recorded a decline from 70.5 to 45.0 and then down to 37.4 per cent.

and the fairly equitous distribution of incomes, leading to a perceptible decrease in poverty levels, until recently had not been complemented with major efforts in the field of human development. It has been suggested (Sengupta and Gazdar 1997: 183) that West Bengal had been doing well in the past and that the LFG policies had not added much to the already reasonably developed health and educational conditions in the rural areas. In the early 1980s, for example the infant mortality rate (IMR) was lower than in most states in the region. IMR in West Bengal was 95 per thousand; in Assam (101), Bihar (114) and Orissa (136), Madhya Pradesh (144), and Uttar Pradesh (159), it was considerably higher. Such a high position, however, was not the case in respect of other indicators of human development. Sengupta and Gazdar (1997: 185–6) nevertheless have rightly suggested that West Bengal had failed to live up to the expectations, and that some progress has persisted in conjunction with backwardness and lacklustre performance:

Political change, and particularly change based upon the mobilization of oppressed groups for their economic claims, can be expected to raise the consciousness amongst these groups of their social rights in other spheres. It has been suggested, for example, that political awareness in Kerala has been an important factor in raising people's awareness of health issues and their ability to demand health services. For all these reasons, political change in West Bengal represented an opportunity for social change and decisive improvements in well-being.

Improvements in well-being and well-feeling have been recorded, but educational levels, child mortality, birth rates and death rates did not develop in a way that was effectively different from what was observed in the rest of India. In terms of the HDI, the LFG, until the early 1990s, had not yet displayed the same vigour as in the realm of agrarian reforms and political decentralization. A comparison with Kerala, the other Indian state where the Communist parties have been in power for various periods from 1957 onwards, comes to mind. Kerala has achieved literacy, fertility, and longevity levels that are quite close to OECD standards. In the next chapter, I shall suggest an explanation for the departure in Kerala that in an important way was associated with the first communist ministry in that state (in 1957–9). The overthrow of that ministry by the opposition parties occurred in the confrontation, associated with street skirmishes, over the reforms in the educational system.[18] In West Bengal, the tension, on the other hand, was focused on

---

[18] Agrarian reforms had been introduced quite successfully, but the focus of the political struggle, which drew in the common people in every nook and corner of

agrarian issues and control over local administration. Health and educational issues were addressed but not under stormy conditions, as in Kerala, and progress was relatively slow.

Statistics on infant mortality, child mortality, birth rate, death rate, and fertility rate in the not so recent past have not been too accurate, and are difficult to compare. In any case, a distinction should be made between the urban and the rural figures, as these tend to vary substantially. The reasonably favourable figures for West Bengal that Sengupta and Gazdar have referred to do not give a disaggregate picture. The high level of urbanization in the state—the impact of Calcutta—had a flattering positive effect on the overall statistics. It is quite probable that, although the aggregate IMR in comparison with the neighbouring states was lower in the 1970s and 1980s, the rural IMR in West Bengal in the past has been at levels not lower than in the neighbouring states.[19]

Whereas West Bengal in the 1980s appears to have remained a middle-ranking state, in the 1990s there has been a break in the trend. Seeta Prabhu (1998: 3) concluded that among the states that she studied (West Bengal, Andhra Pradesh, Uttar Pradesh, Kerala, Gujarat, and Haryana), only West Bengal had a high rank correlation between economic development and literacy and IMR in the 1990s. The IMR in the state has continued to decline, down to 53 per thousand in 1999, but this was not an exceptional performance since the Indian aggregate had also come down to 72. The gap with the low levels reached in Kerala (16 per thousand) is still apparent, and, although West Bengal had reached the third position among all Indian states, just after Maharashtra, the record could have been better.

It is apparent that in the past insufficient attention has been paid to institutional development and conscientization. Two factors may have obstructed further progress. Despite the devolution of many resources

---

the state, was around the issue of the freedom and accessibility of education. Educational institutions were in private hands, controlled by families who stood to loose from the agrarian reforms. By launching a struggle against the educational policies of then communist government, which ultimately led to its overthrow through central intervention, they sought to circumvent the radical agrarian legislation. Education henceforth was at the core of public life and political sensitivity.

[19] Failing to provide the specific statistics, I can make a reference to the crude birth rate (CBR). In the mid-1980s West Bengal recorded a CBR of around 29 per thousand. The CBR in rural Bengal was around 33 per thousand; in rural Orissa it was around 31 per thousand. On the basis of the 1981 Census, Chakrabarty and Pal (1995: 66 ff.) have calculated that in terms of CMR rural West Bengal (103 per thousand) was trailing many of the states, although it was ahead of (rural) Maharashtra, Orissa, Madhya Pradesh and Uttar Pradesh, but not of Bihar.

to the *panchayats*, the health department is still typically run through centrally appointed staff. Conditions in the educational sector are even more complicated: policy is basically the terrain of the teachers' unions, and these unions appear to be more interested in defending their own interests than setting the agenda for a universal (and refurbished) system of education. Neither the state administration (and its ministers) nor the local levels of administration do not have much management control over these institutions. The second factor is the relatively low level of expenditure that the LFG has earmarked for social development. West Bengal currently has the second lowest per capita budget plan outlay (only 58 per cent of the average across the states),[20] and moreover had the lowest percentage (19.3 per cent) earmarked for social services, much below the 26.2 per cent all-India average (Kurian 2000: 543). Social services includes education, health, sanitation, water supply, housing, and other such necessities which critically depend on government finances. The limited financial support, which has been a consistent feature over the last decades, does not augur well in a situation where much of the infrastructural support is not yet in place and where the staff are still largely autonomous from local control.

More progress has been made in the reduction of fertility levels. Although some of the family planning programmes also depend on the presence of a well-functioning and well-furnished health department, fertility levels have come down drastically. By 1999, West Bengal had reached the third lowest birth rate among the major Indian states, after Kerala (17.9) and Tamil Nadu (19.2). Although the family planning idea has caught on in the rest of India as well, more in the south than in the north and more in the cities than in the villages, West Bengal, especially in the 1990s, has done extremely well. This must have been part of an official programme, but it has not been the focus of a public campaign. It is interesting to note that in the official CPI(M) publication on the occasion of the twentieth anniversary of the LFG (Basu 1997), no reference was made to the family planning efforts and declining fertility.

[20] Ahluwalia (2000: 1643) notes that whereas Orissa had the highest ratio of state expenditure to GDP at 7.1 per cent between 1987 and 1999, and had an SDP growth of 3.2 per cent only, West Bengal with the lowest plan ratio of 2.7 per cent had a relatively robust growth of 6.9 per cent. In the 1980s as well, West Bengal had by far the lowest Plan Expenditure/SDP ratio: only 3.6 per cent; the other states had more than 5 per cent ratio, and the other backward states in the region, such as Bihar (6.20 per cent), Uttar Pradesh (6.33 per cent), Orissa (7.41 per cent) and Madhya Pradesh (7.39 per cent) scored even much higher (see Table 8 in Ahluwalia 2000). It would be interesting to do a study on the political economy of corruption and efficiency.

Nevertheless, it is an issue that has seeped down to the villages, for example as an integral aspect of the messages contained in the Mass Literacy Programme. It is a reflection more of agency from below than of initiatives and campaigns from above. The LFG never seems to have taken up this issue as the focus of a mass campaign.

The success in various indicators of human development, a bit late in coming, seems to have resulted from a natural development rather than from a government campaign. Human development has followed in the wake of economic development. It illustrates Amartya Sen's preference for a growth-mediated process, where the increase in economic welfare and the enhancement of the quality of life tend to move together and where the success tends to be more enduring. Economic growth, if based on a just distribution, helps to provide a 'protective security' to the poor people. On the basis of such security, poor families can then avail of the other 'entitlements' in life, such as education. The so-called support-led approach, through priority being given to social services, does not wait for increases in the per capita levels of income. It emphasizes progress in life expectancy, literacy rates and birth control as the basic indicators of quality of life, and as having a high priority. But, Amartya Sen (1999: 48) adds:

It is obvious that the growth-mediated process has an advantage over its support-led alternative; it may, ultimately, offer more, since there are more deprivations—other than premature mortality, or high morbidity, or illiteracy—that are very directly connected with the lowness of incomes [as being inadequately clothed and sheltered]. It is clearly better to have high income as well as high longevity [and other standard indicators of quality of life], rather than only the latter.

Writing on the basis of a close reading of the data available up to the mid-1990s, Seeta Prabhu (1998: 3) concludes that the only state which had a high rank correlation between increase in productivity and literacy rates/infant mortality rate was West Bengal. She ascribed this to the distribution of the benefits of agricultural growth and the decentralized political structure, despite 'the West Bengal government not paying any special attention to enhancing the levels of social attainment indicating the importance of broad based growth in enhancing the prospects for growth-led security'.

Whether the approach has been a conscious one or not, it appears that only the early 1990s have established a trend break in literacy levels and mobidity levels in West Bengal. During the 1980s, the state was not doing particularly well. The literacy level in the state was slightly above the national average, and was clearly ahead of the levels in the neighbouring states, but it was in no way closing the gap with the more advanced states and it was in fact falling behind. A brief look at the Census data will illustrate this. In terms of male literacy, West Bengal remained 3.5 per cent above the national average, but, overtaken by Haryana and Karnataka, it slipped from the ninth to the eleventh position. In terms of female literacy, West Bengal was apparently doing better, increasing its overall percentage from 3.4 per cent to 7.7 per cent above the national level, but some other states, particularly, Sikkim and Manipur were doing even better, and West Bengal slipped from the eleventh to the thirteenth position (among 25 states).

At around the time of the 1991 Census, the government decided to engage in a massive effort to bring adult education and full literacy to the state. Until that time, it was correct to say that 'energetic activism on the agrarian reforms agenda went alongside with a near total absence of initiative in public policy on other factors that influence well-being' (Sengupta and Gazdar 1997: 194).

By the late 1990s, the impact of the campaign was obvious. By 1997, the overall literacy rate in Bengal had moved up to 74 per cent from 58 per cent in 1991, and the state thereby had moved into third place, just behind Maharashtra (Ahluwalia 2000: 1646). The steep increase was very much a reflection of the increasing literacy in rural areas. In 1985, rural literacy was 34.8 per cent, not much above the national average of 30.9 per cent. By 1995, as Figure 6.2 illustrates the ratio had gone up to 52.6 per cent, clearly above the 39.8 per cent national average. By this sharp rise, West Bengal moved from the ninth position to the third place.[21] Table 6.2 has various indicators of that progress in human development.

A trend break with the past can thus be noted. The progress has been very much on account of the involvement of the *panchayats* and the local activists after 1990 when the decision was taken to start the literacy campaign in a big way. That campaign did access the poor people in the villages directly, bypassing the educational institutions. The institutions, whether the ministries or the schools, are staffed by bureaucracy and teachers who usually belong to the upper segments of society and are not benefited, and may even stand to lose from higher literacy and welfare levels. School teachers have been manifestly absent in the mass literacy drive. It is only after, at the party level, and supported by many

---

[21] West Bengal is still far behind the remarkable state of Kerala (which already in 1970 had a 55 per cent rural literacy and by the mid-1990s had achieved universal literacy), and behind Himachal Pradesh which by 1985 had already reached a literacy level of 44 per cent (Fan et al. 1999: Table 12).

130 POWER, POLITICS AND RURAL DEVELOPMENT

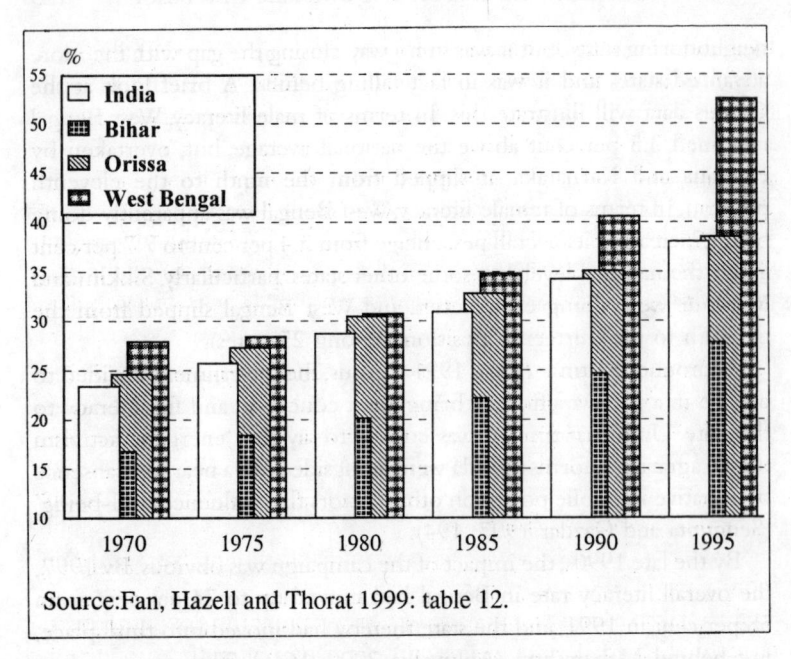

Fig. 6.2: Regional Comparison of Rural Literacy, 1970–95

Source: Fan, Hazell and Thorat 1999: table 12.

Table 6.2: Poverty and Social Indicators in Indian States

	Population below poverty		Literacy, 7+ (1997)		Birth rate	IMR
	1994	Rate of change after 1978	All	Female		
Punjab	21.6	1.4	67	62	23.5	51
West Bengal	26.0	4.2	72	63	22.8	55
Kerala	29.2	3.7	93	90	17.8	12
Andhra Pradesh	29.4	2.9	54	43	22.7	63
Gujarat	33.8	1.0	68	57	25.5	62
Tamil Nadu	34.9	2.8	70	60	19.2	53
Karnataka	37.9	2.1	58	50	23.0	53
Uttar Pradesh	40.2	0.9	56	41	34.0	85
Orissa	40.3	2.7	51	38	26.8	96
Maharashtra	43.7	2.7	74	63	23.2	47
Rajasthan	43.5	1.1	55	35	32.3	85
Madhya Pradesh	44.1	2.3	56	41	32.4	94
Bihar	60.4	0.4	49	34	32.1	71

Source: World Bank (2000: 36).

layers of volunteers, a decision for a literacy campaign was taken that West Bengal started to break away from the low levels of human capital growth.

Conclusions

The long haul of political stability in West Bengal cannot any longer summarily be dismissed as the effect of stronghanded tactics by the ruling coalition and a skilful electioneering strategy. The stability itself is a pointer to the wholesome effects of a regime that has introduced land reforms and has taken the policy of decentralization seriously. It has been argued that until the early 1990s, there was more scope for questioning the positive impact than during the 1990s. In this chapter, I have supplied evidence from various fields (agrarian production, reduction in poverty level, declining inequality, lowering fertility, increasing literature). All the evidence suggests that whereas West Bengal had done reasonably well in the 1980s, the departure in the 1990s has been even more impressive.

It has taken a long time for the LFG to confront the slow progress in terms of human development indicators, long after the production relations in agriculture were tackled and long after deprivation ceased to stalk the countryside. We have suggested that this followed from the specific historical roots of the LFG. Three critical factors combined in the transition of power from the Congress government period to the Marxist-dominated LFG in 1977. The factors underlying the leftist movement in West Bengal were the struggle for land reforms, particularly the sharecropper's movement, the struggle against economic stagnation and deprivation (understood to be associated with semi-feudalism), and the struggle for the restoration of democracy. The organizing practice of the leftist movement, and of the LFG, was directed at these issues. The outcome was fairly successful in terms of land distribution/sharecropping reforms, equitable agrarian development, and a return to democratic practices, particularly the successful decentralization to village *panchayats*. It took, however, a long time before the political agenda came to include policies that were not directly related to the economic sphere. Indicators of human developed started to show a perceptive improvement only well into the 1990s. Reform and initiatives in such fields as education, health care and fertility control were urgently needed but were not forthcoming with the same conviction as was shown when economic and political changes were taken up from 1977 onwards.

CHAPTER 7

Human Development in Kerala: Structure and Agency in History

Kerala is often being used as an example of high human development despite faltering economic development. Many explanations have been suggested to explain for this puzzle. The argument in this contribution is that many explanations have incorrectly excluded the reforms introduced during the first government headed by EMS Namboodiripad. The other argument is that the explanation should go beyond the mere institutional changes and involve the cognitive changes in the wake of an intense political battle and social turbulence.

It basically boils down to assigning a proper place in the making of history to the *kudikidappukar* (hutment dwellers), the *veerompattadar* (tenants-at-will) and other low-class people in the rice fields of Kerala. I shall catch them under a common female name, Kutiamma. Kutiamma stands as a metaphor for all poor people in Kerala, irrespective of religion, occupation, gender, or ideology.

There is a methodological catch in such an analysis. From historical sources, we do know what has happened at the official level in the public domain: legislation, implementation with facts and figures, agitations, inquiries, the intervention by organized movements, pronouncements by party leaders, etc. We, however, do not know what has happened in the private domain, on the inside of the people involved. Such an insight is important if we want to understand the impact on development processes. Mental changes and modifications in the societal memory system add significantly to the direction of social change. It is a change that has a longer staying power than a particular political regime, and it may give a society that qualitative shift which studies of the public domain may not perceive.

More than forty years after the first communist-led ministry was ousted by the federal government in New Delhi, an attempt will be made to assess the long-term effects of the innovative approach followed during the first reign. We have to keep in mind that changes in the memory system and in the discursive understanding have hardly been documented and that much of what is going to be argued rests on extrapolation. We shall relate the impact to the policy interventions in two crucial sectors: agriculture and education.

Human Development: The Facts

The end of the colonial period brought the development debate to the fore. Whereas previously, colonizing countries had put in place only the bare rudimentary of state power which allowed for the legal and administrative classification of the subject people, and for the requirements of international trade, the governments of newly independent states straightened themselves to catch up with the developed Western world. Development became an assessment benchmark underwritten by lofty UN conventions and good intentions. The catching-up process, conceptualized as modernization, initially centred on industrialization and increase in the Gross National Product. Intermitted, however, and especially so since the late 1980s, when the UNDP (United Nations Development Programme) started producing its Human Development Index (HDI), education and health factors were brought into the package of development priorities.

Kerala, which in 1957–9 had attracted some world attention as the first democratically elected—and undemocratically removed—state government in India, henceforth served as a metaphor for a high HDI despite a low Gross National Product (GNP). In terms of literacy, morbidity, child mortality, longevity and fertility, it approaches the standards reached in the developed countries. Even in comparison with China and South Korea, admittedly success stories in human development management, Kerala did much better. Drèze and Sen (1995) have shown how Kerala, for example in terms of rural female literacy, has done better then every individual province in China.

By the turn of the millennium, the state was credited as having reached full literacy of men and women. The gender disparity index, an indicator of the different achievements of males and females in terms of education, longevity, employment, etc., has narrowed down significantly. In terms of rural literacy for example, the female/male disparity has narrowed down to 92 per cent.

Even in comparison with the neighbouring states (see Table 7.1), the performance of Kerala is outstanding. In particular, the low infant

Table 7.1: Some Social Indicators for
South Indian States, 1991

	Kerala	Tamil Nadu	Karnataka	Andhra Pradesh	India
Life expectancy	71.9	62.9	64.7	62.9	59.4
Crude birth rate	18.1	20.7	26.8	26.0	29.5
Infant mortality rate	17.0	57.0	77.0	73.0	80.0
Male literacy rate	93.6	73.7	67.3	55.1	64.1
Female literacy rate	86.1	51.3	44.3	32.7	39.3
Below poverty line (per cent)	17.0	32.8	32.1	31.7	36.0
Per capita income (Rs)	3,843	4,428	4,737	4,722	

Sources: Chakrabarty and Pal (1995); Government of India, Economic Survey.

mortality rate (and consequently the high life expectancy) stands out as a major achievement. The literacy rates, which since the 1991 census have climbed to full literacy levels, form a distinctively positive exception which sets Kerala apart from the other states. Further, the low per capita income contrasts with the low percentage of people below the poverty line.

Explanations

How is this departure to be explained? Lies the secret in the cultural traits or in the (non-) colonial past? Is it because of agency and empowerment in the wake of social movements? Or is it because of structural changes in equity relations? We shall first look at these three modes of explanation which, among others, are represented by Gita Sen and Marti Bhat and Irudaya Rajan, by Amartya Sen, and by Franke and Chasin and V.K. Ramachandran.

Gita Sen's article on 'the origins of Kerala's remarkable social development' has identified three factors: the relative autonomy of Cochin and Trivandrum during the colonial period which allowed the native rulers to spend on health and education, the matrimonial and matrilocal family organization, and, in the third place, the surge of the social and religious reform movement during the latter part of the nineteenth and the early part of the twentieth century (Sen 1992: 263). These three main factors were further conditioned by the commercialization (of cash crops) in the nineteenth century which demanded a work force with a basic education, by the land reforms in the nineteenth century (which gave rise to the commercialization process), and the changes within the christian community, which also started accelerating in the nineteenth century. The contribution of the communist-inspired political movements and the communist-led governments with their policy of structural initiatives has been overlooked (see also Mathew 1999, and Mari Bhat and 'Irudaya Rajan 1990 for similar approaches).

Amartya Sen, one of the most authoritative participants in the debate, has explained Kerala in terms of political agency from below, while at the same time dismissing the political agency from above. The vicious circle of educational inequalities and social disparities, he argued, could only be broken by political action. The weakness in this respect 'of even the parties of the left is striking. . . . The difficulty in getting even "leftwing" parties interested in combating inequalities in education relates to the general atmosphere in India (including the nature of the leadership of the different parties) which take some major disparities as simply "given" and not particularly worth battling against' (Sen 1996: 14–15). He, however, does take notice of the political activism in Kerala and suggests the 'importance of political leadership and initiative and of popular involvement in making a real difference in the realization of basic capabilities of people at large' (p. 16).

More outspoken in associating the positive departure with the communist involvement in the state administration is V.K. Ramachandran. He explicitly rejects the notion that the education policy by the erstwhile rulers and the educational reforms (and conversion work) by the Protestant missionaries could have brought the literacy levels beyond a certain threshold. The monarchy and the upper-caste elite, despite the good intentions of some of them, prodded on by the Protestant resident in the court, constituted an autocratic and undemocratic ruling stratum. The royal support for education created a network of schools, but it did not really reach the lower echelons of society. Their entry into education required radical changes in the status of the people of the oppressed castes as well as land reform, i.e. 'changes well outside the class and caste calling of the ruling elite of the princely states of Travancore and Cochin' (Ramachandran 1997: 303; see also Franke and Chasin 1992: 99).

The Ingredients of a Break: 1957–1959

During the first government run by the CPI (1957–9) some changes have been introduced that have become associated with the Kerala development model. The argument is that changes occur in the interface between government intervention and social mobilization, two institutional factors which feed upon each other. The 1957–9 period accordingly has to be assessed as having backward and forward linkages: the discursive influence of the victorious party had been active before, and would continue to operate afterwards.

The process leading up to the 1957 electoral victory of the CPI, drawing support from 40 per cent of the electorate, fed on and was reinforced by ongoing social changes. There was a shift in empowerment and consciousness, prior to the elections. The social and political work of social reformers in the previous period had contributed in a considerable measure. In particular the impact of the social movements (the breast cloth controversy, the temple entry movement for example, the SNDP, the working class action, and the peasant movements in the 1930s have been crucial elements in this process.

There were forward linkages as well. The changes that were introduced during the first EMS government formed the matrix of the further political and social development. It witnessed the expansion of the youth clubs, the women's organization, the library movement and the mass campaigns of the Kerala Shashtra Sahitya Parishad (KSSP). The performance of the undivided CPI during the first reign also increased its popular support. In the February 1960 elections, the CPI, due to the opposition unity, managed to secure hardly one-fifth of the Assembly seats, but in terms of electoral support, however, the CPI increased its mass base by around 50 per cent (an increase from 40.7 per cent to 43.1 per cent of the votes and aided by a 38 per cent increase in voters' turnout, bringing it to 84.8 per cent of the eligible electorate; see Lieten 1982: 158–61).

Henceforth, the popular support for what the communists stood for could only be disregarded at the peril of being wiped out as a political party. Kutiamma had entered the public stage. The massive participation in the electoral process was a clear sign of the changing character of the public space. Government interventions thereafter had to keep the claims to enfranchisement in mind.

The above argument suggests that the first communist administration cannot be isolated from the preceding and the following period. At the same time, we propose to argue that the first reign contains the ingredients of a break. We shall first illustrate this with reference to two long trend developments of key social indicators, namely the demographic transition and the literacy rate.

Figure 7.1 illustrates that the crude death rate (CDR) in Kerala had been coming down during the previous two decades, and also that it started declining at a sharper rate after the late 1950s. In one decade, from 1961 to 1971, the CDR declined from around 16 per thousand to around 8 per thousand. The decline was very much associated with the dramatic drop in the child mortality rate. T.N. Krishnan (1976) has calculated that the infant mortality declined by about 43 per cent in the period 1956–66. The most remarkable development in that period was the sharp drop in the crude birth rate (CBR), from close to 40 per thousand in 1960 to less than 20 per thousand in the early 1990s.

The acceleration in literacy also took place in the same reference period, i.e. in the 1960s. Literacy in the state was already high, particularly in Travancore and Cochin, but the faster growth occurred in the period immediately following the EMS government. The upward departure was possibly related to the initiatives and the mental changes during that government period. A detailed break-up, the district-wise figures in Table 7.2 (see also Figure 7.2), indicates that in most of the districts literacy of females more than doubled and literacy of males almost

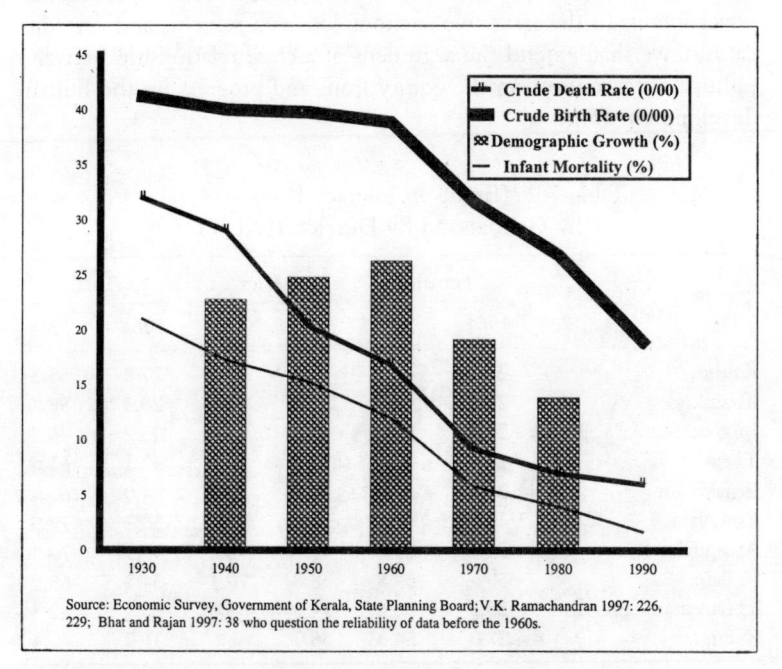

Fig. 7.1: Demographic Transition in Kerala, 1930–90

doubled in the period between 1961 and 1971. For example, in Kottayam, which already had a relatively high rate of literacy, literacy of females increased with 106 per cent above the 33.7 per cent level reached in 1961, and male literacy increased by 97 per cent. In the Malabar area, with a lower benchmark, progress was even more spectacular. In Kannur, female literacy increased by as much as 121 per cent; male literacy, which was already relatively high in comparison with female literacy increased by 'only' 99 per cent. The consequence of the uneven progress in male and female literacy seriously narrowed the gender difference, but since male literacy did increase in a spectacular fashion as well, the gap still remained significant. At the state level, the difference, which had been 26.8 per cent in 1961, had come down to 18.5 per cent by 1971. In the districts with a lower literacy rate and a bigger gender gap in 1961, the difference narrowed substantially, for example in Kannur from 39.7 per cent to 26.1 per cent.

The many explanations, which have been used to explain the high literacy, obviously should, at the very least, include the political interventions which took place around 1960 by the communist-dominated government. In the next two sections (on land reforms and on education), we shall extend the argument of a close relationship between political intervention on the equity front and progress on the human development front.

Table 7.2: Trends in Literacy Rate in Kerala by Gender and by District, 1961–71

	Females 1961	Females 1971	Males 1961	Males 1971	Total 1961	Total 1971
Kannur	21.0	47.1	34.8	63.7	27.8	55.3
Kozhikode	21.3	49.9	35.3	67.6	28.3	58.8
Palghat	20.0	39.2	30.8	54.6	25.2	46.7
Thrissur	27.9	57.2	36.8	66.3	32.1	61.6
Ernakulam	29.8	60.2	38.2	70.5	34.0	65.4
Kottayam	33.7	69.5	38.7	76.2	36.2	72.9
Alappuzha	35.9	65.8	43.9	75.2	39.9	70.4
Kollam	30.7	59.8	38.8	70.1	34.7	65.0
Thiruvananthapuram	25.6	56.5	34.3	68.6	30.1	62.5
Kerala	27.0	54.3	36.9	66.6	31.9	60.4

Source: Census reports as reproduced in Mathew (1999: 2818).

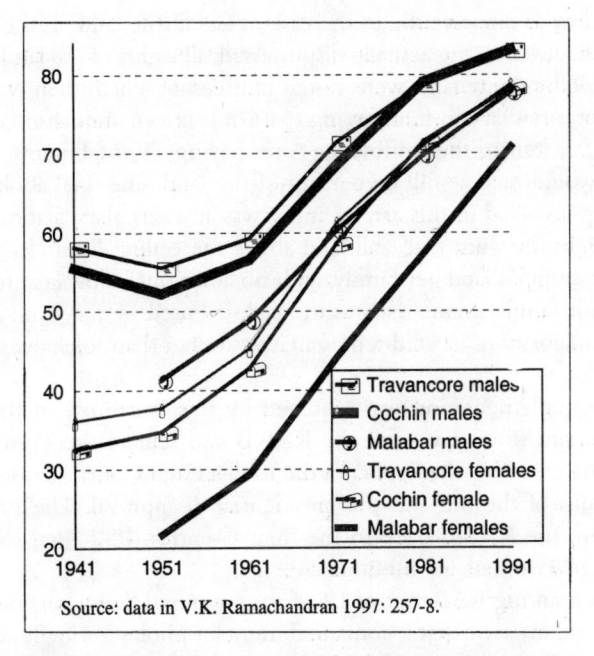

Fig. 7.2: Literate Persons in Kerala, three regions, 1941–91

Land Reforms

The land reforms' strategy, for various reasons, had been built into the programmatic understanding of the Indian National Congress party and of the CPI, but Kerala was the first state where land reforms were firmly put on the political agenda. In the assessment of Nossiter (1982: 147), the land reforms programme indeed was 'the first comprehensive measure of its kind attempted in India; and it tackled tenurial relations of greater complexity than anywhere else in India' (see also Herring 1983; Radhakrishnan 1989).

Two questions can be posed: what changes did land reforms effect in the agrarian system, and what did it do to the social relations and psyche of the people?

The Kerala Agricultural Relations Bill (KARB) was drafted immediately after assuming office. It contained three important features. In the first place, it provided that generally no holding by permanent tenants, including farm servants and mortgagees, would be subject to resumption by the landowners. The rent to be paid by tenants was reduced to a maximum of one-fourth of the gross produce, and to much less, as low as one-twelfth, in the case of less fertile land. In the second place, the lessors were actually dispossessed: all rights of the landlords in land held by the tenants were vested in the state which then would act as an intermediary in transferring (part of) sixteen annual installments of the fair rent to the landowner. After paying all installments, the ex-lessee would receive full ownership of the land. The total abolition of tenancy involved in this arrangement was an exemplary feature of the KARB. In the third place, all land above the ceiling limit (15 acres of double cropped land per family, with no additional allowance for adult or minor family members) was to be distributed by the Land Boards, with a majority of elected representatives rather than solely by bureaucrats.

The implementation was scotched by the overthrow of the EMS government (four days after the KARB was sent to the President of India for approval), the verdict of the Kerala High Court against certain provisions of the bill and the presidential disapproval. The President later sent the KARB back to the then Congress-PSP (Praja Socialist Party) government for modification.

The resulting KAR Act of 1964 was a watered down version of the KARB in the sense that it contained more loopholes for ineffective implementation—for example the bureaucratic composition of the Land Boards and the exemptions for charitable trusts and plantations—but overall, the ideas which the CPI had introduced in 1957 remained intact. The installation of the United Front government in 1967, dominated by the CPI(M), allowed for new legislation to undo the evictions and to remodify the KAR Act, resulting in the Kerala Land Reforms (Amendment) Act 1969 (see Lieten 1977a: 416; Herring 1983; Radakrishnan 1989).

The impact of the administrative intervention in agrarian relations has been mixed. The estimates of surplus land vary wildly from around 2 lakh to around 8 lakh acres. The latter estimates include the huge areas which have been classified as plantations (rubber, tea, coffee, cardamom, etc.). Bogus transfers as well as transfers validated by the Acts of 1964 and 1969, and by the controversial Gift Deeds Act of 1979, had reduced the land size originally thought to be surplus. By the mid-1980s, only 50,000 acres had been distributed to 90,000 households (Radakrishnan 1989 and Ramachandran 1997; Eashvaraiah 1993: 135, gives slightly higher figures). Land distribution was only a rearguard battle. The impact of the legislation had significantly been reduced by the long interval between the ceiling proposals of 1957 and the effective implementation that actually started in 1970. Ultimately, the extent of redistribution amounted to hardly one per cent of the net sown area, and M.A. Oommen (1994: 127) has concluded: 'The performance of Kerala regarding the distribution of surplus land is in no way better than the dismal experience in the other parts of the country.'

In terms of tenancy reforms, on the other hand, the original CPI programme has come to full fruition. Radakrishnan (1989) has reported that close to two million acres were transferred to 1.3 million households. The aggregate area transferred to the lessors amounted to 36.5 per cent of the net sown area in the state, or 42.9 per cent of the area excluding plantation crops (Eashvaraiah 1993: 141). M.A. Oommen (1994: 120) noted with satisfaction that the implementation of the tenancy reforms conferred upon Kerala 'the unique distinction among Indian states of having abolished feudal landlordism lock, stock and barrel'. In addition, artisans, farm servants, and agricultural labourers, who had been living on the land of the *jenmi* and who had been at their beck and call, were henceforth entitled to retain their hutment land. Around 4,50,000 applications for *kudikidappu* (homestead land) were received; around 2,75,000 were accepted (Eashvaraiah 1993: 150). This single initiative must had have a tremendously liberating effect on the *kudikidappukars* who henceforth were in a position to maintain an autonomous existence, freed from feudal subservience.

The impact of the land reforms on landlessness has been enormous. In 1959, one-third of the rural households did not own any land. By the 1980s, 92.2 per cent of the rural labour households owned land (Oommen 1994: 134). The access to land, increasing the entitlement to food and income, decreased the state of utter dependency. Ramachandran (1997: 300) rightly concludes: 'The role must be emphasized of land reforms not only as a process that helped to transform agrarian relations in the state, but also as a facilitator of social change in Kerala.'

The organization from below and the administrative measures from above, helped to increase the bargaining power of agricultural labour. Mass mobilization has been an effective instrument in the policy of land reform implementation, and even in the formulation of policy agenda. Throughout the state, innumerable *kisan jathas* in support of the land reform legislation were staged, and peasants gathered in the village meetings to discuss the merits and shortcomings of the bills, culminating in a special session of the state *Karshaka Sangham* which suggested changes to the KARB. H.D. Malaviya, a senior leader of the Congress party, praised this involvement: 'This popular involvement in the discussion of the Bill is something unique, a parallel to which can hardly be found in any other state in India' (Malaviya 1959: 89). M.A. Oommen (1994: 122) has formulated the impact in the following way: 'the abolition of a rentier class who enjoyed the highest rank in social status in a caste-ridden society not only heralded a new area of relations of production, but ratified a long process of change in social relations as well, especially in the Malabar region'.

Since no anthropological or sociological studies were conducted at that time, and since the life story of Kutiamma was not recorded, the impact on the world view of the people involved can only be extrapolated by logical reasoning. Discussions, arguments on the extent of reforms, the economic impact on the lives of the people, and the social mobilization surrounding it brought scores of people, the so-called underclass, into society. They internalized their right to have rights. One of the rights they could come forward to claim was education.

Educational Reforms

The changes in the educational system shall be focused on as the second important contribution during the EMS government. Nossiter (1982: 168) has succinctly stated: 'No account of the communist ministry could avoid placing the accent on education and land reform'.

The private sector, particularly the education provided by the Catholic and Protestant church organizations, is usually credited with introducing the best educational system in Kerala in the pre-EMS period. The role of the state in the process, and therefore also the intervening privilege of the state, has not been given due attention. In 1957-8, the share of the government in the total educational expenditure was as high as 80.6 per cent, even higher than the 65.6 per cent at the all-India level. It supplied 99.1 per cent of the finances (figures in Lieten 1977b, and 1982: 36; Kuttikrishan 1994: 50-1). The state committed substantial public revenue to education, and had thereby evolved a scheme of direct payment system to teaching and non-teaching employees of aided private institutions right from primary level to collegiate level.

The reorganization of the educational system was needed because education remained the privilege of specific castes and classes. Relatively more finances were applied to secondary and university education. Children from Brahmin, Nair, and Christian families had access to the various stages of the school system and were later on well positioned for posts in the bureaucracy within the state or elsewhere. A majority of the Ezhevas, Kammalas, and Muslims remained illiterate. By the mid-1960s, only 17 per cent of the SC population had finished the primary school; of the Muslims and Ezhevas only 21.2 per cent and 24 per cent respectively had done so (Lieten 1982: 35). The much-acclaimed Kerala model in the past, i.e. in the pre-EMS government period, had a definite class (and caste) bias around it. There obviously was a threshold beyond which the much applauded system could not move.

Reforms were considered necessary to eradicate corruption, maladministration, ethnic discrimination, and whimsical employment conditions, and proposals for changes in the management of education indeed had been prepared by the previous non-communist governments. Two important measures were needed to overhaul and improve the educational levels: a reorganization of the educational system in favour of universal primary education, and a judicial regulation of school management. The Select Committee of the Legislative Assembly, which looked into the draft bill presented to the Assembly in July 1957, and on which the communist representatives did not have a majority, broadly agreed with the proposals, albeit with modifications (Nossiter 1982: 154). The Kerala Education Bill attempted to regulate the salary payment and security of service of the teachers. The bill stipulated that salaries would be paid by the government directly, and that teachers henceforth could only be appointed from a district list of qualified teachers.

The importance of the educational reforms is on account of at least two reasons. It helped to professionalize and to universalize the education system in Kerala. On the other hand, it allowed the conservative forces led by the Catholic churches and by the Nair caste association NSS (Nair Service Society) to launch the so-called Liberation Movement (Vimochana Samaram). The Vimochana Samaram was a coalition of right-wing opposition groups around organizations with a sizable number of the landlords in their ranks. On this second aspect I will focus because in my view, it made much of the difference as compared with other states. Education became a hotly contested issue, and Kutiamma was brought onto the public stage in defence of education.

The opposition to the Kerala Education Bill was basically an opposition along religious lines. Whereas Catholic and Muslims organizations, with higher stakes in the private system, were adamant in depicting the bill as part of a totalitarian effort to enslave the minds of the people, the SNDP and the NSS, the organizations of Ezhevas and Nairs came out in support of the bill. Church authorities launched a venomous attack on the legislative proposals. The schools run by the church organizations stood to lose, financially and organizationally. The public argument, however, was that the communists had set off to brainwash the children along atheist and communist lines, and that, therefore, unless the centre intervened, the onward march towards a totalitarian society would be difficult to stop. In the church sermons, a clarion call for an all-out war against the atheist and totalitarian communist machine was given, and one of the more zealous Catholic priests, father Vadakkan, decided to organize clusters of committed youth. These so-called Christophers spearheaded the stormy demonstrations that were organized within days of the publication of the bill. Later, in March 1959 when the KARB was being finalized, Mannath Padmanabhan of the NSS, who earlier had supported the bill, joined the Liberation Movement.

Kutiamma took part in the demonstrations, on both sides. She was mobilized by the communists who told her that her folk also had the right to education. She was mobilized by the organizers of the Vimochana Samaram who told her that she had the right to free and fair education, and the communists were going to take it away from her. It dawned on her that her children had basic rights as citizens, and for one of those rights she was called into the streets.

The attempts to interfere with the educational system were bound to invite a strong reaction from conservative forces, especially those with vested financial interests in the school management. The recourse to casteism and communalism has been more prevalent among the elite. When their economic interests came under siege, the very same caste leaders who earlier had supported the educational reforms now came forward to use the allegedly communist tyranny as a propaganda weapon in order to organize public support for the hidden agenda, namely the resistance against land reforms.

The communalist-driven frenzy did indeed mobilize large segments of poor Catholic and not-so-poor Nair followers against the communist government. The communist initiatives, on the other hand, also led to an increase in public support in favour of the government. The immense increase in electoral participation, and the increasing popular vote of the CPI and its independent allies, are evidence of this. The intent of the educational reforms is likely to have appealed to the poor people. The intense political movement around the educational reforms has brought the issue of education and the right to education centre stage in the consciousness of the people. This may help to explain the spurt which education got in the ensuing years. At stake was the impact of social mobilization on entitlement. The initiatives of the government in combination with movements from below created an enabling environment in which the hitherto excluded people could avail of their right of access to the educational and the health system. At stake was a process that in modern parlance we would call empowerment.

The intense political battle, with education as the number one item on the political agenda, valourized education as a basic right. The result of widespread discussions, agitational politics and propaganda meetings, was to bring more and more people of the underclass within the ambit of education. The interference with the unregulated private system indeed was followed by a number of interesting developments, which have contributed to the break in the system for which Kerala now stands as a model. In the period after 1959, there was a perceptive decline in the number of privately run schools, probably schools which had been run as business enterprises swallowing government subsidies, and a comparable increase in government schools. As a consequence of the new arrangement, the number of pupils in the primary schools, and especially so in the secondary schools increased sharply. Within one decade, primary school enrolment had doubled, and enrolment in the secondary schools had trebled (Government of Kerala 1976). This information ties up with the data in Table 7.2 that was referred to earlier. Both in terms of gender and in terms of the three regions of the state (Travancore, Cochin, and Malabar), a perceptible acceleration in literacy could be noted between 1961 and 1971.

Conclusion

The preceding section may help to explain the break which occurred in the 1960s, and which established the Kerala model of low GNP and high HDI. The conclusion that the EMS ministry, particularly through agrarian and educational reforms, has played a pivotal role in establishing this model is based on extrapolations. Historical research cannot possibly go back and reconstruct what was happening in the minds of the people. Even oral history would run into difficulties when attempting to construct how thoughts, aspirations, demands, and claims started changing.

In the study of development processes, the changes in mental processes, has not sufficiently been paid attention to. It has been our contention that this change, rather than the various institutional factors specific of the Keralese society, has been responsible for the Kerala model. It has further been our contention that the policies of the EMS government, specifically the land reforms and the educational reforms, have played a major role in creating the enabling environment. Our argument has been that a major impetus in the changeover towards autonomy of the body—that is what control over fertility, morbidity, and illiteracy amounts to—must have happened during this period. The political turbulence involved Kutiamma as an actor. This made much of the difference with the much slower process that has been witnessed elsewhere in South Asia.

Because Kutiamma and her male and female neighbours were drawn into a struggle that sought to establish their entitlement to education, they became actors from below involved in human development. Their agency was facilitated by the structural reforms that at the very same time were introduced by the communist government. Structure and agency overlapped, and gave a big boost to human development in Kerala. This explanation, I suggest, is a necessary addition to the various explanations given by other authors.

CHAPTER 8

Development Priorities: Post-Modernist Assumptions and Pre-Modernist Aspirations

In the world of development theory, after the marginalization of the socialist discourse, two kinds of discussions seem to be going on: the neo-liberal discourse and the post-modernist discourse. The latter brand of development theory has attracted many radical opponents of the neo-liberal and globalizing development model. Over the last decade, a body of literature subscribing to the post-modern paradigm has made its appearance, and has begun to have a considerable impact on West-based development academics, even though some of the major contributors originated from Third World countries.

A few general remarks will therefore be made about the latter discourse as a benchmark reference for a discussion on priorities in the development project. To what extent does post-modernism reflect a field-reality critique of the neo-liberal development model, and to what extent is it therefore a helpful theory in questioning, confronting, and displacing the current mainstream development theories?

Underlying the essence of development as an extraneously-pulled process remains the idea of modernization. It has endured as a persistent approach in the development strategy, not because of a lack of alternative ideas (see Kitching 1989; Hettne 1991), but because of the continuing dominance of North Atlantic capitalism, which in practice determines the direction of development. The old signifier (modernization), which has come under crossfire as a normative and derogatory concept, seems to have been discarded, and has been replaced by a new signifier: globalization. The new concept, as yet hardly contested, essentially refers to the market-induced extension of western production, trade, and culture over the entire globe. Underlying the concept remains the idea that the developing countries shall have to catch up in order to share in the common good which beckons all at *the end of history* as Fukuyama (1989) has envisaged. 'Development' is thus inherently defined as the march of as yet retarded societies towards the economic, social, political, and cultural pattern of the OECD countries. Development is then the closure of the economic and cultural gap which still exists. The twin concept of progress and development serves as a signifier of universal values. In ethical terms, to the extent that these values are accepted, they turn the mission of development into one of an unquestionable benevolence (cf. Cowen and Shenton 1996; Rist 1997).

In the attempts at the closure of this development/underdevelopment gap, new messages have continuously made their appearance and have conveyed the message that the benign intervention by the developed Western world is on the verge of taking the developing countries around the bend towards 'progress and development', and, in the respective periods, have engendered a great deal of enthusiasm.

Such enthusiasm, if confronted with the actual achievements of development, may easily transform into dismay and sarcasm. It is not necessary here to address the various less savoury aspects that are associated with development, both in the First World and in the Third World. The dissenting schools will marshal the facts and figures in any of the fields—enduring poverty, widening gaps, eco-disasters, social disintegration, individualism, materialism, cruelty, civil wars, drug addiction, etc.—to argue that the great narrative of development has betrayed its promises and its pledges.

One such dissenting school of thought, fundamentally criticizing the 'Western development project', is the so-called post-modernist school. Development, the theoreticians of post-modernism argue, is a myth altogether. It is a myth that on the one hand re-assures concerned Western citizens that a more humane alternative is possible, and on the other hand throws the Third World citizens off their bearings and make them chase the unattainable and alien Western dream.[1] It is a formidable critique, arguing that the development rituals, the promises, the new initiatives, the ongoing institutions, the celebrations and the policies seem to proceed in a limbo. They are enacted in a world oblivious of the harsh and worsening reality, and possibly are even meant to deflect from the

---

[1] It is, as put strongly by Gilbert Rist (1997: 239), the imposition of a virtual world in which, like in the heaven of religious beliefs, the common good is being realized or is going to be realized in the not so distant future. The foundation under the development paradigm is the 'believability' structure: 'For every belief gets used to temporary uncertainties, and even feeds off them; anyway, they do not challenge the social consensus'.

harsh reality of further marginalization in a large number of regions of the Third World. It is a radical critique, and a critique that may easily become too radical, overshooting its target.

The critique of modernization and development, it is our contention, has to be positioned within modernization and development, albeit in a redefined meaning. This chapter intends to reflect on the post-modern tendency of 'deconstructing the grand narratives', assumed to be narratives of 'Western' civilization and development. Its deconstruction (debunking) of the grand universal ideas is accompanied by a tendency to subdivide the Third World into a myriad of localized cultures, with localized values and narratives, that are assumed to have an inalienable essentiality that has to be protected and groomed.

Typical for the change that has taken place is the title of the book that has been edited in honour of Andre Gunter Frank. The concept of development of underdevelopment (the exploitative and debilitating impact which world capitalism is supposed to have on the 'dependencia' zones) has been the hallmark of Frankian analysis. Surprisingly, however, the editors in their preface to the book in honour of Frank (Chew and Denemark 1996) write that Frank has coined the opposite phrase 'the underdevelopment of development'. This line of thinking actually has come to Frank only recently. *El Subdesarrollo del Desarrollo* was put to print only in 1991, and constitutes a plain example of reversing the argument in tune with the onslaught of post-modernist thinking. The argument has now turned into an attack on development as such. A queer ideological shift has taken place: underdevelopment of development has been substituted for development of underdevelopment. That is the new ideological position, a post-modern injection into the dependencia theory. It amounts to a rejection of the 'modernization agenda' of the various development schools and of the values that have been associated with European Enlightenment.

The Enlightenment agenda is squarely questioned by postmodernism, and also by the ex-dependencia theoreticians. It is argued that the short-lived European hegemony will come to an end, and will make way for a 'humanocentric' alternative. The available models (capitalism and socialism) are pronounced to be inadequate for development. The assumption is that development is actually antidevelopment and that such development runs counter to the interests of the majority of the people.

Which development are we then waiting for in the aftermath of successful new social movements? The specificities of this rupture, the stages involved, the organizational models, and the inter-societal and intra-societal relations are not worked out. Thus, the humanocentric world view appears to get bogged down in romantic religiosity and does not provide clear answers, clear concepts, clear logic, or clear theory.[2] The longish reference to the work of the new Frank and his colleagues serves the purposes of abstracting some of the essential 'narratives' of post-modernism. The 'solutions' remain stuck in vague appeals for a culturally diverse community-based global humanity without a dominant world system. The predatory nation state, often in the service of the predatory forces of globalization, has to be opposed by 'civil society'. It is assumed that universal concepts, ideas, values, norms, and aspirations are basically western reflections.

Post-modernism, as a reaction to the (over?) industrialized world, is a recurrent reflex in a long tradition, and is reminiscent of the many millenarian and counter-culture movements of the past.[3] Although a cry against the injustice of the world at the turn of the millennium, they fail to give a concrete handle for countering the bane of underdevelopment and neo-colonial dominance. The default is typical of the major post-modernist authors. One of the foremost of them, Arturo Escobar, for example, wants to develop alternatives to development, and he commences his book with the intent of the 'the liberation of the discursive field so that the task of imagining alternatives can be commenced' (Escobar 1995: 14). In the end, he concludes his book with the sober message: 'But it is too soon even to imagine the forms of representation that this process might promote. . . . Out of hybrid or minority cultural situations might emerge other ways of building economies, of dealing with basic needs, of coming together in social groups' (Escobar 1995: 215, 225).

If post-modernism is the theory of debunking the established development ethos, it does not excel as a practical guide to the way forward in (alternative forms of) development. It pleads for a multivariate hybrid world culture. Such a culture should, in the view of Escobar,

[2] In the last article in the book on Frank, Immanuel Wallerstein, when he unwraps the dream, adds to the invention of elusive concepts: *utopistics* is what he recommends. It boils down to some form of equality and some form of participative democracy. Its meaning is 'explained' in a couple of sentences: 'It means we have to engage seriously in the project of inventing the future system—not by a philosopher-king, but collectively. We need to debate priorities and the nature of institutions that could implement them' (Chew and Denemark 1996: 361).

[3] Synchronizing with the onset of (industrial) capitalism, ideological movements have sprung up (see for example Kitching 1989). A common factor of these movements was the search for alternatives in a pre-industrialized provincial past.

Esteva, Homi Bhabha, Ashis Nandy, etc., be based on primordiality, indigenousness, non-coloniality, and even on non-economics: 'In spite of the economy, common men on the margins have been able to keep alive another logic, another set of rules. In contrast with the economy, this logic is embedded in the social fabric. The time has come to confine the economy to its proper place: a marginal one' (Esteva 1992: 22).

For all practical purposes, this amounts to a defence of multiple counter-cultures devoid of any reflection on political economy and actually on any aspect of the daily life of the people in development and under underdevelopment.[4]

From the above, it can be concluded that post-modernism intends to be a head-on confrontation with the economic and cultural rationale of the present world order, but that it fails in providing any alternative whatsoever. It tends to construct a world of longing and a world of belonging, but it remains a world without contours and without priorities to strive for. At the same time, it claims to speak on behalf of the downtrodden and the marginalized, the poor and the needy who are construed as being attached to local cultures rather than to a process of modernization.

The weakness of post-modernism is its esoteric level of theorizing and its disdain for collecting field evidence. Post-modernist writing, essentializing the mysterious naturalness of people in the developing countries, accordingly does not excel in an empirical interest in of the view from below. It often boils down to a neo-Orientalist projection of traditional ways and thoughts. Later in this text, I shall present some of the empirical data collected in villages in Uttar Pradesh, which have much to say about the world view and expectations of the downtrodden and the poor.

Fallacies of Post-Modernism

The search for alternatives, a mission of great urgency, requires a reflection on the available options rather than an abstract commitment to the preservation of a myriad of local cultures, amounting to cultural relativism.[5] The aim is to construct a future world on the basis of those

---

[4] Esteva actually hails the crisis that has hit Latin America for the people that have been alienated in the economic structure of globalization would now be in a position to opt out and live new life, of their own making, outside mainstream economics.

[5] The latter tendency in post-modernism has been referred to as holophobia. In opposition to holophobia, there is a plea for the observance and application of

differences. It proceeds on the assumption of a hybrid world, a reading in which 'the selves of the Third World are manifold and multiple'. Alternatives should be directed at 'the goal of *strengthening those differences* by inserting them into political strategies and self-defined and self-directed socio-economic experiments' (Escobar 1995: 215 and 223, italics added).

It is too facile to subsume all universal values under Western value and knowledge systems. Many development concepts and many of the solutions to problems of poverty and exploitation may have originated in the discursive tradition of Western cultural and political circles, and may have served as instruments of power, formerly described as cultural imperialism. This fact, however, would not automatically disqualify them as development alternatives in a Third World environment.

Post-modernism, however, argues differently. All generalizing concepts, including the concept of development, have been marked as 'a regime of representation' only, not as a concept with an analytical portent that should help us to understand structured reality of how and why the world is what it is. Concepts such as 'development', are assigned the role of producing consciousness and hegemony. In a sense we are back to Hegel, who in the mid-nineteenth century also analysed social dynamics in terms of the emergence and imposition of ideas. The theoretical premise is that concepts construct power, unlike for example the Marxian assumption that economic endowment constructs power.

The 'invention of development', as Escobar (1995: 5, 10) has argued, has produced the Third World as an entity, as a discursive construction which has throttled the potential of people in the Third World to follow an independent course:

Reality in sum, had been colonized by the development discourse.... Foucault's work on the dynamics of discourse and power in the presentation of social reality, in particular, has been instrumental in unveiling the mechanisms by which a certain order of discourse produces permissible methods of being and thinking while disqualifying and even making others impossible.... The notion of regimes of representation is a final theoretical and methodological principle in examining the mechanisms for, and consequences of, the construction of the Third World in/through representation.

---

universal values. Nicholson (1990: 8); Gardner and Lewis (1996: 25); David Washbrook (1997) and Terence Turner (1997) for example have pleaded for a commitment to basic values and minimum standards of normative lifestyles rather than endless cultural relativism.

The power of the West is the power to impose ideas that go against the vision, the expectation, and the roots of the people at the receiving end. The acceptance of the idea of development by people in the Third World has thus resulted in a dependent, self-denying aspiration for modernity: 'Development has relied exclusively on one knowledge system, namely the modern Western one. The dominance of this knowledge system has dictated the marginalization and disqualification of non-Western knowledge systems'. Gustavo Esteva (1992: 9) had argued similarly: *'the metaphor of development gave global hegemony to a purely Western genealogy of history, robbing peoples of different cultures of the opportunity to define the forms of their social life'* (italics added).

The political agenda following from such a Hegelian analysis is clear. The concepts of development, progress, modernization, and universality of basic values are assumed to be embedded in a system of dominance and in turn to be contributing to that dominance. Therefore, the sooner the non-Western people are liberated from the alien world views of the dominance of the West, the better.

The assumption in post-modernism is that objectifiable knowledge is bad to start with since it centres on reason, and reason deflects from the innate human nature. The programmatic understanding of 'development' will then reside within pure subjectivity. For many contributors in the post-modernist frame, it also entails a 'deconstruction' and rejection of the Enlightenment ideas that are said to underlie the developmental project. The objection to Enlightenment, i.e. the set of ideas around fraternity, equality, and liberty, is actually presented as having a progressive ring around it since Enlightenment by its very essence is European. Enlightenment is deconstructed as the twin of colonialism, alienation, and oppression. Development is deconstructed as the imposition of neo-colonialism.[6]

Summing up this short theoretical roundup, we want to focus on two assumptions which need to be tested. Post-modernism tends to delineate the micro-cultures as homogeneous, irrespective of class, gender or age, and freezes them as sacrosanct expressions of an ancient past. On the other hand, it posits the non-universality of basic expectations.

---

[6] In typical post-modernist jargon, Neera Chandhoke (1998) establishes that 'the narrative of post-coloniality' actually is the narrative of coloniality that continues to operate through the national elites who have inherited the reigns of the state. The national elite is bent on continuing the predatory process that once was embarked upon by the colonial elites, annihilating the local cultures. They can do this by constructing the ideology of developmental modernity.

Post-modernist authors claim to speak on behalf of the people, more specifically on behalf of 'civil society' against the imposition of an agenda by the predatory post-colonial state. Ashis Nandy (1992: 56) even argues that any modern state is a pathological deformation. He regards 'an indigenous modern state as a contradiction in terminis'. The assertion is that the people in society below the state structures have their own awareness, hopes and aspirations, and that these are opposed to the development agenda of the modern state. We shall take up these assumptions for investigation in a concrete village setting in North India.

Listening to the People

Various incidents which appear as warp and woof in village life, and which have found their way into innumerable studies, reflect underlying antagonisms, jealousies, factionalism, etc. They suddenly appear to erupt from the tranquillity of village life, a tranquillity in which villagers have learned the processes of situational adjustment in social action and in public utterances. From such incidents, one learns that the dominant views on the social order and on the path of development do not have general acceptance. What we find at the local level is a contested world view rather than a homogeneous culture. Most attempts at essentializing such a culture gloss over the world views and aspirations of the powerless, and impose on them a normative model (of development). The understanding and the preferential lifestyles at the lower end of the social order require a careful, patient, and emphatic listening. Down below, usually outside the purview of the administrators and the planners, a distinct view of development is available.

My contention is that this distinct view, i.e. a class and gender specific view, by definition, despite all the positive departures in the management of development projects, is not solicited in the formulation and reformulation of development priorities. Development priorities indeed are closely following the agenda drafted by the neo-colonial power centres, coordinated in the International Monetary Fund/World Bank policy strategy. This agenda is based on a macroeconomic model that generally incapacitates the many and the weak, even when economic growth takes place. Post-modernism has challenged this process of imposition, and has opted for the opposite extreme, indigenous essentialism, a position it claims to be taking on behalf of the indigenous people and their culture.

In both approaches the usage of concepts as civil society, shareholders, empowerment, agency, local culture, ownership and grass roots have become common practice. *Participatory development*, captured by a variety of appealing concepts since the mid-1980s, has been embraced by NGOs and World Bank circles alike.[7]

The veracity of the view from below is difficult to ascertain. Various factors may interfere with a coherent and dependable access to the *developees*. Awareness of the local differences helps us to remind ourselves that findings from local fieldwork settings may not be extrapolated to cover entire areas. Nevertheless, carefully planned and executed fieldwork sheds the light on those spots where post-modernism is extremely weak: the discourse of the people down below. How do they see development?

Two Villages

In order to uncover the social cognition and the world views behind the public stance, three series of surveys in combination with in-depth interviews were conducted in three different areas of Uttar Pradesh, the most populous state in northern India. The purpose was to gauge the reaction of the people to the ambient ideological changes that have come with the process of social and economic modernization. The research was part of a bigger project, which aimed at studying the socioeconomic changes in the context of village councils and devolution (Lieten and Srivastava 1999). In a follow-up study, two adjacent villages, with around 130 and 220 households respectively, were selected in Faizabad, a relatively poor and isolated district of the same state. The female literacy (27.8 per cent and 11.3 per cent) as well as male literacy rates (62.6 per cent and 46.5 per cent) give an indication of the differences between both the villages. The higher literacy in village A is associated with a dominant Brahmin population; in village B does not have a single upper caste family.

The majority of the households owned less than 1 acre of land. Only

---

[7] One of the recent trail-setting contributions was Lawrence Salmen's work *Listen to the People*, pleading for 'an effective way to bring people into the planning and implementation of programmes that affect their lives' (Salmen 1987: 125). His work, like the one of David Korten and Michael Cernea was indicative of the World Bank catching up with the participatory ideology which the NGO, in the footsteps of Paulo Freire, Robert Chambers, and others, were proud to claim as the new panacea.

40 families (11 per cent of the households) owned more than 2.5 acres of land. The bigger landowners reside in village A; one-fourth of the cultivators in that village have irrigation pumps in their fields. In village B, where only 4.8 per cent of the families owns more than 1 acre of land, irrigation pumps have been installed by only about one-tenth of the families. In terms of occupation, 226 of the 362 households could be classified as poor peasant households, and a further 29 and 20 households respectively were middle and rich peasants respectively. In addition, 39 families derived their income from agricultural labour and 27 households were active as artisans. The occupational classification reflects the agrarian orientation of both the villages.

There is a typically strong correlation between land ownership and caste. Whereas the ex-untouchables and Muslims are dominant among the landless and marginal landowning families, rich peasants are almost exclusively Brahmin. Particularly in the Brahmin-dominated village, inter-caste inequalities are severe: land ownership per individual Brahmin was 6.5 times higher than the ownership per individual member of the ex-untouchable castes. The fairly uneven access to land is exacerbated, but in a sense also rectified, by labour migration, which connects many of the families with the industrial centres in the country. One Brahmin extended family with 29 members staying back in the village, had as many as 6 male members serving in government jobs in various cities. Unlike their illiterate wives, they all had good educational degrees. The income from migration, in addition to that from a reasonable fertile land, has helped most families to improve their economic condition.

Most of the agricultural labour and small peasant families are still in poverty. Particularly when diseases or deaths occur, when marriages are to be financed and when the number of dependents increases, deterioration into abject poverty will follow. Among these families, I found that one quarter of the families do not possess any durables and for their clothes and even for their food often have to negotiate a loan, at 5 per cent to 10 per cent interest a month. On the other hand, when the ratio of earning members *vis-à-vis* dependent members has increased, and when some migrant labour earnings contribute to the running of the household, these families are able to pull back to normal conditions of poverty. The survey of all the poor households indicates that the appreciation of the changes in the economic position is more or less in balance between the positive and the negative cases.

On the basis of the assets (house, vehicles, agricultural equipment, durable goods) in combination with land ownership and the occupational diversification, we have divided the households over five status groups, ranging from very poor to very rich (see Table 8.1). The picture that emerges confirms the continuation of upper caste dominance. Together with some lower caste families and some elite Muslim families, they account for the rich and very rich families in both the villages, and do not have a single family in the poorest category.

In both villages, after the socio-economic mapping, we wanted to get an idea of the conception of development priorities among the villagers. We selected 137 respondents (86 males and 51 females), who were evenly spread over the various age and status groups and over the kinship groups (27 Muslims, 39 SC, 41 OBC, and 30 upper castes; see note to Table 8.1 for explanations).

My intrusion into their lives made many not feel at ease. They were not immediately appreciative of the purpose of the visit and of the informality of the session. Confronted with general questions such as the meaning of development and the changes aspired for in the village, answers were often difficult to get, and they feigned indifference or ignorance. This initial response, it turned out, was a cover-up for fear of public defiance. In real life, their opinion was hardly ever asked for

Table 8.1: Village Status Groups (% Caste-wise)

Status group	Total N	Brahmins	OBC	SC	Muslim
Very poor	58	0	10.3	58.7	31.0
Poor	203	7.9	35.5	36.4	20.2
Middle	65	23.1	15.4	24.6	36.9
Rich	31	49.7	24.5	0	25.8
Very rich	5	100	0	0	0
Total	362				

Note: For all practical purposes, the Indian caste system has three division. At the bottom are the ex-untouchable castes. In the Indian legislation, for the purpose of positive discrimination, they have been referred to as Scheduled Castes (SC). Above them, but also low on the Hindu scales of purity and respect, are the Other Backward Castes (OBC) who in the early 1990s have also been provided with some measures of positive discrimination. Above them, we have three strata (Brahmins, Kshatriya, and Vaishya) who together form the upper castes and used to control much of the economic, political, and administrative power.

and, if solicited, they have learned not to defy the views of the village strongmen. They therefore initially wished to comply or to indulge in the politics of silence. When the informality and the confidentiality of the discussion were established, opinions were expressed.

The State

What was expressed was very much in line with conventional developmentalism. Roads, schools, a hospital, handpumps, sanitation, and irrigation were the more tangible wishes; a return to the village ethics and freedom of insecurity were the more abstract wishes.

The return to village morality is not to be construed as a confirmation of the post-modernist agenda of a return to a tangible pre-colonial indigenousness. It is rather related to an ambivalent reaction in the midst of changes. On the one hand, there are the material goods like clothes and two meals a day, and the infrastructural provisions, like education, sanitation, health schemes, and transport, which have made life less cumbersome and gloomy. The appalling levels of material deprivation, illiteracy and morbidity of the past have been overcome. On the other hand, economic individualism, decreasing cordiality, and the influx of new lifestyles have brought disorder and even insecurity. The worries and anxieties which this process has generated is also likely to be associated with compensatory illusions, i.e. the mental resurrection of the proverbial harmonious past. Under circumstances of injustice, disorder, and misery in the present *kaliyug* or dark age, the projection of a past era of justice, honesty, and rectitude can bring succour.

Roads and schools are seen as the key into a world of more development, opening the avenues for communication with the outside world, and bringing in work opportunities and new knowledge and technology.

The development that has taken place has been a class-specific development. It was based on the capitalist market economy, which fostered a lopsided growth, and was underwritten by a state that had close links with the dominant rural classes. The developmental state is being run by a bureaucracy that by and large originates from these classes and accordingly has put in place development projects which benefited the haves more than the have-nots. The poor villagers are keenly aware of this biased development model and of the domination of the rich over the instruments of state power. References to the works undertaken by the government departments are accordingly often accompanied by sneering remarks about the money that has gone down the drain.[8]

Nevertheless, the acceptance of *sarkar* (government) as the major and more reliable development actor is unequivocal. Government is generally not despised for what it does, but for what it does not do, namely its inactivity in eradicating corruption: 'When dishonesty will disappear, poverty will end.' Several statements, particularly by the poorer people, indicate that the government is doing its best, but that the middlemen have occupied the space at the delivery point, and that the all-pervasive corruption prevents the benefits from reaching the people. The government is assessed for what it claims to be doing, namely providing general facilities for rural development and target oriented facilities to the poorer sections, and it is taken to task for what in practice it allows to happen: the fragmentation of the resources among its strategic support base.

There is no suggestion that the state is an alien body, at loggerheads with the community in the 'civil society', and that autonomous space should be regained from the interventionist state. The priorities of the poor, it appears, are particular and personal, but also, unlike the assumption by Chambers (1983: 148), general and abstract. They include the eradication of corruption so that the benefits of the government schemes may reach the target group. This in fact suggests that the need is for more government intervention rather than less.

In this sense, the dichotomy that in much post-modernist writing has been posed to exist is not reflected by this segment of the Indian civil society.[9] The idea of a local community with its set of rules, its reciprocity, and its self-sufficiency does not have many takers, particularly not among the poorer classes. The state, in the wake of economic and political changes extending over many decades, has filled that space. The

---

[8] Numerous have been the complaints by the respondents that although the expenses may have been duly entered into the books, most of the money in fact has gone to line the pocket of the local administrators and of their friends, with a further cut for the higher echelons. It is often suggested, and sometimes illustrated that much of what comes from the government, is snatched away by the influential people.

[9] The fulmination of post-modernism, in line with anarchism and with the neo-liberal credo, against the state, does not appear to be echoed by the people in many other villages which we studied in northern India in the past (see Lieten 1996b, 2001a, 2002a; Lieten and Srivastava 1999).

entry of the state into the local arena as a matter of fact, as Pranab Bardhan has argued, is not all the modernizing and predatory elite's doing:

The community institutions have been in decay for quite some time, at least partly out of internal reasons. . . . With the decline of the hierarchical authority and with the moral and political environment of age-old deference to community norms changing, [the] state's penetration was thus partly in response to invitation to fill an institutional vacuum. (Bardhan 1997: 190)

The resurrection of those communitarian, inward-looking local institutions is not what the low-caste and low-class villagers are pining after. Popular demands for more equality and material comfort have brought the modernizing state to the remotest corners of the country, and despite the many misgivings about corruption, malfunctioning, and inappropriate, elite-oriented development projects, the supra-local state is conceived as a potentially helpful ally. We may infer that the presence of the state as a development agent is based on a popular mandate.

Priorities

If the state is accepted as a development agent, in what direction would one expect it to formulate policies? The obvious answer would be that it should have a policy that brings welfare and happiness to the highest number of people. Depending on where one stands philosophically and politically, the economic agenda shall have different features. In the midst of the debates on development, where do poor villagers stand, and do they in a way bemoan the developmentist departure which they have experienced?

We have learned earlier that the village people suggested development initiatives belonging to the conventional pattern: roads, schools, hospitals, sanitation, etc. In order to get some idea of priorities, we confronted them with five choices, and asked the respondents to prioritize these five forms of development intervention. Sequentially, they were asked to choose between one type of intervention and each one of the other four types, i.e. twenty choices had to be made. Each choice was marked with a positive and a negative value. For example, if education was preferred to development finances, to land reforms, and to a clean administration, but not to employment generation, it would receive a +3 score, and the others, except for employment generation (+1), would receive a 1 score. After all the scores were averaged by the number of respondents, an aggregate idea of the development priorities could be had. Table 8.2 reveals the overall preferences and the distinctive differences between the various status groups.

Table 8.2: Class-wise Development Priorities

	All (N=137)	Very poor (N=15)	Rich (N=18)
Education	−2.00	−3.60	−0.11
Development finances	−1.88	−1.96	−1.55
Land reforms	−1.50	+0.13	−3.22
Clean administration	+2.87	+2.87	+2.66
Employment generation	+2.51	+2.56	+2.22

The findings are interesting on many counts. In the detailed discussions with selected families, we have been in a position to elaborate further on some of these choices. At this stage it is interesting to note that there is a concurrence across the classes on three types on intervention: employment generation and particularly the institution of a transparent and clean administration have high levels of support; financial support programmes on the other hand score rather low. Foremost as a poverty eradication instrument is employment. A few people do see some solution in loans for self-employment, but at least one-third of the suggestions argue for regular employment in factories and rural industries so that particularly landless families will be able to get one job per family. The class-wise disagreement relates to education and land reforms. Whereas the poor households do have hopes for land reforms and do not see much benefit in education, the richer households take the opposite view.

These findings are striking for various reasons. Much of the development effort since the 1970s has been channelled through individual financial support programmes. After the lead taken by government institutions (e.g. the Integrated Rural Development Programme), the idea has been re-invented by The World Bank and by the NGOs under the banner of micro-credit programmes. It is probably the personal experience of the poor people that much of the money disappears in wrong hands. It is probably also their experience, and the experience of the middle groups, that the financial obligations which come with the (subsidized) loans impinge on their future earnings and in the balance, given the constraints of the market, may not add to their security. Probably, the adverse opinion of development finances is directly linked to, and caused by the corrupt, arbitrary, obnoxious, inaccessible, and negligent bureaucracy. The call for 'good governance', a World Bank prescription since the early 1990s, is apparently echoed at the village level, but it carries a more mundane meaning.

Villagers across class, gender, and caste seem to realize that a clean administration, somewhat more responsive to the needs and expectations of the people, is a prerequisite if employment programmes and target support programmes are to function. The transparency and fairness in public development planning have their bearings on the 'development planning' of the individual households. These findings are actually in line with the general reliance on the state as a development actor as we alluded earlier. The opposition is not to state development programmes, but to programmes executed by a state bureaucracy which, in line with the basic character of the state, looks after the interests of the elite. The interception of the resources by the elite is the issue to be addressed. Chambers (1983: 138) has used the image of snakes and ladders: more snakes than ladders at the bottom of the board, keeping the poor poor, and more ladders then snakes at the top, helping the rich to get richer: 'The problem is to reverse the trend—to load the dice differently, to make more ladders near the bottom.'

Ladders to modernity may be a gruesome thought for postmodernist thinking, but not for the poor villagers in a northern Indian district, who appear to be striving for modernity. However, modernity need not be a Western modernity. Some crucial features are associated with modernity has. They have to do with education, health, emancipation from material deprivation, a certain degree of freedom and mobility. These features have been found to be very much in the vision of the villagers in the locality under study.

The assumption that all modernity is Western and that as a matter of fact it is a Western ploy of dominance and further suppression, constitutes the basic fallacy of post-modernism. As such, modernity can even combine with a re-invigoration of tradition, which is what makes the villages all over the world differently, and in a sense similar.[10] The academic construct of an otherness, which is also essential to postmodernism, does not tally with the mundane wishes that we have just

---

[10] The fault with post-modernity is that it assumes a closed system of cultures and denies the inevitability of historical changes, changes which have their causal origins within internal mechanisms and extraneous influences. David Washbrook has rightly argued that there is not one invariant model of modernity, but that modernity expresses itself different in different contexts, with a high degree of continuity with tradition manifested in them. There is 'a tendency to hypostasise *the West* as possessed of an original and authentic culture and history, which distinguishes it absolutely from all Other and Traditional cultures and histories' (Washbrook 1997: 410).

observed in the 'non-Western' setting. What we have observed in the sample villages is rather more commonness than otherness. Differences between cultures do exist—with gender, class, age, and neighbourhood variations—but universal features common to people living under different social relations, economic systems, and cultural peculiarities may very well co-exist with the differences. General principles of fairness, justice, equity, and freedom are likely to inform the innate human condition. The urge for 'development' would follow from such a condition. The adherence to universal principles and the grand narrative of development need not be in contradiction with respect for multivariate cultures.

Concluding Remarks

Generally, there is a conflict around the direction that development should take. Post-modernism in recent years has become an active beacon in the debate, attracting to its side many scholars concerned about (non—and lopsided) development in a globalizing world. Its forcefully formulated dismay of development is not matched by the formulation of an alternative beyond reiterating that the alternative should be embedded in community cultures, unsoiled by development. In the process, post-modernism also questions and jettisons any possibility of universalizable ideas. People in Asia are not supposed to have ideas on progress, democracy, secularism, equality, and solidarity that are similar to the ones in the 'Western world'.

The anti-modernist school of thought ascribes to the non-European people an essential otherness (typical of the dichotomy constructed by the Orientalists during colonial times). It is the otherness of an ancient culture, of harmony and solidarity among the people, of communal living and respect for nature. In homogenizing and romanticizing the indigenous mentality, it constructs an ideal type pattern that is devoid of an economic and political analysis. In a normative sense, its denies the local communities the choice to an alternative in development along a modernist path.

We have stated that post-modernism is strong on ethical assumptions and projections but poor on locally informed perspectives. How do their theories about perceptions in civil society, as opposed to the state ideology, square with the views held by the people below, in this case a rather backward village in northern India? The material presented in this chapter shows that villagers in a randomly chosen area in northern India generally appear to have aspirations, hopes, wishes, and visions very much akin to, and as divergent as, the views and aspirations in the more 'developed' part of the world.

The controversy about development, a controversy among learned scholars, operates at the local level as well. The views in the villages are differentiated across age, class, and gender, generally are also aligned to the normative expectations of development into modernity.

The questions which, in post-modernist theories, have been raised about this modernist path, about its multiple ecological, social, moral, and political deformations, in the end may be more logically and urgently addressed to the agents of globalization—the destructive imperialist institutions—than to the local institutions of the state and to the Third World villager. This villager is still looking for solace in more development rather than less. The extremely radical critique of development, rather than of the specific form of development, which is being pushed by the international financial, industrial, and military complex, deflects from an analysis of, and a confrontation with, the real causes of non-development and lopsided development. It pre-empts the formulation of alternatives in development based on equity and fairness, which is what the (poor) villagers are waiting for.

CHAPTER 9

Women, Caste and Religion in a North Indian Village

The area around Sisauli in Muzaffarnagar district constitutes an ideal setting for the study of rural development and its impact on changes in the socio-cultural parameters. Earlier (Chapter 3), we have studied the (non-) functioning of the *panchayats* in this area. In the present chapter, after describing the historical and economic specificities of the research area, the focus shall be on the contrast between the deficiency of the democratic structure and the numerous divergent views, challenging and contesting each other.

A Green Revolution Area

Skirted by the Ganga in the east and the Jamuna in the west, Muzaffarnagar district in western Uttar Pradesh, as a square perched between Meerut and Saharanpur, has established its mark as one of the most successful Green Revolution areas in the country. The remarkable success of the district is associated with a highly fertile soil, an ancient irrigation system, and a peculiar land system, the so-called *bhaichara* system.[1] The *bhaichara* land system facilitated the emergence of a class of peasant cultivators who were ready to physically engage in agriculture and who had sufficient resources and sufficient land to apply the indivisible input package. In western UP generally, rich peasants (with at least 7.5 acres of land) on the eve of the Green Revolution may have represented one-fourth of the peasant households and may have operated three-fourth

[1] The term *bhaichara* applies to villages owned by descendants of a common stock (Crooke 1989: 134). The villages had been granted rent-free, or had been occupied by force. Ownership of the land had gone into the hands of the (sub)lineages of the original settlers. By custom (*chara*), the clan council of the community (*bhai*) would supervise the land use and manage the land revenue (Pradhan 1966: 34–6).

of the land (Saith and Tankha 1972). The land reforms decade did not alter this iniquitous access to land (see Saith and Tankha 1992 for figures on a neighbouring district). The rural population has been neatly divided between middle and big peasants on the one hand and the landless service class on the other hand. The agricultural labour-peasant ratio has increased from 0.63 in 1971 to 0.82 in 1981 and 0.84 in 1991 (see also Singh 1992: 40–64).

The district has an excellent irrigation system, which actually dates from (pre-)colonial times.[2] Most of the soil has a highly fertile loam structure, which in combination with irrigation facilities on much of the land allows for two abundant crops per year, mainly rice and maize in the *kharif* season and wheat in the *rabi* season. Sugar cane has replaced cotton as the important cash crop. Sugar cane crushers and sugar mills have been erected in the vicinity of most villages.

The population of the district (2.2 million in 1991), in the last decades has become more and more urbanized: from 13.9 per cent in 1971 to 21.7 per cent in 1981 and 24.6 per cent in 1991. This does suggest that as a consequence of the process of depeasantization, an increasing number of people have been pushed out of agriculture, and have moved into the secondary or tertiary sector in the cities.

The agrarian dynamism in the wake of the Green Revolution is not reflected in the human development variables. The crude literacy of males of 45.5 per cent in 1991 (40.7 per cent in 1981) was roughly at the average UP level. The literacy rate of women was almost three percentage points above the state average, but the low level (23.5 per cent) and the slow progress in comparison with 1981 (17.5 per cent) indicate that no radical departure has materialized in the wake of economic expansion and entrepreneurial dynamism. The conservative attitude is exemplified in the relegation of girls and women to a dependent and serving role. The continuing low sex ratio in the area may be a reflection of this disregard for women. The area, ever since the first Census Reports in the second half of nineteenth century, has been infamous for its low sex ratio: 857 in 1891, 825 in 1941, and 861 in 1991. Since

---

[2] The modern irrigation system superseded an ancient irrigation system which had provided the area with a relatively dense irrigation network, namely the Yamuna Canal and Ganga Canal systems, even before the onset of colonialism. The canal construction by the colonial government had proceeded on the assumption that the area was 'populated by enterprizing peasant cultivators who possessed a relatively large resource base in terms of land and finance and who could be expected to obtain the maximum benefit in terms of increased production' (Clift 1977: A83).

scheduled castes usually, at least during the last decennia, had a sex ratio of close to 900, it is safe to assume that the Jats and upper castes in the area had a sex ratio close to 800.[3]

Muslims form a sizeable minority: slightly more than one-fourth of the total population, and more than one-third in the cities. The proportion has hardly changed between the mid-nineteenth century (Atkinson 1876; Census of India 1891 and 1921) and the late twentieth century. The Partition in 1947 also does not seem to have had much effect on the composition of the population. In the nationalist movement, Muslims and Hindus had united within the INC (Indian National Congress party) umbrella, and at the time of the communal violence in 1947, the traditional *jati* and village *panchayats* joined forces in beating back the fanatics (Pradhan 1966). Religious strife appears to have been absent from the district.[4]

The cultural and religious life in the district has not only been void of 'bigotry', it was also religiously amorphous. The Hindus by and large did not have much identification with and loyalty to the grand religion of the Brahmins. The many instances of paganism and fetishism indicated to Atkinson (1876: 80) that the Hindu tribes 'prove Hinduism proper to be a name. Brahmanism is something quite above the comprehension of the masses.' Especially among the lower caste, the Brahmanical pantheon and the religious idiom from *karma* to *moksha* did not find many takers.[5]

After this short introduction, I intend to go down to the individual perceptions that exists in the villages in the area. Reactions to village

[3] This conclusion can be established by the figures of the 1921 Census when specific figures, caste-wise and religion-wise, were available. In Thana Budhana, which includes Sisauli, Muslims had a sex ratio of 872; Hindus had a sex ratio of 807.

[4] The secular tradition goes back for many decades. Atkinson (1876: 77) reported that 'there is none of that religious bigotry which is so characteristic of the relations between Musalmans and Hindus in other districts'. Many of the Muslims were converts from all sections of the Hindu population, and carried with them many of the rituals and popular beliefs of Hinduism. Jats, Dhobis, Ranghads (ex-Rajputs), Julaha weavers, etc., are some of the *jatis* which in the course of history have converted to Islam (Blunt 1931: 200–3).

[5] Polenda (1983: 241) reports that before the reconversion work of the Arya Samaj, the sweepers caste in the area worshipped a Muslim saint, and 'in ritual, the gestures and forms of worship were largely Muslim'. Jats until the adoption of the Hindu Marriage Act in many respects deviated from the standard Brahmanical rules. See also Muzaffarnagar Gazetteer 1980: 66; Pradhan (1966: 87).

politics and to the socio-economic developments in general have been canvassed among a random sample of 149 households in two villages in Shahpur block.[6] The purpose was to gauge the reaction of the people to the ambient ideological changes which have come with the process of social and economic modernization. In the process, some understanding should emerge of the various ways in which the caste system and the religious values are perceived, and how they are practised, and of the motive forces in social and political engagement. Since it is assumed that the area is known for its male Jat power and dominance, special attention will be paid in a later section to such central issues as the position of women and the position of lower caste people.

Economic Progress, Social Corrosion

On one issue, practically all the villagers are in unison: despite the economic progress (or because of the economic progress), the social quality of life is deteriorating. One of the eldest women in the Bhangi *biradari* knows it for sure: this is the *kaliyug* age. The reasons given for the alleged deterioration are manifold. Some people blame the growing materialism and selfishness. Others see pitfalls in the interface between the commercial development of agriculture and the financial risks involved. Women often blame the failure of the family heads to instil traditional values and on films and television programmes. Some rich peasants blame it on the population explosion.

The changes in economic activities have a manifold impact on the social praxis, although it must be remembered that these changes have been handed down from a previous generation. Already in the 1960s, Pradhan (1966: 18) wrote: 'Individualization has eroded the traditional values of simplicity, equality, honesty and kinship. . . . In short, Jat society is changing'. The traditional *bhaichara*, which had an economic as well as a social and political function, is on the wane. A number of family ties has snapped under the pressure of wealth and envy. Even in the past, the traditional solidarity (within the *biradari*) may have been more fiction than fact, but the differentiation which has occurred in the wake of the Green Revolution has made the break in solidarity more tangible.

---

[6] The sample of 124 males and 25 females included 10 Brahmins, 72 Jats, 28 Backward Castes, 29 harijans and 10 Muslims; 63 families were landless, 19 families had less than 2 acres of land, 38 families had between 2 and 6 acres, and 27 families had more than 6 acres.

Despite the complaints about the deterioration of the mores and norms, Jat peasants generally prefer the village life to city life. The village, they say, offers space, healthy air, abundant food, and still more cordiality than the city, but they also are uneasy about the insecurity. The major complaint, not only by the SC people who traditionally have been at the receiving end, relates to the surge of *goonda-gardi*. One Brahmin, an ex-teacher summarises, his views on the so-called village cordiality and tranquillity as follows: 'Crime, theft, dacoit, murders and rapes. Even in daytime, there is insecurity, but in any case, people want to reach home before the night falls.' The low-caste people complain that Jat *goondas* are moving around with pipeguns, and that it is better to keep out of their way. The women complain that it is not safe to go to the fields to attend to the call of nature, and that if they do not move in groups, they may get accosted. People from all groups, males and females, complain that the teasing, dacoity, and kidnapping are so widespread that it is risky to send the girls to continue their studies after class IV in the nearby town.

The discourse on insecurity and criminalization mainly deals with virtual reality. The collective assessment of decreasing cordiality and increasing insecurity is likely to be based on real stories of the immediate neighbourhood, on twisted stories of adjoining villages and on invented stories of the wider area. In the case of the dominant castes, it is probably also induced by the declining caste dominance. Whereas hitherto there was compliance and order, nowadays there is some defiance and therefore disorder. The reference to insecurity is thus likely to be a reflection of the corrosion of the old mechanism based on dominance and fear. The word often used for cordiality and kindness, which is supposed to have balanced village life in the past, is not *prem* (love), but *prem bhoy* (love and fear or respect).

The assessment in terms of insecurity, however, particularly in the case of the lower castes, is also likely to be associated with compensatory illusions, i.e. the psychological need for a mental construct which makes misery and distress bearable by transcending it towards a golden past or a heavenly future. Since the lower castes, as we shall see, by and large do not countenance the idea of comfort in heaven (*moksha*, or release from bodily existence), the mental resurrection of a more harmonious past helps to kindle the hope for a better life. The present age is known and experienced as the *kaliyug* age. Under circumstances of injustice, disorder, and misery, the memories of the *satiyug* age of justice, honesty, and rectitude can bring succour.

The imaginary of a recent golden past indeed serves, to quite a few as an antidote to a life of poverty and powerlessness. The village happens to be the place where they make a living and its has a mixed bag of attractions. To some, city life seems attractive. The city provides employment at higher wages and better educational facilities, and in addition, it is also free of the injustice and the harassment which they have to undergo in the villages at the hands of the Jat and Rajput landowners. Neither the open space and the clean air nor the cordiality and abundant food, which the richer villagers tend to evoke, carry much meaning for the poor people. In the words of one Chamar dwarf peasant: 'Village life actually is only good for landed property holders. Here we are gulam (slaves). In the city, there is no harassment on the basis of caste, which is good for us.' If he did not have his land, he would seriously consider moving to the city. His stand is ambiguous though, for he realizes that the city as well has its pool of insecurities. Ali Raza, an elderly labourer, explicates that apprehension and points at the advantages of a small scale environment, such as a village: 'Social life has deteriorated, I agree, but even then it is better than in the cities because here we know each other and whoever wants to create riots and do injustice to us, he will not dare to do so since others will not like it. So we are safer here.'

Ali Raza is a Muslim, and he knows that in the cities, given the raking up of communal fires by forces allied to the Bharatiya Janata Party (BJP) life and property of Muslims are at stake (cf. Jeffery and Jeffery 1994 for a neighbouring district). In the micro context of the village, however, his safety depends on giving due respect to the power holders, and sometimes, depending on the class position, continuing to live the life of a *gulam* (slave), as some maintain. Asymmetric reciprocity, dependency on patronage, is the key to protection. After all, most of the lower castes depend on the powerful Jats for employment. Straightforward caste suppression, as we shall argue later, has eased substantially.

More open forms of class relations and class suppression may have entered, but also, in the wake of increasing mobility, many landless households have left the village, or migrate seasonally. It helps them to a higher (buffer) income and exerts pressure on the local agricultural wages. It has also helped a number of them to economically escape abject dependence.

One such person is Rampal Singh, used to work as a sweeper, until during the Indira Gandhi days he got a tiny piece of land that he now cultivates, he supplements the income from the land with daily wage work. The wages are not always paid on time and in full, but he refuses to accept the idea that he is still a *gulam*, and that the social environment has deteriorated. Rampal is absolutely illiterate, but he appears to have a good sense of dialectics in the historical process:

There is not so much difference between city and village. Crimes, violence, harassment, all these things go on everywhere. There is not much caste in the cities, but also here it has become much less rigid. You see, when our country became free, I remember that we were then allowed to take water from their well. Once such things are done, they cannot be undone. Many other such changes have crept in. A few people have started it, others have opposed it, but in the end the environment improves, becomes more free.

Freedom and helplessness, like poverty, are relative and dynamic concepts, operating at different levels and in different societal fields. The absolute dejection and semi-bondage in which the lower caste agricultural labourers and seasonal industrial workers used to live, belong to bygone days. That at least is the picture which is transmitted by the standards of living. Whether the expanding economic opportunities indeed also have led to a rearrangement of the traditional social structure, will be dealt with in the next section.

Churning and Bewilderment

The bewilderment in civil society, which clearly erupted around 1990 and led to calls for the strong and benign ruler, has been compounded by the collapse of the political party consensus. The party support in the past had been fluctuating, but generally the strategic interests of the farmers, i.e. the Jat farmers, were looked after. After the death of Charan Singh in the mid-1980s, his mantle was taken over by Ajit Singh, his son, and by Mahendra Singh Tikait, the emerging peasant leader. Their fight for the command over the peasantry in western UP led Tikait to call for supporting the BJP in the 1991 elections. One particularly source of dissatisfaction with the Janata Party was on account of V.P. Singh who introduced reservation for the backward castes. 'It was good that he was thrown out,' says a 50-year old Jat peasant, 'because he had started to give too much attention to the lower castes.'

The unearthing of the report of the Mandal Commission, and the decision to introduce a system of positive discrimination for the Backward Castes was one of the reasons for Ajit Singh to move away from the mother party and for many potential supporters from the middle and upper castes to abandon V.P. Singh in favour of the BJP. To hardly any Jat whom we talked to did *Hindutva* carry any religious or cultural meaning. Instead it was the Mandal Commission which preoccupied their minds. A Jat is not concerned about the construction of a temple or about the niceties of the *dharma* involved. The class source of the BJP victory in the 1991 and later elections was clear: 11 of its 18 supporters in our sample at that time were rich peasants, and all its supporters with one exception had made it to the grade of TV owners. The two small peasants who had opted for the lotus symbol had done so because Tikait had asked them to do so. In view of the dissatisfaction with Congress and Janata Dal, the BJP at that time was looked on as an alternative delivery system. The BJP reaped the windfall, but real commitment to the party came with a motorbike.[7]

Motorized BJP-wallas like Kalyan Singh claim that the Hindus had been sleeping. Kalyan Singh has only 2.5 acres of land, but as a government employee in a strategic position, he earns a good living. The motorized Hindu speaks the ethical language of Hinduism and civilizational values, and expects the government to be stricter by exhorting that the government should profess more *imandari* (honesty): *Yata raja vata praja* (So the king, so his people). Furthermore, he maintains that these days, even children are defying the elders, and it will be necessary to go back to the proper Hindu traditions. Although he agrees that the interests of the *kisan* has been hit by the BJP, he still favours it as 'it is a party of businessmen':

Yes, the Jats were awake, but not in religious matters. The Hindus were sleeping. The temple in the village was lying unused. That has changed now. We have purchased a sound installation, and every morning *kirtans* are being sung for the solace of the whole village. Mohammedans and Christians have always been conscious about their religion and have propagated it. We also should have priests to do that.

Two of his rich peasant neighbours have also taken this line and have converted to Hinduism in a new way. Unlike Kalyan Singh, they are also conscious of the material advantage (*labh*) which the Muslim-Hindu conflict can bring them. One of them shares 8 acres of land with the families of his three brothers; with all the children growing up in the joint household, the search for outside jobs has started. Although the BJP may not help the peasants, under its reign, he feels, the Muslims will

---

[7] One write-up in the *Times of India* (24 October 1990) with a sneering reference to the upper middle class car owners of the urban BJP support base had the heading 'Toyota Hinduism'. In Muzaffarnagar, the staunch BJP backers, without exception, own a motorbike.

be 'sent back' to Pakistan, or they will loose their rights in India, and then 'we will get their jobs'.

The Jats, although not imbibed by Brahmanism, by and large are staunch defenders of the caste system. Even those who repudiate it, at least in official discourse, are opposed to a policy instrument such as reservation. They argue that reservation is wrong because it clashes with the universal values of fairness. The more conscious individuals among the lower castes on the other hand also have doubts about reinforcing the caste identity, in the wake of reservation policies and agitations, but they proceed from the basic reality on the ground, namely caste suppression in its various manifestations, i.e. politically, socially and economically. Thus, while they decline to regard the reservation as a panacea, they insist that it will help in balancing the economic disparities between castes, as a consequence of which a social struggle for societal equality can proceed. Total social and economic equality will be possible only, one of the Kahar teachers argues, by a political struggle and for that struggle the poor people need their own party. This party then, in the second half of the 1990s, somewhat later than in the rest of UP, emerged in the form of the BSP (Bahujan Socialist Party). The emergence of this party appears to have bolstered caste as a social institution and may have sustained the segmentation of society in locked hierarchies.

Caste

Traditionally, the economic and social texture of Indian villages has been perceived through the prism of *jajmani*. Its various interpretations (among others Wiser, Dumont, Leach) have been dominant in the 1950s and 1960s, and have informed sundry village studies undertaken in Uttar Pradesh. Many of these studies were undertaken by American scholars—Marriott, Lewis, Gould, Beidelman—and also by Miriam Sharma (1979) and Saith and Thanka (1972). Another scholar, Pauline Kolenda, on the basis of her field work in Muzaffarnagar in the 1950s, concluded that the demise of the caste system as a system was imminent.[8]

[8] Kolenda (1983: 72) argued that the village was no longer an isolated fortress, and that, since the dominant caste was increasingly oriented towards commercial agriculture, the disintegration of the *jajmani* obligations would follow: 'While during the Village Fortress period whatever food was produced could be distributed to hardworking and loyal lower caste retainers, during the Commercial Farm period, food can be sold, and other crops can be raised for monetary profit.'

In retrospect, it would seem that the confidence in the fading of the caste system with the weakening of the master-servant relationship was inappropriate. Caste retains its palpable importance as a social and political category, if not as a craft category; the positioning on the *varna* scale remains largely congruent with the class position and the system continues to regulate marriages by means of *jati* endogamy. But does it also remain the signifier which gives meaning and direction to life, to lifestyles and to social conduct?

Kolenda, on the basis of her study had already provided material to suggest that positions were shifting in the 1950s. Since it was difficult to find ideal types—ideologies of each respondent were 'a complicated set of views, displaying inconsistencies [and] ambiguities'—she mapped the views and expectations around four 'main anchorages' or clusters. One of the clusters was still defined in terms of caste hierarchy, pollution, reincarnation, *dharma* and *karma*. Ideas about the desirability of social and economic advance by the lower caste and about the need for inter-caste equality, however, were clearly ingredients of the other clusters. Despite the presence of the equality paradigm, none of the key respondents could visualize the abolition of caste:

None of the men is able to envisage a social order free from restrictions on inter-caste social intercourse. Only the Chamar could imagine people of different castes eating from one plate and smoking from one pipe. The Sweeper is all too eager to discriminate against other castes with respect to food restrictions, and the Rajput opposes inter-dining as a violation of ancestral rules. (Kolenda 1983: 123)

Ideas on the significance of *dharma* and *karma* in the 1950s differed, but common to all the anchorages, as suggested by Kolenda, was the religious sanctioning of the position in society. Religious concepts were clearly the signifiers which helped to explain the social positioning of the *biradari*. Kolenda did a re-study of the same village in 1984. As in the previous study, she worked with a limited number of (male) respondents only. From this limited selection, she learned that a new word *parivartan* had entered the village discourse. The word contained not only the expectation of change and progress, but also of progress with equal rights for everybody. The defiance of caste as an ascriptive social system had thus emerged as a mainstream ideology. Economy and society were felt to be in change, in progress, and the ascribed functions and professions of the older society were in question. The elderly folks, in their sixties and seventies, could still argue that the casteism (*jat-pat*) was good, but this was never the case among the younger respondents 'all of whom pronounce jat-pat a *kharab* [bad] or *bahut bura* [very evil] way of ordering society' (Kolenda 1989: 1836).

Around the turn of the millennium, the caste ideology appears to be more problematical and enduring than Kolenda has suggested. Discourse and practice, explanation and expectation definitely have changed, but the change is not as clear-cut as suggested. A generalization about a rejection of *jat-pat* by the younger generation *versus* an acceptance of the system by the older generation is not warranted. In our sample, excluding Muslims and some Chamars who preferred not to give an opinion, 75 people rejected the caste system ideologically, but as many as 49 still did consider the system as a beneficial, justified, and useful way of ordering society.[9]

The range of opinions on the origins and on the functioning of the caste system is vast. The range of ideas reflects the intra-caste individualization. It can be referred to as a myriorama of views, multiple images on the horizon. The various shades of opinion can be arranged along a continuum. On the one hand, a group of people, mainly Jats, particularly female Jats, argue that caste is a God-ordained system, which is directly related to reincarnation. On the other side, a small group, belonging to various *jatis*, holds that the caste order is a suppressive system of class exploitation. This group further argues that it should be actively undermined by inter-caste marriages and other frontal attacks against its norms and practices. Between the two extremes, various intermediate positions are the rule. Younger people generally tend to take a dismissive and secular attitude; women of middle and upper range *viradaris* generally take a positive and sacral attitude.

The thesis that educational progress will lead to a questioning of the caste system (Kolenda 1989) is not reflected by the evidence: educational levels do not appear to make much difference in the way people look at the caste system. The most important variable is the position in the caste system itself: none of the SC respondents has any appreciation neither for the origins nor for the continuation of the caste division. Only one elderly OBC peasant does consider God as the source of all good and all evil, and therefore also as the creator of the caste system, but yet he is unable to understand 'why God has created such a bad and wicked system'.

---

[9] Since Kolenda had only a limited number of 'key informants' and did not try a sociological survey, we can not compare our percentages with her, but one may suggest that opinions may not have changed that much.

The caste system as a creation of God is an idea which still appeals to a number of Jat and Brahmin women, but apart from them only the proverbial exceptional Brahmin male thinks along the lines of a God-ordained *dharma* and *karma*. The ideas underlying this strand of thought of some Brahmin males are explicitly stated by a retired Brahmin teacher: 'The caste system is based on karma. It is the creation of God, and it has helped our society. Any society needs an hierarchy of superior and inferior people to run the society. People who want to change this will not succeed. They will only bring chaos and caste war, but the system will prevail.'

The handful of people who defend the caste system as a divine construct are only a minority. The religious sanctioning, which in Brahmin dominated areas may underwrite the acceptance of the system, is feeble and does not provide sufficient moral or economic grounds for a defence of the system. The males who defend the continuation of the caste system usually do this with a reference to *parampara*, the tradition as constituted by society itself. They appreciate it as the tradition of the ancestors who have created the system, and those elders 'must have done so after careful consideration' in order to divide the work functions. In this way, in the course of history, the caste divisions got related to positions in the production process. The religious concept *karma* has become secularized in the sense that the membership of a *jati* is not associated with the deeds in a previous life, but with the present position in the labour process. This superiority and inferiority as based on the work one does is a basic argument in the majority explanatory discourse on caste. The neat classification of people according to functions in the labour process in the past has played a positive role in developing India as a golden bird (*sone ki chiriya*), and the decay which has gripped society in the *kaliyug* age is interpreted as a consequence of the amorphous modernizing system which the government wants to impose.

External attempts to subvert the system, for example in the form of government intervention through reservation, are castigated by this section of the village, mostly if not exclusively the higher castes, on other grounds as well: the government should reward the industrious, the bold, and the courageous, i.e. they should reward the Jats who are working hard. It is the Jats who have the *garam khul* (the hot or positive qualities), qualities which they have inherited from their parents and which they have applied to the economic development of the country. Rather than providing benefits like jobs and houses to the Dalits, the government should ask these people 'to first show their muscles'. The insinuation is that they will not be able to prove their mettle, since after all these lower caste people are *kamdila* (weak-hearted) people. Ganesh Singh, who is one of the richest farmers in the area, candidly defends the caste system as the fountainhead of order and work ethos:

> The caste system was created by society for its own betterment. It has put the best brains at the top, and then the *dildar* (courageous) people. There is no injustice in it, and those people who now oppose it are wrong. Hierarchy is a must in order to run society properly. If you abolish this, poverty and chaos will increase.

It is a system which the ancestors have created, and which allows for the continuing appropriation of the labour power of the lower castes by the dominant castes. Such a phrasing of what the caste system means in economic practice is not usually expressed publicly. Some of the bigger landowners, however, do so. The continuing imposition of the hierarchical system is one of the means by which the emergence of a free labour market is sought to be prevented. In the words of Arvind Singh:

> If it finishes, then it will be impossible for us to get the work done. No labour will be available. It will be disastrous for society. So, that is why we have to keep the rules intact. I shall not even accept a *bidi* from a low caste person, and I shall not allow him to sit with me on my charpoy. Before you realize, they will get married to your daughter, and you will have to start working in the field.

Caste segregation is associated with class differences and village practices associated with it. Particularly within the village, it is of paramount importance that the hierarchy is maintained. The crumbling of that caste-anchored hierarchy could significantly reduce the imposition of power by the landowners in their dealings with the labourers, who usually are lower-caste. One middle-aged Jat shudders at the idea that he would have to drink tea in a local restaurant and sits on the ground while the low-caste worker sits on the *charpoy*, but he agrees that while travelling in a bus it has become impracticable to ask a Dalit to get up and move somewhere else.

Changes in this respect are taking place. Caste-neutral services, including food catering services, are accepted as a fact of modern life. Whenever they move to the city, the mantle of caste inhibitions are taken off. At the supra-local level the normative social structure is replaced by a social limbo which can be referred to as recurring *rites de passage*.[10] Ambivalent and contradictory positions are the rule rather than the exception. Jats and Brahmins do not have much social contact

---

[10] At the interface between the still traditional and the already new, we get liminal situations as the seedbeds of new symbols, models and paradigms. Victor Turner (1979: 21) explained this as follows: 'These new symbols and constructions then

with harijans, and when they do, rules are applied in various ways, as one SC man explained: 'Caste rules are crumbling. Almost all the households offer us food on their plates, and they will wash them. Possibly half of the people will allow us to sit on their charpoy and may come to our place if the food is prepared by a *halwai*. Only around one fourth will come if the food is prepared by us.'

For younger people, particularly if they have made inter-caste friendships in school, it has become normal to move around together in their spare time. The spare time of their fathers and grandfathers is spent on the *charpoys*, *hookah* at hand, and this is not the place where an average harijan male would like to go and spend his spare time. But in Khedi Sundyam, the research village that is numerically dominated by Jats, with only a few SC households, caste proximity does occur. Even regular intermingling between Jats and Chamars does take place in the case of a couple of Chamar families. Of these richer SC families, a number of Jats say: 'They are rich people, and are educated, and have stopped doing labour work. They are the persons whom we allow to sit with us on our cot.' The common class position which they share with these families but also the constraints in the labour market (there are not many SC families to draw from) may have helped to reduce the social space between upper and lower castes. The following story, told by a Chamar, tells of the pride the villagers have in the inter-caste relations in the village:

The system is more relaxed here. Last year I was invited to the wedding of Brahmin N's daughter. While I was sitting on the cot, one Rajput from another area came to know about my identity, and he asked me to leave. So N had to intervene and told him to impose his views on untouchability in his own village, but not in our village. That is the way we live, he said, and don't disturb our cordial relations.

Some modifications are apparent in the way the higher castes (Jats are actually just above the OBCs) deal with the lowest castes. The lower castes do appreciate the relaxation, but it hardly goes far and fast enough; they reject the system completely. None of them was prepared to accept it as a creation of God. Like a number of other people in his Chamar neighbourhood, one young labourer, who has finished secondary school, is quite clear about the repulsiveness of the system, but

---

feed back into the "central" economic and politico-legal domains and arenas, supplying them with goals, aspirations, incentives . . .'.

he does not know how it has come about or how it will be ended:'I can't think of why it is there. But it is a great injustice and it is against humanity, and thus it cannot be the creation of God.' The religious theory with its emphasis on *dharma, karma,* and ritual purity, is resolutely dismissed by Chamars and Bhangis with the sarcastic statement: '*Upperwale kutch nahi banaije*' (The One Up There has not made anything). The religious configurations have been replaced by an economic theory which emphasizes the creation of social and ideological systems in the light of class requirements. Caste is explained as a model for social ordering. Specifically among the young Chamars and Bhangis, it is not possible to find takers of the religious underpinning of the *varna* system. If God is referred to as The Creator, then it is only to make it clear that He has created two species only, or rather, as one landless OBC explained, two and a half species: 'God has given us life. He has made males, females and *hijra* (eunuchs). We have added the *biradari*.' A recurring criticism against the social order is that 'the caste system has been created by the rich people in order to dominate us'. The general idea is that in the course of history a division was created between the rich people and the poor people, or between those who work and those who do not, and that then the Brahmins, 'with themselves nicely put on top', have codified this division of labour. If the caste system is a class system which helps the economically dominant class to reinforce the class division, then it may have a self perpetuating dynamic of its own. The system will then tend to be reinforced in order to underwrite the symbolic, political, and economic dominance of the ruling class segments.

Not all anti-caste people are confident that it will ever be possible to eradicate the caste system. They have seen some positive changes, but a frontal confrontations is unfeasible. Even an open discourse, an expression of intent, virtually amounts to a multiple confrontation with a sanction-loaded society. Egalitarian ideals and expectations are muted, in the formulation of R.S. Khare (1984: 142), because action is confrontational. It thus involves a prior calculation of the odds involved. An active intervention against the system takes place in a no-win situation. Any radical deviation from the accepted lifestyles may attract harsh sanctions, and it may therefore be better to allow things to improve by themselves through economic development with more opportunities in the labour market. The call for a direct struggle by the downtrodden people therefore finds favour with a handful of SC people only, usually the well-off section. They are a vanguard, supporters of Mulayam Singh Yadav, Kanshi Ram, or of communist leaders, and as an outspoken vanguard, they may be voicing the hidden expectation of others. Openly, however, many SCs, especially the elderly, are pessimistic about the possibility of change. Changes for the better have taken place, but people at the sharp end of the system will remain at the sharp end of the system.

The ultimate step, and the only step which may ultimately abolish the caste system, the inter-caste marriage, has the blessing of only five non-SC males (two teachers, two businessmen, one landless Jat), on condition that the partner will be 'educated and cultured'. The implications of such an ultimate step are tied up with family property and inheritance rules, and with the position of women, to which we shall now turn.

Women

The continuation of the caste system is intrinsically, and possibly exclusively, linked to the continuation of caste endogamy in arranged marriages. In the majority of families, the opinion of children may be sounded, but the marriage scouting and contracting is the work of the parents. Tied to the arranged marriage is the question of dowry, and in a more general sense the subordination of women.

Despite some attempt to do away with *dahej* (dowry),[11] the practice continues. The rich people are setting the trend, and will continue to do so with the argument that since the daughter is not inheriting the property, she may take with her some of the family wealth when she leaves the households. Landless Chamars, Bhangis and OBCs, who do not have family property, claim that they are not paying *dahej*. Although a negotiated *dahej* occasionally does occur, in other cases no contract is negotiated, but some presents, 'to the extent that they can afford', are nevertheless sent along to the in-laws' household. This is usually more than the household budget can bear, and at least some of the debts, at 2 per cent to 5 per cent monthly interest, have been contracted for marriage purposes.

It is argued that it is better to pay some dowry, or a hefty dowry, rather than keeping the daughter unmarried: 'one cannot play politics over the

[11] On the issue of dowry, the Balyan Jat *biradari* in 1952 and 1956 had issued strictures. The ban was reiterated by the BKU in 1988 (Singh 1992: 115). The BKU had wanted to do away with *dahej*, and replace it by 'the presentation of clothes and utensils only'.

back of one's daughter'. One possible way of getting rid of *dahej*, a system which many people do denounce in no uncertain terms, would be the implementation of the personal law, specifically the legislation on inheritance rights. Except for two persons from propertied families, all others who claim to favour equality of women and men, however, want the women to have co-ownership in the property of the in-laws only.[12]

In principle, a number of males and most of the females agree that women should have equal rights. The possibility of equality, it is felt, can only arise when women have acquired educational standard comparable to those of the males. This actually is hardly a way-out for most of the girls, who are thus maintained in a vicious circle. Girls usually attend the first four years in the village school, but thereafter the problem starts, especially if they have to attend the higher forms in neighbouring places. Many fathers and mothers complain that girls are insulted, molested, and even kidnapped. At least, they have heard stories to that effect, and consider it safer to keep the girls at home well before the time that puberty sets in. These stories usually affect the behaviour of the poorer families, who have nothing to lose but their virtue and thus are extra careful to keep their daughters out of harms' way. In the cities, they claim, girls can grow up peacefully, but in the village, there is always the risk of them being accosted by youngsters from well-to-do Jat families, and it is wise and prudent to pre-empt the possibility of a conflict, which they are bound to loose.[13]

Equality for men and women is not a controversial issue for SC males. Some males argue that, unlike many Jats, they don't treat their females as kitchen animals. But inequality does prevail, not only in the preferential education facilities for boys. The division of labour, assigning the household chores to the females, is seen as a natural division. In addition, in most households, the husband remains the master, and often

---

[12] The view follows the stand taken by the Jat Biradari Sangathan which has further prescribed that divorced women should be given a subsistence allowance (*guzara*) from the property of her ex-husband.

[13] In a recent incident, a class VII girl was 'kissed' by a senior boy while proceeding from the village to the school in Sisauli. Thereafter, the village '*panchayat*', i.e. the traditional *panchayat* of influential Jats and a sprinkling of others, met and decided that a sweeper should beat the young offender with his shoes. The offender happened to be a young Chamar, and the girl happened to be the granddaughter of one of the village patriarchs. The lower caste people argue that if it had happened to their girls, and especially if the offender had been a Jat, no sanctions would have been taken.

may behave in an unjust and dominating manner. Women tend to covered all the injustice, neglect and even violent behaviour with the mantle of privacy. Since women prefer to keep their household problems within four walls, male dominance is more difficult to fight. This was succinctly conveyed by Kamal, an elderly Bhangi:

> I want to be known as a honourable (*izzatdari*) person, and people from the outside think that I have a respectable life. That is how it is, even after tortures by husbands, we do not dare to disclose it because we want the *izzatdari* of the family intact. Those women who disclose it, and those women who run away are considered bad women.

Among the SC respondents, there usually was a gender similarity of views on the respective position of men and women. Among Jats and Brahmins, opposing views are the rule rather than the exception. In our discussion with them, the women often started by claiming that, as far as they are concerned, they have equal status. For them, equal status implies that the husband does not discriminate in gender terms and that the housewife is in charge of the household affairs. When interview circumstances allowed for a more confidential exchange of views, additional information on the actual differences emerged. The discussion then uncovered many hidden levels of dissatisfaction. The discussion with Javitri Devi developed as follows:

JD: Women are below the males, and that is justified because the men are working hard; they produce the food which we eat.

Q: Don't you work hard then?

JD: Yes, we work harder, but the men are known as the hard workers. And also, they can manage everything much better. We are an uneducated lot.

Q: But your husband is hardly literate, then why is he more educated than you?

JD: That is true. You see, that happens when you have to stay inside the household all the time. It is only by going outside that you develop, but we are left with the household chores.

Q: Does your husband help you?

JD: How can I ask him to help me. The whole village would laugh at him. He will be *beijati* (outcast, marginalised).

Q: You could go and work outside.

JD: That is not possible. I can't go for service, and I have to put on my veil if I move outside the neighbourhood.

Q: I can't understand why things are not changing here. It now appears that you are not satisfied. Are you accepting everything?

JD: No, no, and things have changed. Earlier it was bad. Nowadays, the prestige of women has increased. In those days, the gents used to beat the women for not doing the work properly, and that has stopped.

Q: Really?

JD: I know that it is true in my case, but we are still under the control of the men. You see, in the cities, women can also go for a walk, like men do, but here, there is always the household burden.

The improved status that Javitri Devi appears to have reached, does not provide for freedom in the public space. Hence the jealous reference to the women in the cities who have their own money to go to the movies. Over half of the Jat, Brahmin, and Muslim males have no problems with the denial of independent access to the public space, now (as daughters) as well as in the future (as women). Women should be kept in their present (subordinate) position. A couple of Muslim women and two Jat women concur with this position. The other half of the Jat and Brahmin males do state to favour equal rights, but with a few exceptions. They make it clear that equal status does not imply that women could join service.

The exclusion from service is partially defended on the same grounds as the reasons for withdrawing girls from school. It boils down to the argument, mentioned in different wordings though, that the chastity and loyalty will be at stake. But there are many other grounds as well. More rights to women and more education are generally seen by the males as the root cause of family fights and the corruption of old values. Were women to start working, then the entire scaffolding of the social order would come down: women would get the jobs and men would become unemployed, they would just be gossiping rather than working, the economy would suffer, and it would be difficult for them to do the household work. All these problems appear surmountable. Insurmountable, however, are the developments which will follow and which the males claim to have seen happening with relatives and friends in the cities: after the women start getting a salary, they also start bossing over the males and will demand freedom to go out on their own. Such a future, they confide, has to be blocked.

Girls may go for education, but they should not do so for many years; definitely by the time they are fourteen year old, they should be observing *pardah*. The minimum level of education is needed in order to help in the upbringing of her children, but otherwise she should be under the control of the husband. Such control is necessary because it is felt, if left to themselves, at least half of the women would 'go on the wrong path' and would start 'corrupting' society. The bridling of the sexuality of women for the good of society, for the good of themselves, and possibly also for the good of the males is justified as follows by one of the bigger landowners (who had just spent Rs 1.5 Lakh on the marriage of his daughter!): 'If they are given equality and freedom, it will be disastrous for society. The ship will sink in the sea. Women are inferior to men because they can go to any extent to satisfy their selfish interest.'

Another rich Jat, one of the richest in the area, has additional reasons for denying women access to the public space:

I support the male dominated society and it will be better if the traditional caste structure continues and if women remain where they are. Tulsi Das has written that Sudras, the drum, cattle and women [nari] deserve to be beaten. Those lines from our tradition are still correct. Sudras are stupid people and women have less mental capacity than males. So how can you expect equality?

The reference to women at the level of drums and cattle flows from the mouth of one of the richer and more influential Jats. He is a typical example of this class of people. Their obsession with dominance and order, the key elements underwriting patriarchy, apparently stretches all the way from cattle (means of production) to lower castes (servants and labourers) and to their married women who look after their offspring as well as their nutritional and sexual sustenance.

Concluding Remarks

Various ideational issues have cropped up. Some more fragments of the world view could have been taken, but the overall conclusion would point in the same direction. I have called this the myriorama of views. All these divergent views (or cacophony of opinions) are clustered along the caste (and class) hierarchy. Each opinion is a shade different from another opinion, but overall they fit universal axioms and caste and class consciousness. The divergence is embedded in a process of a multiple refraction of universal axioms and judgements. That refraction is also coloured by the fact that each individual person usually has an ambiguity, a conflicting mix of views and convictions. Treatises that have been written about the structuring of ideas by the material infrastructure or by the culture often have assumed monolithic belief systems or a confrontation between conflicting belief systems. This at least has been the basis of Orientalist scholarship. Such a dichotomy between the Western world view and the Eastern world view does not appear to exist. Archetypes of either traditional or modern thinking tend to be what they are: theoretical constructs. In the living persons, the archetype is hardly ever embodied.

One could set out a number of ideal types in a matrix, but not many respondents would fit any of them. A male Brahmin who states that the caste system is a despicable social structure, who applauds the Babri Masjid destruction, who considers Muslims and their religion in an ecumenical fashion, who allows his daughters to study but considers his wife at par with a house servant, etc., is only one of the numerous cases of an ambivalent values system.

The multiple refraction of universal ideas, however, does not take place at random, in an absolute vacuum. Some broad correlations can be observed. The minimal degree of religious belief and religious practice, and the absolute rejection of the caste system by the lowest castes is one such correlation. The inimical attitude towards a *Hindu Rashtra* is also widespread, although the expression of this position is often mitigated by political considerations.

Javeed Alam has looked at the numerous causal chains emanating from the stunted and retarded capitalism in order to explain the different social forms and ideational features. He argues that many cultural, social, and political expressions, which should have been swept away by the modernizing processes of capitalism have, in fact, been given a new lease of live. Although he agrees that even in full-fledged capitalist societies, monolithic value systems are missing, the multiplicity of ideas is exacerbated in developing societies: 'An infirm capitalism needs crutches and therefore it sits awkwardly upon and feeds on the pre-capitalist forces in society in a parasitic relationship' (Alam 1989: 245). The interpretation of the myriorama of world views in terms of the churning between two systems in the transition from feudalism to capitalism is not without merit. For a more adequate explanation, however, we shall have to elaborate on ambivalence and contrapoint, two concepts that have been developed by Wertheim (1976: 127–32, 138–42). Wertheim explicitly questions the assumptions by modern Weberians that societies have dominant value systems that lubricate and unite the social system: 'Simultaneous endorsement and rejection . . . is a consequence of the instability of the value alignments.' A range of ideological appellations is continuously shaping and reshaping the minds of people. The specific alignment in terms of gender, caste, class, religion, politics, etc., is subject to various developments, forces, and signifiers.

In Muzaffarnagar, despite the restraints on civic freedom, new ideologies have been wafting in and have addressed the various individuals in different ways. A redefinition of each individual's position on caste, class, gender, religion, nation, and many other categories that demand a normative stand, is taking place as a continuous process. On some issues it appears that the area is still steeped in tradition, particularly in respect of women, marriages an to an extent caste, but overall it is clear that the traditional social systems and belief system have waned or are in the process of dissipation. As many villagers stated: *parampara tordia*, the end of tradition.

CHAPTER 10

Hindu Communalism around Ayodhya between Caste and Class

In December 1992, tens of thousands of Hindu fanatics stormed the Babri mosque in Ayodhya in order to reclaim the area for a Hindu temple. The vandalism and the days of ethnic cleansing, which followed, especially in Mumbai, were the culmination of a fairly recent turn towards religious strife in India. The development has motivated many scholars to search for the cause behind the sudden rise of the so-called 'communalism'.

In an excellent study, Eric Kolodner has noted that post-Independence India was 'an experiment in multi-religious, multi-cultural, multi-ethnic, and multi-linguistic nation building' (Kolodner 1995: 234). A unified Hindu movement for a long time had been impeded by the religious pluriformity within the broad parameters of a Hindu culture, and by the 'hierarchical, anti-egalitarian and divisive nature of the caste system. . . . Paradoxically, therefore, what is probably the most fundamental element of traditional Hindu society, caste, presents the largest impediment to mobilizing Indians to create a unified "Hindu" nation' (Kolodner 1995: 237). The rise of Hindu nationalism, and its possible demise, should therefore be located outside the realm of religion. Hinduism could ascend to centre stage because of social dislocation in the wake of uneven economic development and because of the political and ideological void in the wake of the moral decomposition of the long ruling Indian National Congress party (INC or Congress):

Promising to clean up politics and to stabilize the country, Hindu nationalists surged into this moral, political and ideological void. They exploited the weakness of the ruling elite and capitalized on the fears and insecurities of the Hindu majority. Channelling the economic and social frustrations of Hindus, they were able to appeal to many diverse groups of Hindus with a broad range of disparate messages. (Kolodner 1995: 242)

Although not explicitly stated, it is assumed that the earlier impediment (the caste division) has weakened and that the Hindu majority, i.e. inclusive of the lower castes, has fallen for the baits of psychological security and material improvement that the Bharatiya Janata Party (BJP) and Hindu unity could provide. In this chapter, I shall investigate this assertion, and shall argue for two modifications. The first modification is that the BJP did not exploit the weakness of the ruling elite, but that it emerged as the new strategic party of the ruling elite. The second modification is that the lower castes by and large have remained outside the appeal of communalism and Hindu nationalism, and that recent developments have thus accentuated the division within Hindu society: communalism has remained a movement mainly relying on the upper castes.

I shall attempt to construct an argument along secular lines, i.e. religious strife will be explained not on the basis of religion but on the basis of political strategies based on class interests. This will be followed up by illustrative material from an anthropological survey among villagers in Jaunpur district in eastern Uttar Pradesh, an area 150 km to the southeast of Ayodhya.

Compensatory Illusions

The arguments to be constructed rest on the axiom that religious and ethnic strife are not the product of particular types of religion or particular types of culture, but that there is a common trigger which is neutral to religion.

Hinduism, it should be added, offers more scope for strife and conflict than any other religion, since it has within itself, a strict hierarchical order, which is defended with abundant dogmatism. The authoritarian caste system socially disintegrated the Hindus into an ever increasing number of groups and sub-groups which were made to consider themselves as inferior to those above them and superior to those below them. This authoritarian system was built on religious, social, economic, and political inequality, and any attempt to change that inequality attracted repercussions, often violent, from the upper castes.

Whereas internal strife (casteism) has been intrinsic to Hinduism, open confrontation with other religions has been relatively absent. The explanation for the absence is not an assumed intrinsic tolerance of Hinduism (as opposed for example to Catholicism and Islam), but the non-existence of Hinduism as a unified religion. Until fairly recently (until the nineteenth century), Hinduism was more an umbrella indication for the various religions in the subcontinent beyond the Indus. The so-called semitization of Hinduism (the formation of one doctrine with a definite set of Gods, an ecclesiastical structure, and the codification of holy texts) is actually still in progress as a political project.[1]

One feature of modern societies is the absence of a directly interacting community. The notion of the community (nation, people) has to be constructed through mental processes. This is what Anderson (1993) refers to as the *imagined community*. The constructing of the self usually involves the constructing of the other. Perceptions and stereotypes about the other are structured and passed on from generation to generation and thus turn into a material force. Religion in this sense helps to organize the emergence of communities, and in that sense may be considered as a social good. Edward Said (1993: 212) has suggested that religion actually absorbs social ideals: 'A social ideal may be expressed not only in secular but also in religious form. However, the fact that it assumes a religious form does not necessarily mean that this social ideal is backward and reactionary, just as a secular form does not always means that this social ideal is oriented towards the future.'

Religion as the opium of the people helps in overcoming the thrall of earthly existence and to organize social life. But religion also helps to separate people from the economics of society and may then serve as an instrument in the hands of the economic and political elite. It may be used as an instrument of power used by the secular elite with the intent of controlling political power and of continuing their economic privileges. Religion then, as opium for the people, helps to lead the people away from the issues of exploitation and suppression. The ruling class usually shows indulgence in allowing the deflection of class conflicts and economic grievances into community oriented or communal contentions.

This estrangement, within a state which has to legitimize itself, leads to what could be termed the *illusory consciousness*. Consciousness is structured by ideological reflexes which do not unilaterally and directly

---

[1] Since even today, there are so many religious beliefs, the semitization of Hinduism is fraught with many problems. The BJP and its religious front organizations aim to create a semitised Hindu religion and identity (*Hindutva*) and then to mobilize all the Hindus in a political movement to the exclusion of the other religions and in confrontation with them. This brand of communalism thus appears as a political project.

reflect the material basis, but which are also, to various degrees, influenced by direct interventions from the dominant ideology of the ruling elite which is in control of the state. Illusory consciousness thus depends on the antagonistic class basis which fosters it for its own legitimacy and survival.[2]

Religion usually serves as the medium through which national identity is shaped and reinforced. It may provide a positive stimulus to emancipation, but it usually also creates new command structures. The 'ambiguous fertility' of nationalism, a term borrowed from Basil Davidson, in the words of Edward Said (1993: 322) creates not only the assertion of a once incomplete and suppressed identity (under colonialism), 'but also the inculcation of new authority' through new doctrines and new myths.[3]

Contextualization

Although it has never been altogether absent from the political scene, during the 1980s religious nationalism emerged as an important political movement. The new movements have tried to emotionally integrate Sikhs, Muslims, and Hindus under the banner of religion. Behind the religious banner, however, the issues at stake were secular. The secular grievances, which they thrive on, are formulated in terms of the constructed ethos of one's community. Religion as such is only 'a powerful instrument in the hands of those interests which seek to play their game through it' (Engineer 1989: 2). In fact, as I shall try to establish later, the symbols of contention (like the Babri mosque at Ayodhya) were used by upper class (and upper caste) leaders in order to deflect the

---

[2] In *The German Ideology*, Marx and Engels have argued that alienation is always connected with the appearance of 'compensatory illusions'. Under conditions of class division, this illusion takes the form of the 'illusory community'. The construction of the imagined community, i.e. the common interests assumed to rest on communality of language, religion or ethnos, not only tends to efface class antagonism, but also constructs the other (within or without the state borders) as the (imagined) adversary of the common interests. Put differently: a ruling class will be interested in supporting and financing religious organizations rather than (working) class organization. The former will help to sustain 'false' consciousness, the latter will foster class consciousness.

[3] Such new authority, legitimizing the control by the state, need not derive from an appeal to religion. As a matter of fact, in the course of Indian nationalism, both in its anti-colonial and its post-colonial phase, the religious identity has hardly ever played a dominant role.

people from anti-establishment activities. In that sense the new religious movements were communal.

Communalism (like casteism) in my reading is not the emergence of contradictions in underlying ethnic structures, but is generated within a competitive socio-economic context. It is used as the instrument of political intervention aimed towards vertical multi-class solidarity as a safe substitute for horizontal class solidarities, i.e. to ensure the continuation of upper class against the background of emerging lower class consciousness and organization.

The question to be asked at this point is why communalism could emerge at centre stage only so late in the history of independent India. Earlier, there had been communal eruptions but each time they remained local and were clearly related to local economic and political conflicts. After the middle of the 1980s, and culminating after 1990, Hindu communal organizations mushroomed and the BJP, increasingly on an overt communal platform, emerged as the second largest political party. The explanation for this sudden rise will be given in terms of the cardinal political and economic changes prior to the emergence of communalism and not in terms of the religiousness, fanaticism, backwardness, or whatever cultural traits which have overburdened our perception of people in the Indian subcontinent.

Until roughly the late 1970s, India had been a reasonably stable country. The Indian National Congress party had been in power for most of the time in most of the states, and had held aloft the promise of national and class emancipation. Politics was characterized by consensus, carrying forward the ideals of the nationalist movement. It was accepted policy that the downtrodden masses should be uplifted through special reform and welfare measures; it was agreed that the power of the big industrial companies should be restrained and that small-scale entrepreneurs should be stimulated and protected; it was decided that India should not integrate with the Western capitalist world and that the multinational companies should be kept under strict control. It was a policy acceptable to most segments of Indian society. Even to the poor people, the Indian state under the leadership of Jawaharlal Nehru and Indira Gandhi was a relatively benign institution: various measures, however inadequately executed, prevented the excessive polarization between rich and poor people and provided a certain degree of protection to low-caste labourers and poor peasants.

This view of India in terms of a consensus has to be understood in a relative sense for consensus politics at the same time operated within a state structure dominated by the monopoly bourgeoisie, landlords and rich peasants. The ultimate practice of state interventions and non-interventions bore all the signs of this class dominance, although in a mitigated form.

The continuation of consensus economics came under severe strain in the 1980s. The fortunes of the Indian big bourgeoisie as well as the rich peasants had grown considerably and they wanted to get rid of the constraints imposed by the earlier consensus politics. Their urge for liberalization of the economy coincided with the policy changes imposed by the International Monetary Fund.[4] The policy of liberalization, the rolling back of the state and integration in the capitalist world economy had serious repercussions. Many of the protective institutions of the state (for example food subsidies, health expenses, credit-based development programmes, and job creation) were trimmed down.

The prime victims were not only the poor people, but also many lower middle class families in cities and the countryside. They increasingly had the idea that they were left to their fate. There was, as many people were ready to tell us during our field work in the countryside, a growing sense of *asuraksha* (insecurity) and this insecurity in turn made for a relapse into primordiality: emotional sustenance, patronage, and economic survival could be found by tapping the powerful within caste or community.

The other side of the coin, however, was that emancipatory carvings had continued to expand. The INC, as well as most other parties, had promised caste and class emancipation, and had fought many elections on that platform. The end result was that the act of political balancing between rich and poor, which the Congress party had always excelled in, became awkward. The poor electorate was growing conscious of its rights and parties on the Left and caste-based parties were increasingly stealing the thunder from the multi-class approach which had been typical in the consensus model.

The continuation of consensus politics, already under strain by the radical changes in the economic policy of the ruling INC, came under irreparable strain during the short-lived Janata Dal government (1989–90) of V.P. Singh. Under this government, the Mandal Commission

[4] In 1980, India had contracted a massive loan from the IMF, and, in the wake of repayment problems, was increasingly ready to accept the so-called Structural Adjustment Policy of the IMF. The financial crunch in 1990 led to a drastic change in the economic policy in exchange for (or as the price for) a new IMF loan that bailed the country out of its foreign exchange crisis.

Report, which had been lying with the government for over a decade, was resurrected and translated into legislation. This legislation provided for a hefty reservation of government post and educational seats in favour of the so-called Other Backward Castes (OBC), i.e. the castes just above the untouchables in the Hindu caste hierarchy. The latter group, which is referred to as the SCs (Scheduled Castes), had received preferential treatment already at the time of Independence. With the additional reservation for OBCs introduced by the Janata Dal government, more than half of the government jobs would be out of reach of the upper castes, which traditionally had monopolized those jobs. The outcastes and backward castes, who always had been relegated to the lowest economic positions and de facto had been excluded from advances in education and from access to government institutions, now appeared to be standing on the threshold of claiming their rightful place in society.

The reaction to the introduction of the Mandal Commission Report in the summer of 1990 was chaos, street violence, and mayhem. A general disturbance held most of northern India in its grip for weeks altogether. The BJP as a party was not involved in the street agitation—it could not risk of antagonizing the OBC and SC electorate—but was preparing for the movement which aimed at reuniting all the Hindu Indians behind one issue. In September–October its supreme leader L.K. Advani led a *yatra* (procession) through most of the Indian states, starting in Gujarat and culminating in Ayodhya.[5] The final days of the march to Ayodhya and the weeks thereafter produced something which was unique for post-independent India: communal riots and attacks which spread simultaneously over the entire country and which left many hundreds of people dead. The Janata Dal government collapsed and the legislation on reservation for OBCs was temporarily deferred.

The belligerent call for the destruction of the mosque and the construction of a temple thus not only removed a government responsive to the interests of the lower castes, but also opened avenues for reuniting all Hindus across caste and class behind an alluring call for action.

The BJP could now hope to consolidate its gains. Its call for the defence of Hinduism had brought the party into prominence, but it would be too easy and moreover not correct, to ascribe it to the religiosity of the Indian people. From the local village data given later in this chapter,

---

[5] Ayodhya is the place where a mosque was supposed to have been built in the mid-sixteenth century after destroying a temple, which had been erected there in commemoration of the mythical Lord Ram who is claimed to have been born there in the ancient past (Sushil Srivastava 1991).

we shall gather that religion was not a major motive force. The BJP was helped into prominence by the fact that the other party, which had given stability to the country and had acted in the strategic interests of the ruling classes, the INC, as a consequence of internal bickering, corruption and the unmitigated abandonment of the old consensus policy, was forsaking its hitherto reliable role. The BJP leaders were in a position to tap this disquiet and sense of disappointment with the INC which got hold of the ruling classes.

Fatal Intra-Hindu Divide

The BJP's attempts to reunite the Indian people politically and socially, however, was obstructed by the fact that most of its leaders belonged to the highest castes. Particularly at the village level, these leaders and their families for ages had exploited and suppressed the lower castes. It was a lifelong experience which the members of the lower castes, given the face to face encounters in the villages, could vividly remember.

The lowest caste population, variously referred to as untouchables, SC, harijans, and Dalits in fact have always been outcastes, both in a religious sense and in a social sense. The high caste strong men in the villages had ostracized them from social life in a systematic and culturally ordained manner, possibly unequalled anywhere in the world.[6] Until fairly recently, it was the rule rather than the exception that they had to keep sitting at a safe distance from the village well and wait for a member of the Hindu upper castes to be so kind as to pour water into their vessel. The analogy with a dog waiting for the master to do the same will easily come to mind. Unless one argues that the outcaste people were also having the mental and intellectual capacities of dogs, one may assume that, despite all the outward signs of compliance, they must have internalized a deep-seeded caste/class hatred for the upper castes and for the religion they were practising. The inhuman discrimination, resulting from the brazenly imposed caste hierarchy, added to the tinderbox of discontent which, if unchecked, could lead to an ignition.

The introduction, after independence, of parliamentary democracy and of elected village councils, was bound to mitigate the caste segregation and oppression. The political factor, rather than any other factor,

[6] The apartheid regime in South Africa and the slave economies in the USA and in Latin America were based on racist segregation between different ethnicities. In India, the segregation was within one ethnicity and was based on the religious legitimation of inequality, which is the opposite of what one finds in all other religions.

a special note in the 1931 Census on the United Provinces forecasted, would bring about caste emancipation: 'If Hindus wish to include these millions in their community for political reasons they cannot logically exclude them socially, and what is more, if they persist in excluding them socially, the depressed class will completely throw over Hinduism' (Census of India XVIII: 630).

The political project of all parties had to come to terms with this factor. Although most political parties, all of them with a leadership basis among the high castes, failed to transcend the caste divide, the BJP had never really attempted it. The party had always been known as a party of high caste Brahmins (the priestly caste) and Vaishyas (the Banias or trading castes). Through the homogenization of the Hindu population in one belief system, and through its positioning against the other (the Muslims), the wealthy Brahmins and the Vaishyas in the BJP attempted to build cross-caste political support by a recurrence to communalism. In other words, by constructing a communal idiom and the image of underlying injustice and unfreedom (caused by the other), they envisaged to pre-empt low caste mobilization.

The attempt, as we shall argue later, was generally unsuccessful because the SC continued to be excluded, or had the feeling that they were excluded socially: *Hindutva* and casteism were considered as coterminous by the lower castes. When, towards the end of the 1980s, the BJP emerged as a major political party, it was brought face to face with the forecast made in the 1931 Census report: its politics of *Hindutva* was confronted with the intrinsic problem of a caste-wise and class-wise divided Hinduism. Its electoral appeal was clearly conditioned and constrained by that division. For indeed, in the meantime, the lower castes/classes had been attracted by other political formations which promised them economic and social emancipation. As we have indicated earlier, the danger of a further political polarization was one of the grounds for the recourse to *Hindutva* after the demise of the earlier Congress consensus model.

The strategy seemed to have paid off. Since the BJP had fought the 1990 elections on the single issue of *Hindutva* sentiments, the victory in those elections not only came as a thunderbolt, but was also explained as a vindication of Hindu unity. During the 1990s, *Hindutva* has set the agenda in Indian politics. Despite the electoral successes, growing from an insignificant representation in parliament to the dominant government party within a couple of years, the Hindu project in the above sense, however, has not been very successful. The latter conclusion, and some of the other statements in the preceding section, is based on overall election analysis[7] and on strong evidence from a number of field studies conducted between 1991 and 1995 in the western zone of Uttar Pradesh (Muzaffarnagar; see for example Lieten 1994a), in the central zone (Amethi) and in the eastern zone around Ayodhya (Faizabad and Jaunpur; see, e.g. Lieten 1994b).

We shall produce the results from a number of villages in one specific district, Jaunpur, in the second part of this article. Jaunpur district of course has some specific features, and cannot be assumed to stand for developments in the entire state, leave alone the entire country. But since the findings in the four areas have produced by and large similar results, the Jaunpur findings may hypothetically be construed as valid for the state.

Lower Castes to the Fore

In comparison with the western areas of Uttar Pradesh, Jaunpur is rather backward, both in terms of general standards of living and in terms of capitalist development. Semi-feudal sharecropping arrangements are still practiced and the landed class has not taken to investment in agriculture in a big way. Most high caste (Brahmin and Thakur) landowners, however, are doing well, with incomes from various sources: sharecropping, self-cultivation, government service, teaching, local shops and moneylending, business in far-flung places, etc. In the areas which we have studied, 5 per cent of the families owned around one-third of the land. On the other side of the scale, the bottom 50 per cent of the families owned only around one-tenth of the land.

The acute class division correlates strongly with the caste division: at both extremes in the caste hierarchy, the correlation with class is almost perfect (see Table 10.1). Whereas only 2 of the 80 Thakur and Brahmin families belong to poor households, practically all very rich

---

[7] In the 1991 elections, the BJP had taken Uttar Pradesh by storm. From a marginal position in the 1984 and 1989 elections, the party was catapulted into the top position in 1991. On what was perceived as the Ayodhya *Hindutva* wave, the party secured 31.6 per cent of the votes, and formed the government. The BJP had constructed itself in the language of Hindu ethnicity as the self-proclaimed authority of and over the Hindus. In the next elections, two years later, the BJP support, however, stabilized, and the government fell into the hands of an alliance of the Socialist Party of Mulayam Singh, with strong support among the OBC and Muslims and a caste-based party with strong support among the SC (BSP). In later years the BJP again came to power, through alliances and horse-trading.

Table 10.1: Correlation of Caste and Class in a Jaunpur Village

Economic status caste	Upper caste	Middle	OBC	SC	Muslim	Total
Very poor	1	1	11	36	1	50
Poor	1	8	32	16	4	61
Middle	34	5	31	1	1	72
Rich	32	2	7	1	0	42
Very rich	12	1	2	0	0	15
Total	80	17	83	54	6	240

Note: The information in this table is based on a sample study, in three phases, in 1992, 1993, and 1994, in a dozen villages in the north-eastern corner of Jaunpur district.

families are of upper caste vintage. On the other hand, with two exceptions, the SC households can be classified as either poor or very poor. The SC and to a certain extent also the OBC belong to the poorest households of agricultural labourers, sharecroppers and poor peasants. A wider sample would slightly blur the quasi-perfect correlation, but probably would not substantially alter the correlation.

The caste-class correlation may lead to a political confrontation, dividing the so-called Hindu population. The inference of the fact that the voting pattern runs along caste lines in that case may very well be that at stake is a class assertion rather than a caste assertion. The BJP successes camouflaged that the Hindu *pariwar* had remained largely what it had been before: a beacon of upper-caste Hindu rather than a *pariwar* of all Hindus.[8] Electoral success have fluctuated and indicate the importance of socio-economic and political environment rather than the frenzy for *Hindutva*.

The 1989 assembly elections in the constituency in the research area had been won by Janata Dal (32.6 per cent), very closely followed by the INC (32.3 per cent), and then at a distance by the CPI (13.9 per cent) and of the BJP and Bahujan Samaj Party (BSP, appealing to lower castes and Muslims) with around 6 per cent each. At that time, the desertion of the INC had begun, but the political attraction of the BJP (and the BSP, a party which would come into prominence by winning the state

[8] The term Hindu *pariwar* (family) refers to the network of political parties and front organizations around the BJP (and Shiv Sena in Maharashtra).

assembly elections in December 1993), according to out first field-level data, had not yet started. The next elections (in 1991) started the churning process which led to an ignominious collapse of the INC. The Congress electorate then was still in the process of shifting its allegiance: the poor people towards the Janata Dal, the rich people towards the BJP.[9]

The data in Table 10.2 illustrate the class/caste divide in political preferences. In the run-up to the 1993 state assembly elections, there appeared to be a perfect shift of upper caste and upper-class votes from Congress to BJP. There was also a shift of lower caste and lower-class votes to the (ex-) Janata Dal parties (Janata Dal of V.P. Singh, the Socialist Party of Mulayam Singh) and the BSP. At the November 1993 hustings in the constituency, the BSP attracted 36.9 per cent and V.P. Singh's Janata Dal 17.3 per cent of the electorate. The fortunes of the INC had been plummeting, and would plummet further until the party could secure not more than 5.5 per cent of the votes in the Assembly elections later in the decade.

Table 10.2: Class-wise and Caste-wise Political Preferences, 1993

Socio-economic status	Janata	Congress	Communist	BJP	None	Total
Poor	73	8	6	6	8	101
Middle	32	10	4	13	1	60
Rich	13	11	2	23	1	50
Brahmin	0	14	4	31	2	51
Thakur	9	4	0	1		14
Bania	2	1	0	9		12
OBC	68	3	3	1	2	77
SC	33	7	5	0	6	51
Muslim	6					6
Total of the sample (%)	55.8	13.6	6.6	19.8	4.6	
Elections in the Constituency 1993 (%)	64.5	5.5	–	28.0		

Note: The information in this table (and in the other tables) is based on a sample study, in three phases, in 1992, 1993, and 1994, in a dozen villages in the north-eastern corner of Jaunpur district.

[9] In the urban context, the BJP *Hindutva* has been referred to as Toyota Hinduism, in the sense that its main support came from the motorized upper middle classes. In the rural context also, the first adherents of the new political ideology were the rare owners of television sets or motorbikes.

The arguments by the wealthier villagers for their shift towards the BJP were sometimes coached in terms of Hindu sentiments, but, as we shall argue later, this often was an allegoric reference only. The reasons for their shifting away from the INC were more often coached in economic policy arguments, for example the rising price of fertilizers which the BJP was expected to rectify. Occasionally, the discussions revealed an underlying caste/class syndrome, as the following interview with one of the Upadhyaya landowners (U) exposes:

U: During the Congress regime we were not getting fertilizers, but Kalyan Singh's government gave it to the *kisan*. Congress made us repay the loans, even if we had not received a loan. Under the BJP, the administration was just and strong and nobody dared to harass the *kisan*.

Q: But how does it help you? You are not really a *kisan*. Almost all your land is cultivated by sharecroppers.

U: The wind has changed, and all *kisan* people are united against Congress. I must change with the people around me.

Q: But then why have you supported Congress for so long?

U: Nehru, Indira, Rajiv, Shastri, they were the great leaders. They have done the good things and the bad things, but now they are gone, and after the Janata only the bad things have remained.

Q: Mandal, you mean?

U: Congress had already started it, but now it has been extended even further. This we cannot tolerate. The Brahmins and the Thakurs are in trouble. Nobody listens to them any longer. They have been downgraded socially and economically. None of them can get a job.

Q: Because the jobs now go to the SC and the OBCs?

U: Exactly.

Q: But in this village, there are not many jobs going, isn't it?

U: I have five sons; they should like to get jobs in the city, but now their future is being ruined. And here in the village itself, the *chhotolok* have become too demanding and too *dhristi* (arrogant).

Q: But in the meantime, you seem to be doing well!

U: Yes, yes, if you look it that way, economically and educationally, we are doing well, but socially, the whole structure is falling apart. We cannot tolerate the *shudra* rule, and that is going to be the reality unless we do something about it.

Communalism

The bottom line behind the concept of 'communalism' is that two communities form separate denominations, and that the separateness is based on differences in religious belief. Communalist leaders on both sides, in order to make the identification with the religious community click, will use ethnic markers (in respect of dresses, habits and rituals, but also in respect of stereotyped mental characteristics). Many similarities, even in rituals, religious sites, and saints, which Muslims and Hindus in many rural areas do share, in addition to common class, gender, linguistic, and regional interests, on the other hand are markers of the commonness. Communalist leaders will harp on the differences: 'Each side can produce a closed or circular account which creates a hostile, frightening "Other" to justify pre-emptive strikes or violence in response' (Jeffery and Jeffery 1994: 555). In doing so, the communal leaders, as the self-appointed representatives of a homogenized community, 'arrogate to themselves a proprietorial right to define what Hinduism means' (Basu et al. 1993: 1–2).

In the specific case, the communalist position involves the separation of Hindus and Muslims first as separate ethnic identities, then as separate nationalities, and finally to argue that Hindustan belongs to the Hindus. Muslims at the time of the separation of India and Pakistan in 1947 had been given the opportunity to leave the country for their new motherland. Those who have stayed behind as guests in Hindu India should accept the Hindu character of the country, in the law and mores.

While Uttar Pradesh seemed to be disappearing behind the smoke and dust of a communalist frenzy ignited by this type of argument, and while the BJP media propaganda hyped the onslaught against 'disoriented secularist' and 'leftist intellectuals', we asked the question of 'us' and 'them' at the local level.

In two rounds in early 1993 and late 1993, 220 respondents were questioned. An additional 30 respondents were visited in early 1995. Only ten answers sheets had to be eliminated from the sample since these respondents were unwilling or unable to express their opinion.

We confronted the sample population with three statements, in a positive or a negative clause, and interspersed with other dialogues suggesting

1. that there are no differences between Hindus and Muslims,
2. that Hindustan is a Hindu country, and

3. that Hindus and Muslims should have equal rights as citizens of Bharat.

The reactions by the respondents belonging to the respective caste grouping reveal significant variations. The aggregate score of OBC, SC, and Muslim respondents, on a scale of 1 to 5, was 4.7 (accepting that there are no differences), 1.2 (disagreeing with the concept of a Hindu country), and 4.9 (agreeing with the equal rights argument), which indicates a very strong agreement with the secular position. Among Thakurs also, the secular position was dominant.

The hesitation of some of these respondents on the first statement is due to the fact that they realize that the religion and the religious practices of Hindus and Muslims are different, but even then, repeatedly, it is explicitly stressed that the blood of Hindus and Muslims is the same and that 'We are all children of God'. One of the elder Pasis (the caste of swine herds) felt that while in his youth also there were Hindus and Muslims, he did not understand why it had become a problem now. He suspected that long before his time, a very long time ago, 'something must have happened which divided society, but the God remains the same, and He wants us to respect all His children'.

Statement 1: Hindus and Muslims as Citizens of India

	India belongs to Hindus	Basically, Hindus and Muslims are not different	Hindus and Muslims should have same rights
Brahmin	2.9	2.7	3.3
Thakur	1.9	3.8	4.1
Bania	3.1	2.6	2.8
OBC	1.3	4.7	4.9
SC	1.2	4.7	4.8
Muslims	1.0	5.0	5.0

Note: A value close to 1 signifies strong disagreement; a value close to 5 signifies strong agreement.

On the three statements relating to the rights of Muslims *versus* Hindus, Brahmins have a score which hovers around 3.0, which suggests a neutral stand. The aggregate score actually is the statistical average of almost as many Brahmins who take a secular position as compared to Brahmins who want to treat the Muslims as second-class citizens.

Among the Muslim-baiting Brahmins, we encountered many young intellectuals who are no longer steeped in religion. Although they have doubts and are still somewhat afraid that *Bhagwan*, if he should exist, may punish them, they have taken to 'a scientific explanation of the world'. Their *Hindutva* therefore has nothing to do with religion, but rather with economic competition, as one young graduate inadvertently divulges: 'In 1947, the Muslims were given the option, but many stayed on, and now they try to establish their rights, and in service they benefit from positive discrimination. That should be stopped. We can't get jobs although our qualifications are superior.'

Among the Brahmins, the secular position sometimes also combined with an atheistic world view and with an association with progressive parties, but more often it derived from an ecumenical attitude: *Allah* and *Bhagwan* are considered as the *avatar* of one Supreme Being: '*dharm ek hi hai*' (Religion is one).

Among the Vaishya Bania castes, the communalists have a clearer edge over the secularists. Guptas and Jaiswals often take the most extreme position, and have no scruples in declaring: 'Muslims should be asked to leave India and to go to Pakistan or to the Arabian countries.'

The rich landowning class and the trading class, more or less congruent with Brahmin and Vaishya, have a pronounced communalist slant. In politics, they have decided to play the religious trump card. In order to play this card, they should publicly be prepared to accept religious leaders as their mentors. Even if Brahmins can vaguely be associated with a priestly caste, and possibly have some sympathy for the *sadhu*, *yogi* and *pandit*, the Bania definitely cannot be expected effectively relinquish his power and earthly wealth to religious leaders. We have formulated another three statements around the idea of having more interference by religious leaders, and the *dharma* imperative, in the running of the administration, or, in more abstract terms, the *Ramrajya* (the Kingdom of Ram).

In Statement 2, we present the scores on two such opinions, namely the contention that politics should be based on, and be inspired by religion, and the contention that more religious leaders should get involved in politics.

The Bania caste, it appears, feigns a high degree of religiosity and theocracy. Most of them declare that politics should be based on *dharma* and religion and that religious leaders should be involved in the running of society and the administration. Brahmins tend to agree with the first position, but not with the second.

The OBCs and SCs apparently live in a different discursive world.

Statement 2: Politics must me based on Dharma and Religion

	Religion should enter politics	Religious leaders should enter politics
Brahmin	3.5	3.1
Thakur	2.1	1.9
Bania	4.1	3.5
OBC	1.3	1.2
SC	1.1	1.1
Muslim	1.5	1.5

Note: A value close to 1 signifies strong disagreement; a value close to 5 signifies strong agreement.

Their religious world view and practice is in opposition to the Brahmanical belief, and they have understood, or have come to understand, that religious leaders operate hand in hand with the interests of the *punjipati* (rich people, capitalists). They understand that the *Hindutva* slant of the traders, rich peasants, and administrators is not induced by religious piety and undefiled sodality, but by a basal political instinct: religion as a means of evoking loyalties against the dangers of a civic emancipatory process. Repeatedly, this is the specific discourse which illiterate and poor men and women have utilized when described to me why they did want religious leaders to be in politics: 'It is a dangerous ploy of the rich; if they succeed, a big storm will come, we will be suppressed and shall have to work without pay.'

The support for a theocratization of politics, based on the *imam*, the *sadhu*, and the *pandit*, is generally ruled out, with some exceptions though. The exceptions are not related to class or gender, but to age. The ten lower caste people who would like politics to be based more on religion are in their fifties and sixties. Religion in their case is appreciated not as a dogmatic system around Gods and rituals, but as a system which stands for ethical values and justice. Only 4 of these 10 people also approved of the demolition of the Ayodhya mosque.

The Temple of Faith

Here we come to the central case in the BJP argumentation in the months preceding the destruction of the mosque in Ayodhya in December 1993 and in its war of attrition on other mosques: the imperative of the Hindu faith over the constitutional and legalistic arguments. An important aspect of communal politics, argues Javed Alam (1993: 51) is 'to seek sanctions in a domain outside of human reasoning. Priority is accorded to beliefs and institutions over which the presiding power is that of God or some other super-natural force.' Legislation enacted by the Indian Parliament (*sansad*) necessarily had to be superseded by the edicts proclaimed by the so-called *Dharam Sansad*, the religious parliament (i.e. the self-proclaimed advocates of the Hindu religion). Since the Hindus did believe that Ram was born on that very same spot in Ayodhya, and that the infidel Muslim ruler Babur had destroyed the temple erected on Ram's proclaimed birth place, the Hindus, according to the BJP argument, were entitled to rectify the historic wrongdoing.

Although the argument is utterly ludicrous and lethal in a democratic system, the question which concerns us here is whether the edicts of the *Dharam Sansad* indeed reflect the 'The Hindu Belief', or whether it possibly was only a small minority asserting its Might Is Right principle. For answering the question, we can rely on two sets of data referring to the same area of research. The first set relates to 162 elected members of the village councils (*panchayats*), and the second set is the opinion survey among 240 respondents.

The fieldwork among the *panchayat* members, from August 1990 through October of the same year, indicated that only 5 members had BJP leanings. Four of them were rich peasants. Many other Brahmins were still siding with Congress, but the political support was collapsing. The extension of job reservation to the OBCs in the summer of 1990 was commonly condemned by the Brahmins, Thakurs, and Banias as unjust and detrimental to the progress of the country. While the immolation politics of Brahmin students made many regions in northern and north-western India sink into chaos, the BJP hit upon a novel idea to re-unite the Hindu masses: Ayodhya. That idea gave the Brahmins an ostensibly non-selfish bandwagon to jump on: in addition to 27 Brahmins (slightly more than half of the Brahmin membership), we found only one Thakur and one Chamar who supported the idea of demolishing Babri Masjid in order to construct the Ram Mandir. Their shift to the BJP followed.

Three years after the interviews with the *panchayat* members, in the months preceding the destruction of the mosque, it was still mainly the Brahmins who supported the destruction (see Statement 3). By and large, opinion remained locked at the 1990 positions, with a further polarization though. The Brahmins had moved closer to the Banias and the BJP, and further in the direction of the Hindu belief that the temple

Statement 3: Temple Politics

	Religion is misused for political power game	Temple should be built
Brahmin	2.8	3.5
Thakur	4.4	1.9
Bania	3.6	3.2
OBC	5.0	1.1
SC	5.0	1.1
Muslim	4.8	1.0

Note: A value close to 1.0 signify strong disagreement; and a value close to 5.0 signifies strong agreement.

should be built, and that the destruction of the mosque had been fully justified. A majority of them argued that the courts are politically motivated and that new excavations had established beyond doubt that the mosque had been built on a sacrosanct Ram Mandir. Around one-fourth of the Brahmins tended to disagree with this line of argument, and would have preferred the rule of law to prevail. They, however, were in a tangle after the demise of the Congress party, and the emergence of the BJP as their new class party. The dilemma was expressed as follows by one of them after the demolition of the mosque:

> I had voted BJP, but frankly speaking, I did not expect them to do it, and now I feel hurt in my religious feelings. After all, God is one; the ways to approach him are different, and to destroy a religious place and to create tension and fights, all this is *adharmik* (non-religious). And it is illegal also, and a-historical. The rule of the country has been violated, on the basis of Tulsidas, but the *Ramayana* contains so many contradictions that it should never have been taken as the basis for this Ram business. Somewhere he says that women, drums and animals should be beaten; somewhere else he says that women and God should be worshipped. The temple may have been there, and Babur may have done the things he is accused of, but those are bygone days of feudalism. Now we live under democratic rule, and this drama politics cannot be allowed.

By the end of 1993, a dramatic reconsideration took hold of the OBCs: whereas in 1990, around half of them had agreed that a temple could be built, the new position was clearly that a temple should not be built. This actually followed from the position taken earlier that a temple could be constructed side by side with the mosque, but not at the expense of the mosque. The OBC segment, virtually collectively, had shifted against the iconoclasts.

The revulsion against what they generally regard as *kursi ka khel* (chair game, politics) is shared with the SC respondents. They despise the political games and condemn the violence in which it is usually the poor people who get killed. Many of them, especially among the younger generation are indifferent to God and thus are not concerned either with the masjid or with the mandir. The elder generation, which does have some respect for the *paramshakti* (the overarching power, basically tradition) is not concerned with the temple either: 'Our body is our temple'.

Occasionally, one does meet a male SC or OBC who claims to approve of the demolition. Usually, the interview takes a hilarious turn, like in the following case of a young Teli (T):

T: Yes, absolutely, the temple should now be built.

Q: Why?

T: Because of Hindu Rashtra.

Q: So, you want India to become a Hindu Rashtra?

T: Yes, we are the majority and we should be allowed to live as Hindus.

Q: Did you go to Ayodhya?

Y: No, but I fully approve of it. They have done a good thing. The mosque should not be there where Ram was born.

Q: Why are you so concerned about Ram? What else do you do for him?

T: Nothing much actually. Sometimes in the morning I may say Ram Ram, but usually I am too dirty, and too tired.

Q: Do you actually believe in Ram, or in God?

T: Not much, no. What can he do to us? At the most he can take our life. But my mother believes.

Q: Does she pray to Ram?

T: Maybe, but once in a while she invites a Brahmin for *shlokas* (i.e. mantra prayers).

Q: What are they about, these *shlokas*? Are they about Ram?

T: I don't know. They use a strange language.

The young Teli has been hobnobbing with some Brahmins of the village, he has read the rabidly communal Hindi newspapers, and may have started talking their idiom, impaired by his alter ego. His more dominant ego, it turned out, was a choice for Mandal, against mandir, and thus for Janata/BSP against the BJP. The OBC and SC electorate has, practically unanimously, disapproved of the political skirmishes at Ayodhya as a religious disaster and has clearly pointed its finger at the guilty players: the Brahmin *punjipati* of the BJP.

Conclusions

This chapter began by stating our intention to construct an argument along secular lines. Communalism was to be explained not on the basis of religious idiosyncrasies, but on the basis of political strategies based on class interests. Religion is a useful instrument since it possesses a dual use: it helps to shape social life, but it also subjects individuals to power centres which may strive to divide societies, and to deflect from class conflicts and economic grievances. Religion then may serve as an appropriate instrument in the hands of the economic and political elite. As 'opium for the people', it helps to safeguard the economic privileges, and to lead the lower class people away from the issues of exploitation and suppression.

We have also suggested that, in order to make communalism click, upper class lobbies, more often than not working behind the smokescreen of religious officiates, attempt to construct the uniqueness and harmonious interests of the imagined religious community and oppose it to the inimical other. We have further asserted that such a recourse to the religious subterfuge has followed in the wake of economic liberalization and in the wake of spreading lower class consciousness and political mobilization. There may even exist a direct correlation between liberalization and globalization on the one hand, corrupting the social and political texture of post-Independence India, and the emergence of communalism as a major social phenomenon.

We have also argued that the rapid growth of the BJP coincided with the withering of the INC, and have assumed that the process at work was the transfer of support by important sections of the ruling classes to the Hindu communalist party. The essence of the BJP then has to be explained in terms of its reincarnation as the strategic party of the ruling class, a function which the INC had performed till the late 1980s.

In the second part of the chapter, the relevance of the theoretical explanation on the basis of material from anthropological fieldwork in an area close to Ayodhya has been illustrated. We have first noticed a near perfect correlation between caste and class, and a deep sense of distrust among the lower castes (SC and OBC) towards the higher castes. The BJP's upper caste leadership, steeped in caste hierarchy and caste suppression, could therefore not possibly epitomize the new political Messiah for whom the lower castes were waiting. Both in the voting behaviour as well as in the ideological stand, a abyss exists between the lower castes and the upper castes. Among the trading castes of Banias and among the dominant landowners (mainly Brahmins), we found the ardent followers of the BJP and of the militant iconoclasm. It is significant that among SC and OBC respondents on the other hand, we found hardly any takers for the hindutva view. They, by and large, considered Muslims and Hindus as equals in a secular and tolerant India, and almost unanimously were opposed to the demolition of the mosque in Ayodhya and the erection of the Ram Mandir on that very same spot.

The findings do show that it is the rich and the powerful, mainly from among the upper castes, who have taken to 'militant obscurantism'. Amartya Sen has argued that religious gullibility and the political use of 'people's credulity in unreasoned and archaic beliefs' did not come as a surprise in those parts of India where even elementary education is at a very low level: 'While illiteracy may not be a central feature of communal fascism or of sectarian nationalism in general, its role in sustaining militant obscurantism can be very strong indeed' (Sen 1993: 17). The allusion is not warranted: it is precisely the illiterate men and women from the lower class/caste background who have refused to accept the 'opium for the people' handed out to them by the emerging political formations of the very much literate ruling classes. *Hindutva* was rejected as an antithesis to empowerment.

CHAPTER 11

Rural Development in West Bengal: Development of the Weak

Since 1977, the Left Front Government (LFG) has been in power in the populous state of West Bengal. It is by far the longest ruling democratically elected (communist) government in world history. Its policy in matters of rural development has been based on land reforms (a moderate ceiling, tenancy reforms and preferential treatment of small peasants in access to inputs) and on decentralization to the village level through the *panchayats* (village councils). With a few exceptions (D. Bandyopadhyay 1993; Mallick 1993; Rogaly et al. 1999), most studies do agree that the rural development policy of the LFG has done fairly well on many scores.

The tenuous hold of landlords and rich peasants on rural politics and economics has been breached, and the *panchayats* have helped to channel the state resources to the needy beneficiaries, and have prevented too much leakage towards non-target groups. The LFG experiment of land reforms and technological intervention targeted at the poorer households has made rural development happen. The process of polarization and pauperization also appears to have been reversed. Poverty remains, but destitution is less apparent. Agrarian production has grown significantly.[1]

D. Bandyopadhyay, a retired bureaucrat and in the late 1970s Land Reforms' Commissioner with the LFG, was quick to argue that the *panchayat* system had become bureaucratized: 'The elan and vitality with which the panchayats had started in 1978 got dissipated and it became in many a place a lifeless and sterile elected administrative structure' (D. Bandyopadhyay 1993: 18). He further argued that the contractors, usurers and middlemen have started waiving the red flag and

[1] Bergmann 1984; Nripen Bandyopadhyaya 1988; Kohli 1987; Lieten 1992a, 1996a; Eashvaraiah 1993; Harriss 1993; see also Chapter 6 in this volume.

have taken over the *panchayat* power: 'That is why we find the Panchayats running out of steam in terms of ideas, innovativeness and emphatic response to major social and economic issues which confront the poor and the less affluent' (D. Bandyopadhyay 1993: 20).

These words came as a stern warning. The fact that in the later elections the CPI(M) again improved its tally may suggest that conditions were not as bad as D. Bandyopadhyay suggested. Around that time, I did a number of field studies on the working of the *panchayats*. Although I noticed in some *panchayats* the deformations mentioned in the article, by and large my conclusions were more positive (see Lieten 1996a).

In this chapter I shall study the views of the local people and let them speak out on how they see the functioning of the *panchayats* and the changes that have come about in their live over a period of 15 years of LFG.

Changing Public Space

Until the 1993 elections, it could still be argued that the low-caste and low-caste people had entered the *panchayat* structure, but that the real power remained in the hands of the *bhadrolok*. The land-slide change which the elections of 1993 (and of 1997) have brought about makes such an argument less obvious. In the popularly elected village council, more than a proportionate number of the earlier marginalized castes and classes have taken their seats. The public space is increasingly being occupied by poor peasants and agricultural labourers. In terms of strategic power, the important functions all too often may have remained with the male *bhadrolok* members, but the overall impact of the changing composition of the *panchayats* yet may have beneficial to the poorer sections in the villages.

The radical changes that have taken place, I shall illustrate on the basis of research findings in one block in Barddhaman district.[2] In my pre-1993 study on Memari II Block (Lieten 1992b; see also Lieten 1988), I concluded that the progress in 1988 in comparison with the earlier elected bodies was 'remarkable': the SC/ST presence in the *panchayats* was 30 per cent. I should have reserved my qualification 'remarkable'

---

[2] The study (Rural Development and Changing Socio-Cultural Systems in the Context of Devolution of Power), which was financed by the Indo-Dutch Project on Alternatives in Development, has been conducted in three districts of West Bengal (Barddhaman, Medinipur and Jalpaiguri) and Uttar Pradesh (Muzaffarnagar, Rai Bareilli and Jaunpur).

for the *panchayats* elected in 1993 and thereafter: 50.4 per cent belong to SC/ST communities, well above their proportion in the population, and only 36.5 per cent hail from the so-called general Hindu castes. Also, and this is the next significant positive development, whereas previously women were virtually absent from the elected bodies, this time they represent 34.9 per cent, just above the statutory required minimum. The net consequence of the female and SC/ST ascent is that in the block under survey, male non-SC Hindus had had their presence in the *panchayats* sliced to around 20 per cent. One may agree with the projection that women will not immediately start running the show, but in view of their mere numbers, the colour and the agenda of the *panchayats* is bound to change.

The *panchayat* leaders in Memari whom I interviewed, at least to the extent that they belong to the CPI(M), painted a rosy picture of the positive changes and of their role therein. The members owing allegiance to the Congress party cautioned against gullibility and indicated weaknesses and malpractices in the system. The view from the top has to be regarded with the customary circumspection. Collecting data from below will help to come to a more balanced, and in any case a more informed assessment. It may help to explain why the LFG has maintained its popular support basis and has continued to win the *panchayat*, state assembly and national elections from the state ever since 1977.

Three adjacent hamlets in Bohar *panchayat* and two contiguous villages in Kuchut *panchayat* were selected for collecting the view from below. The villages are situated at a distance of about 2 km from the *panchayat* office and from the traffic roads. In a random, qualified sample, with a preference for the poorer households, interviews were organized with 112 men and women, representing approximately 20 per cent of the households: 58 agricultural labourers, 10 artisans and small traders, 22 small peasants, 13 middle peasants, 10 rich peasants, and one government employee.[3]

The political preferences were spread as follows: with 85 supporters the CPI(M) is clearly in the driving seat; the 24 supporters of the Congress party are mainly rich peasants and middle peasants with a sprinkling of poor peasants and agricultural labourers; the 3 BJP neo-converts are middle peasants who have started disliking the *panchayat* leaders because 'all the facilities go to the Muslims and to the SC/ST people'.

[3] Of the 78 males and 34 females in the sample, 70 were landless or near landless, i.e. with less than 0.5 acres of land. Twenty peasants had up to 2.5 acres of land, and seven families had more than 7.5 acres.

Rather than shifting to Congress, which in their mind is still the *ghooskhor* (bribe takers) party, they have pinned new hopes on the rabble-rousing reincarnation of the old Hindu Mahasabha and Jan Sangh which had been reasonably influential in some of the neighbouring areas in the early 1950s.

Benefits

Some of the dissatisfaction in the villages which does occur, and which provides Congress and other parties with a continuing electoral base, is often associated with the distribution of IRDP loans. Villagers may feel disgruntled because loans have not come their way but instead, they apprehend, have found their way to people closer to the party. Leakage of facilities to non-target families may aggravate the case against the claim of fairhandedness by the *panchayats*. The *panchayat* members in Memari deny that this is the case in their area, and argue that the prevalence of CPI(M) sympathizers among the beneficiaries logically follows from the nature of the poverty alleviation schemes. Since loans, as per the rules, are to be distributed among the poor and marginal peasants, with a preference for SC/ST, there would necessarily be less Congress sympathizers among the beneficiaries.

Benefits may accrue to individual households in different forms: allocation of land, employment in public works, rural development (IRDP) loans, minikits for agriculture, etc. The allocation of land basically meant land for housing plots.[4] The limited stretches of land allocated to landless families were the barren plots of *panchayat* land. They have been provided as homestead land to 42 families, i.e. covering practically all agricultural labour families with a plot ranging from 2 to 11 *katha* to erect a dwelling. Most of them are SC/ST families.

Around half of the agricultural labour families have also been provided with an additional income from public works programmes, ranging from one week in the Kuchut *panchayat* to one month in the Bohar *panchayat*. The additional income thus turns out to range from being quite minimal to moderate, but most villagers, however, do agree that there has been *beshi unnoti* (much improvement) through this extra work in the lean agricultural season.

[4] Although the area is dominated by rich peasants, the land in their possession has generally been below the ceiling limit. The biggest area owned by one peasant was found to be 14 acres, and although one elderly peasant cultivated more than the ceiling limit, half of the land belonged to his brother on whose behalf he cultivated all the land.

The appreciation refers more to the nature of the works than to the incremental income associated with the programmes. The female inhabitants are particularly pleased with the drinking water. Numerous handpumps have come up in the proximity of the houses, and are usually in good working order. Electricity though is still absent from most of the hamlets. This, a number of poor villagers explain, is not so much due to the inactivity of the *panchayats*, but to the commercial stipulations imposed by the Electricity Board.

At the general level, virtually all villagers agree that drinking water supply, the local school management, health conditions and communications have improved significantly. Health workers make their regular injection and family planning rounds. They are assisted by a village level worker who gets a stipend of Rs 50 in order to keep a check on epidemics. A number of homeopathic practitioners take care of the minor ailments at low costs. Hospitals at a reasonably short distance take care of the major ailments.

Road construction has made a major difference in the approachability of the villages. Both research areas are located at a distance of approximately two kilometres off the tarmac road from where buses provide regular connections with Memari and Barddhaman town. Many inter-village roads have been surfaced (the so-called *morrum* roads). The roads, in combination with improved drainage, have put an end to the seasonal inaccessibility of the villages. Visits to hospitals, educational institutions, the block headquarters, and the *hats* have become easy. Earlier, during the rainy season, explains one of the richer peasants, they had to carry the cycle on the shoulder all the way. He is appreciative of the new roads, but the way in which the roads have been constructed evokes his bitter resentment.

The *panchayats* have namely taken recourse to the principle of *shromdan* (voluntary labour). Rich and middle peasants unwilling to contribute manual labour, considering it below their dignity, are provided with the alternative of providing food for the payment of additional labourers. Most rich peasants are resentful of these levies which are calculated on the basis of the extent of land ownership and which they claim is used by the party leaders to pay for the labour so that they can pocket the money which they receive from the *panchayat*. The richest peasant in Modhupur village is particularly annoyed: 'Oh *baba*, we have to give it to them. If we don't give for their party fund, they withdraw their labour supply to us. So, there is no way out but to contribute whatever they ask for.' He has more complaints. Although he cultivates 14 acres of land, and has to look after a small family only, he claims that his economic position has seriously deteriorated. His worries are partially of a financial nature: the loan for the tractor is still to be repaid and for the agricultural operations, he had to engage an additional Rs 25,000 loan at 5 per cent monthly interest. His main worry, however, is that labour is not submissive and available at his beck and call, and that he cannot claim any benefits from the *panchayat*:

The British period was the best; then came the Congress period. There was at least peace then, but this period is the worst, *onek kharap*. I asked them only for a minikit, but they only give it to the party people, and they told me that I am a *jhumidar*, and that I don't need it. An IRDP loan, I haven't even asked for. I know that it only goes to their friends, for a consideration of course.

Loan Politics

The number of families who have received IRDP loans during the six years preceding the field work turns out to be on the high side: 46 families, i.e. 41 per cent of the sample. A vast majority of them are CPI(M) supporters. Statistics, however, also tell another story: more than half of the party supporters did not get a loan, and around one-fifth did not get any direct benefits at all. Closeness to the party and *panchayat* leaders need not be an advantage, because while allocating the loans, the repayment position is taken in consideration.[5]

It is sometimes difficult to sort out fact and fiction without taking into account the psychological factors. Political allegiance and economic position may act as selection criteria, but psychological factors may activate some families to make a rush for the cheap loans, and others to relinquish them. Among the former are the greedy who will take whatever comes their way and who never will be satisfied: 'Nobody is doing anything for us' was the opinion of the Hazras. It is also the opinion of a Muchi small peasant. His application for an IRDP loan for a shop was rejected because, in his words, he did not do enough *telomoro* ('oil massaging', flattering). Now he does not like any longer these 'bastards' who only give when you put enough oil on their head, and he had made up his mind to shift back to Congress. We suggest that he could

---

[5] The requests of two persons, quite close to the party secretary in the Bohar area, one of them a bit of a drunkard, were not accommodated with the argument that they would not be able to repay. Some others did not want to apply for a loan for this very reason. Although we shall see later that quite a number of loans were not utilized properly, repayment as a rule has taken place. Six loans went to beneficiaries who had voted for the Congress party. Publicly, they may not have been known as such.

have financed the shop himself because, as he told us, he had spent Rs 18,000 for his daughters' marriage. It then turns out that he partially footed the bill from a loan which he had received three years ago for rice trading, the total amount of which remains outstanding.

I could establish that the loans have almost exclusively found their way to landless labourers and marginal peasants. In five cases the beneficiaries had 10–15 *bigha* of land (4 to 6 acres). Their SC/ST status may have helped them to get the loan. In one case (a Congress family in the Kuchut area), a loan was granted to a reasonably well-to-do family for setting up a shop. The loan was repaid within two years, and the family moreover had enough resources to spend on the marriage of the daughter, in their estimate Rs 1,00,000. Thus, although not much leakage to non-target groups appears to have occurred, some leakage has taken place. One should add, however, that these loans, for irrigation pumps and shops, were among the few loans that were put to productive use. It is amazing to discover how many of the loans were used for consumption needs. On the basis of the distribution of the loans, one would expect the village to float on the activities of cattle traders, vegetables hawkers, and rice traders. In family after family we were informed that the loans were granted for these purposes, and in family after family we were concurrently informed that the business failed. Some of them seriously tried to get into the trading business, but found the going tough.[6]

Before taking the loans, a reasonable amount of deliberation takes place. Some are not interested in the loan because they foresee repayment problems. Some others are in dire need of a pump, a cycle van, or weaving material. They usually waste no time in exchanging the loans for the goods they need. Most of the beneficiaries, however, appear to bet on two horses: to use the money for the most immediate household needs in anticipation of some savings in the future with which to repay the loan and to start the business at a future point of time: '*Suru kori ni*' (I haven't started as yet) is the oft repeated refrain.

Some are more perceptive than others, and spread the loan over different headings. A typical example is Kumkuma, a young SC labourer-cum-tailor who recently got married to a Kayastha girl, very much to the dissatisfaction of his father and attracting empathy from the

---

[6] With the improving accessibility of the villages, the profit margins have narrowed. Advance payments for rice which then turned to be of bad quality, closed the option for a number of agricultural labourers who had planned to turn to trading. In many a case, however, the option had already been foreclosed by the misappropriation of the loan for marriage expenses.

panchayat member. He was offered a loan of Rs 9,000 for a vegetable business. With Rs 3,000, he opened a savings account in the bank; almost the same amount was used to repay a debt to a trader; Rs 1,300 was used to buy a cow, and Rs 1,800 was repaid immediately which left a debt, net of subsidy, of only Rs 2,700. This debt he is confident of repaying within three years.

The calculations lead to ill-use, possibly even misuse, of IRDP loans. This is actually what can be expected within such a programme where the beneficiaries are selected on an individual basis and have individual needs and considerations. The money once received would be used in a manner they would think best. Apportioning of blame for the misuse of funds therefore has to start at the root, namely the philosophy itself behind the IRDP. The programme is a family-centred financial assistance scheme, assuming that poor families have the entrepreneurial spirit and abilities and that there is a conducive socio-economic environment which allows for risky investments. The policy also abstracts from the immediate consumption needs and outstanding usury obligations which may interfere with the appropriate employment of the loan. The LFG, when the programme was introduced in the late 1970s, therefore argued with the Union Government that assistance would not reach the poor families, who usually were bereft of the necessary physical means to participate in the scheme. It proposed to route the money through the *panchayat* which could then act as a catalyst of development and redistribution:

> To this end, the Panchayats were to be given the powers to obtain both the subsidy and the loan component of assistance, acquire the physical assets and hand them over to poor families, undertake the development of infrastructure, acquire elementary machinery and agricultural equipment, livestock, draft animals, etc. The equipment and draft animals were to be hired out to beneficiaries on a no-profit-no-loss basis. (Gumaste et al. 1987: 96)

The state government, after initially opposing the family-centred approach acquiesced and thereby foreclosed the option which would have allowed for a much more productive use of the money in a cooperative farming scheme and other village-centred programmes.

A Change in Class Relations

The changes in the countryside have to do with the benefits that have come in the wake of land reforms, rural development programmes, infrastructural works, productivity increase and employment generation, some of which have been mentioned in the preceding section. How are the changes appreciated?

The changes can be assessed at two levels, namely improvement in the material circumstances and improvement in the social circumstances. I was interested to find out how the circumstances in the mid-1990s compared with the circumstances in the mid-1970s, i.e. before the establishment of the *panchayat* system with the advent of the LFG. When villagers are asked to assess the changes, the time span may be too too long. Individual families may also have the impact of a growing dependency ratio (in young families with many children) or just the opposite. Depending on the political colours, respondents may also exaggerate the positive departure, or rather stress that, if anything, things have deteriorated. With these caveats in mind, I now turn to the major section in which the assessment of the changes by the villagers will be presented.

In terms of changes in economic well-being, Figure 11.1 illustrates that a majority of landless labourers, small peasants, and middle peasants

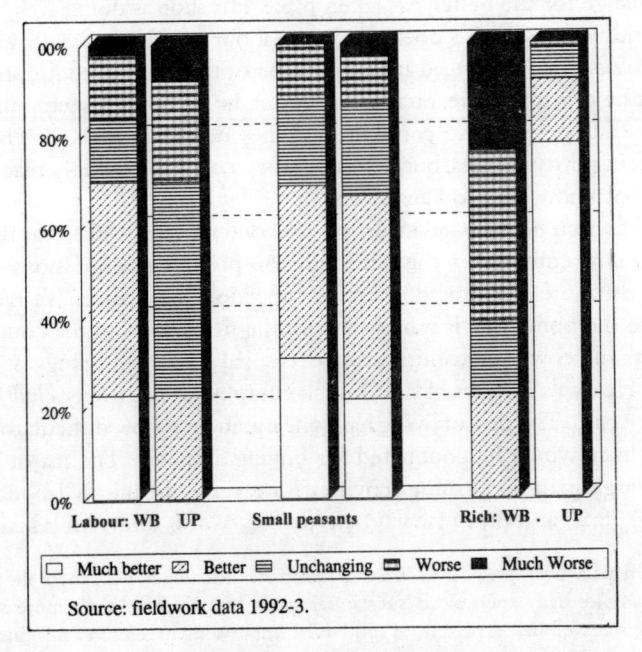

Fig. 11.1: Perception of Economic Changes. Class-wise Appreciation in Barddhaman and Muzaffarnagar

have a positive and even very positive assessment. On the other hand, a majority of rich peasants claims that they have regressed economically. In the Fig. 11.1, I have added the results of a similar exercise that I did in Muzaffarnagar, a Green Revolution area in Western UP, around the same time. The differences are striking.[7]

The unanimous opinion of the rich peasants is that the Marxist party interferes with the agricultural work and is creating too much disturbance. In terms of income, they have not done badly and, from my observations, have not experienced an absolute decline, as they claim. The decline is more in terms of a loss of power and status. With the political landslide in the late 1970s, the curtain ran down on the *dapoth*, the unchallenged authority of the landed elite, and they hope for a return to the olden days. In the pre-LFG days, the rich peasants with their hoodlums were riding roughshod over the poor villagers, especially when they were related with the leftist peasant organizations. Such *jhamela* (disturbances) has now gone, and some rich peasants agree that it is a good thing, but their declining power is difficult to stomach. Asit Mondal, one of the Congress leaders in the Kuchut area, agrees that a change for the better has taken place. His shop is doing well, and as a middle peasant, he does not have labour problems. Stability, loans, minikits, and homestead lands are some of the many accomplishments that he can appreciate, but on one count, he harbours resentment: 'The low caste people have come up, and they don't behave well. They are wearing dirty clothes, but nowadays they come to our holy places and do not know how to keep it holy.'

The rich peasants, as a rule, are malcontent. They claim that the *jhamela* now comes from the other side. All possible transgressions effecting them are mentioned: coercive collections take place, fish is stolen from the pond, rice is removed from the fields or from the courtyard, goats and cows are roaming around, etc. JM is one of the biggest farmers. He owns 14 acres of land, but claims to be in dire straits: *khub kharap* (very bad). The cost of living has gone up, and it is now difficult to repay the loan, which he contracted for buying a tractor. The major factor impinging on his farming activities, however, is the unruly labour class. *Bhoy* (fear) and *chinta* (worry) are the key words underlying his story:

---

[7] In his two sample villages, Webster found that not only 85 per cent of the poorer households had experienced 'substantial' gains, but that half of the more affluent groups as well had experienced substantial improvements. He uses this finding to conclude that 'it reflects the increasing non-antagonistic nature of the Left Front government's agrarian strategy and therefore its reformist, even revisionist, class nature' (Webster 1992: 108).

The wage rate for the labour class has gone up, and that is a good thing, I agree, but they should work as hard as before. But now there is laziness all around. They work for only six hours a day, and if you ask them to do something, they may beat you or stop working and go somewhere else. That is my major worry. There is a tremendous labour problem here, and we are scared to talk to them. The labour class used to be submissive, but now they talk too much. All norms are gone. Everything is bad. Nothing is done in the village. Look at their adult education centres. Great! They are getting educated and are not working in our fields. What then is the use of education for these people? Labour is the major problem, but also, we do not get any help. All service goes to the lower classes. They just give it to the people they like.

Some other rich peasants disagree with the bleak picture painted by JM. In some of their admissions, while claiming to have constant *bhoy* and *chinta*, they also admit that whenever there are labour problems, or problems with collections, they approach the party leader for help, and his intervention usually solves the problem amicably. For TM, the owner of 13 acres of fertile land, a tractor, and a television set, live is very hard under the new regime of leaders who 'are obstructing the peasants' and who 'pocket the panchayat money'. It is an uphill struggle to retain his earlier status, he claims, but till now he has been able to skirt around major labour problems. Problems can be sidestepped if the leaders are approached properly:

I sometimes have problems with the labour class. They don't work hard enough, and put forward excessive demands, but when I go directly to Krishna Babu, he tries to help me out. He has helped me with a ration card, with certificates, and so on. I actually like his *toshon niti* (conciliatory policy) so that problems are solved whenever they arise.

The *toshon niti* showed up in one of the incidents during the fieldwork. The incident exemplified how a relatively minor incident becomes the talk of the village, with interesting variations on the basic theme. Just before we reached the village, a boy was beaten up while stealing potatoes from the field of a Mondal. The labourers went on a lightning strike. The Mondal families approached a BJP lawyer in Memari who prepared a case. The Mondals, bereft of their labourers, initially started working the field themselves but then ultimately had to apologise to the workers. It was 'a one-sided judgement', says one of them, 'and even then, despite our apologies, the strike continued'. But did a strike ever take place, and how was the conflict solved? Anyway, had the boy been stealing potatoes? No, others argue, he was just picking up some stray tubers, which had been left behind when the crop was harvested. He should not have been beaten for foraging, is the opinion on the middle ground. When in search of more light on the incident we move closer to the *para* of Bagdi and Santal (low caste and tribals), the incident changes colour. No potatoes were involved. Neither was their any involvement of Sadgopes, although they were affected by a strike, which actually was less of a strike, and more of a disturbance. For the linchpin in the story, one had to look at sex rather than at class. One Bagdi boy had developed deep sexual desires for a Santal girl, and had accosted her. The girl's father confronted the Bagdi family, and the case was settled with a payment of Rs 1,000, but when a few days later a Santal family member crossed the Sadgope field where the Bagdi had been harvesting potatoes, he was beaten up by the Bagdi, repaying him blow after blow for the money which was unfairly extracted, for after all, as the Bagdi boy shouted: 'The girl wanted it'. Tempers ran high, and work came temporarily to a standstill. It took a major effort and negotiating skill by the party leader to re-establish the working relationship.

The use of banal incidents in political propaganda runs as a base line through the stories of this kind. Such stories are used by the rich peasant (in their own version) as an argument to lambaste the undemocratic behaviour and ruinous economic policy of the CPI(M). But generally, verbal confrontations of this kind are not entering public space. In public space the opposite groups in the class divide have learned to accommodate each other. One explanation could be that the rich peasants have learned to accept their place in the new political configuration, and, in a balance of fear and tactics, refrain from causing a scandal or getting involved in a tussle. I actually almost caused a tussle when I suggested to a young Bagdi labourer that they had become lazy, and were working only six hours for a full day's wage. He insisted that I tell him the name of the rich peasant who had told me such an obnoxious lie:

Are they still thinking of us in this manner? Tell me, and I'll go and teach him a lesson. Everywhere in Memari, we work until the sun sets, from 6 a.m. with a two hours' lunch break, and if we turn up after 7 a.m., we are asked to return home, or the work has been given to immigrant labour from Bihar or Medinipur. It is a good thing that we are not beaten any longer and that we can tell them straight in the face things which we don't like. That is one thing. But the other thing is that it is still *khutni* [toiling] what we do, possibly not double *khutni* like in my fathers' day, but *khutni* nevertheless.

The Bagdi's version of the long working time is an exaggeration: effective working time is closer to seven hours, with usually no overtime allowed. *Panchayat* and Krishak Sabha (peasant union) leaders anticipate that if overtime were allowed, the workers with lower physical strength (women and elderly people) would fall by the wayside.

Figure 11.1 has shown that the agricultural labour class, as well as poor and middle peasants, have subjectively experienced a perceptible improvement in material conditions. Many of them are still in meagre circumstances though: one-third of the sample households possess neither a cycle nor a radio or another gadget. Material well-being is mainly seen in terms of sufficient money for food, clothes, and housing. The graph indicates also that the position of some of the agricultural labourers have gone from bad to worse. A serious illness in one nuclear family and the splitting into new family units explain for the five families who have experienced a serious deterioration.

Family planning in most of the newly constituted households has helped to balance income with expenditure. One exception is a Santal family, which migrated from the Dumka area in Bihar in the early 1980s. The family of six children depends mainly on the daily wages of the 30 years' old man. Family planning, adult literacy drive and party politics remain blind spots in his perception. He had come to Barddhaman because life in Bihar was a hell. Compared to those days, he agrees, life has improved, and the deterioration he talks of is really the deterioration over the last years, with the growing household burden as a consequence of the increasing family size.

Overall, people are satisfied that the conditions of dire poverty are a thing of the past. Even those families, who stated to have experienced a slight decline or at most a status quo, however, also agreed that in the earlier days they were *ekbela* (once a day meal), and now were at least *duibela* and usually *tinbela* people.

Social Changes

The positive assessment of material conditions of life is an important factor to explain for the groundswell support for the CPI(M). Usually, however, less tangible changes in the quality of life are given a prominent place. Words like *sukh subidha* (comfort and contentment), *khomota* (influence), *shantipriyo* (peace loving) and *maan morjada* (respect and dignity) are some of the terms used to express why a wide cross-section of villagers supports the new political alignment in the village. One reason why many people made the initial shift to the CPI(M) in the

1960s and 1970s was the discontent with the beatings (*maramari*), and the disturbances (*jhamela*). On example is Siburam, heading a family of nine persons and a man of all trades. He works as an agricultural labourer, earns a bit extra as a hawker, and cultivates 2 acres on barga. He vividly remembers the power of the *morols* in the earlier days:'We really were in a bind. Police would come and pester us. The morols would take my goat, and if I dared to protest, I was beaten. I tell you, we really suffered under the *zulum raj* (coercion) of those days. Nowadays, we can speak our own mind, and what is more, they now address us with *apni* and not with *tui*.'

There is probably more to it than the honorific and the inferior mode of addressing. It symbolizes the promotion from servants and *chhotolok* to normal human beings. The statement also implies that there is more tranquillity and law and order in the village and that daily lives are not continuously in danger of being harassed. Although thefts do take place and women are not absolutely safe (in a remote Bohar village a Santal girl was raped by a dozen Santal boys in retaliation for her mother's affiliation with a non-Santal), the general feeling is that rice can be left outside, that women can move around safely, and that misuse of power has by and large disappeared.

The picture of general satisfaction as described in the previous paragraph applies to the villages in Bohar. In the Kuchut area, conditions are slightly different though. In that area, the cooperative is malfunctioning (Congress *bhadrolok* still have a big finger in the pie), school attendance is less than universal, monthly interests on usury loans range between 4 per cent and 5 per cent, and some vested land has not been distributed. In one of the two villages, unease with the previous high-caste *panchayat* member who was said to neglect his *panchayat* work and to move around too much with the *jotdar* class, had led to his replacement by a young Bagdi *bargadar*. Together with the other member of the village, a Santal labourer, he seems to be performing adequately well. In the other village, however, the 45 years' old Mondal, for the third time in office as a non-party member, had not yet been replaced, despite harsh disapproval of his ways and his neglect of development work. People bitterly complain about the behaviour of this Marxist-supported *panchayat* member. He is a rich farmer, with 15 acres of land, and also runs a lorry business. He seems to have feathered his own nest rather well. The people in the para complain that even a pump was not placed in the hamlet but rather next to his house, and it has stopped working anyway. The agricultural labourers in his constituency give a running commentary on his misdemeanour: he hardly shows up at the meetings, he is quarrelsome, he does not attach his signature even when loans have been sanctioned, and, what is worse, he uses them as free labour when public works organized by the *panchayat* have ended early in the day. In short, he is a real *shubidabadar* (opportunist). The only positive remarks concerning his person were obtained from some Congress-minded peasants.

Despite such a quarrelsome opportunist as a leader, most labourers did not entertain the idea of shifting to Congress because they see their strength in the unity of labour. They only hoped and expected that next time round a better candidate would be made to stand, which ultimately did happen. Quite a few, however, were not so sure about their lasting loyalties. Since they have moved with the times, the choice for the CPI(M) was a logical option. Since the others in the village shifted away from Congress, they have followed suit, but not wholeheartedly, and they will change again when the others change, which may happen anytime when the leaders of the CPI(M) take the path of bureaucratic neglect and personal enrichment. The philosophy underlying the attitude of these fence-sitters is that they are poor people and as such have to make sure that they are on the right side of the power balance. Or, as Ashok explains:

I have a big family to look after. I cannot take any risk and I will support any government so that I can profit from them. All government is good, but we have to toil. Otherwise I cannot fill my stomach. Anyway, why choose? All leaders are the same. The CPM is good, but they have not done anything for me. Anyone going to Lanka becomes a Ravan [jejon jai Lanka sei hoi Ravan].

Negative utterances were more difficult to come by in the Bohar villages. The party leaders there seem to be of a more informed and a more committed type. The party supporters were quasi unanimous in their verdict: the leaders are good, are working hard and are giving proper and impartial judgements. Such judgements are also forthcoming in the case of people, like Anjali, who have not received any direct benefits. Anjali runs a small grocery shop. She tried a minikit for the 2 acres' plot of land and an IRDP loan, but did not get any. They told her that she should use her own money. She can appreciate the judgement, and like her parents and her husband, she is definitely not planning to change sides. She is proud to have an independent judgement: 'Kharap, kharap bolbo. If something is bad, I'll tell it. I may look shy, but I have my own mind. Even if you make me think very hard, I can't think of anything which is even a little bit bad. The local leaders here are doing their best, they are among us and have not tried to play tricks and become rich.'

Gram Sabha

In addition to the *panchayat*, the council with elected members from various villages or hamlets within a cluster, there is a general meeting of all the adult villagers. This meeting, the *gram sabha*, is called twice a year and is required to discuss the budget allocations and the major works to be undertaken (see also Ghatak and Ghatak 2002 for an interesting case study in 20 villages). In the Bohar villages, more than in Kuchut, the leaders maintain a close contact with most of the households. For many people, this is a reason for not attending the *gram sabha* meeting. Since the leaders come to their place regularly, just for *golpo* (gossiping) or for *olochana* (discussions), they can express their complaints and their desires. It turns out that most of the people who go and attend the *gram sabha* keep quiet. What they had to communicate, they say, they had already communicated in private.

Whatever people's attitudes to the *gram sabha*, they all know about its existence. About 55 per cent of the sample explained that they usually attended. Attendance among women was less than 40 per cent. The people who did not attend usually gave one of two reasons. Often we heard the allegation that they were not invited. The allegation does not hold since the meetings are announced by circulars and by loudspeakers. Others argue that it is no use to go and attend the meetings since everything has already been decided beforehand. An additional reason may be the simple fact that the meetings are usually dominated by the followers of the Marxist party and attendance would usually amount to public defeat if one were to intervene. They actually are caught in a cleft stick: not attending results in leaving the political arena to the Marxist party.

Among the Marxist party sympathizers, canvassing is organized prior to the meeting so as to get as many people as possible. Those who attend do it for two reasons. One reason is explained by Pratimo Bag, a small sharecropper: 'If we don't go there, the government will fall. We have to keep being active and united.' For his uncle, who considers himself too old to attend literacy classes, there is a more immediate reason to attend: 'I'm getting old. It is time for calling on God, not for learning to read and write. But attending the *gram sabha* is a must. Otherwise, the *jotdars* will not give us work. The leaders told us that if we do not join together, we will be out of power. So I attend.'

Like many others he attends and listens. The women who attend, with one or two exceptions, do just that: attend and listen. In this way, they state, they get *gyan* (knowledge, consciousness) and this knowledge can than be transmitted to the people back home. For some, the *gyan* is a question of going to school or taking care of hygiene, for others it is the development on the loan front or irrigation pumps, for others it is information on the new wage rates, etc. Their justification for not speaking up is that the leaders are much more abreast of the situation, and as long as they take just decisions, there is no need to butt in with remarks which may be off the point. Actually, some of them frankly admit, they are afraid of saying something wrong or stupid.

Such feelings indicate that the style of the discussions is still a top-down one. The format of public meetings has been standardized: a raised platform, occupied by the big leaders, is the place from which the 'addresses' the lecturing (*boktrita*) take place.[8] In the *gram sabha* meetings, the issues are usually down-to-earth, and although the *boktrita* culture is not altogether absent, participation takes place. Around one-fourth of the males stated that they take active part and occasionally speak up at the meetings. Webster has come to similar findings in two Barddhaman villages, although in his case SC males, almost 80 per cent of whom attended the *sabha*, rarely spoke up. They just went there to listen. Webster (1992: 99) rightly attaches importance to the follow-up:

Having said this, it is important to recognise that these meetings do take place, that the attendance is high, and that the subsequent nightly discussions amongst householders in the poorer *paras* serve as a secondary forum for expressing views which later can come back to the *gram panchayat* via members or, as is more often the case, via local *Krishak Samiti* members. Finally, the few poorer men who do speak are often seen to do so on behalf of their locality, presenting points or criticisms that have been raised by neighbours.

Concluding Remarks

The research findings do show that, by and large, the poor people in the villages feel that their power over village affairs has increased and that, partially because of the *gram sabha*, their knowledge of rural development programmes has expanded. They have come to occupy the public space on optimal terms. The terms are not equal in the sense that

---

[8] Some have called this culture of public meetings a *boshomo* (a command performance) which is meant to be unidirectional. The leaders are there for lecturing the faithful and the not-yet-so-faithful. This lecturing (*boktrita*) does not induce the addressed crowd to participate in a dialogue or in questioning the policy. Depending on the orator's skill and sensitivity, the message may come down and settle in the minds of the people or float in the air.

economic disparities and advantages continue to exist, but these disadvantages definitely do not weigh heavily against the poor any longer.

It has also become clear that especially the poor people are satisfied about the changes that have taken place and that they have developed countervailing power against the rich peasants. The latter clearly are dissatisfied because of the loss of controlling power over their labour force rather than because of diminishing economic returns from agriculture. They have learned to accept the changing balance of class forces in the countryside. Small peasants and agricultural labourers are conscious of their rights and they intend to show it if need be.

It may not be warranted to extend these findings to all blocks and districts. The continuous hold of the LFG over the rural electorate in vast areas of West Bengal does, however, indicate that the situation in many areas may be similar to the one in Memari. It is probably correct to conclude that the LFG parties, and the CPI(M) in particular, have lost influence in those villages where they have distanced themselves from the poor agricultural classes and have started misusing power for their personal or partisan ends. In that specific sense the analysis of Bandyopadhyay quoted at the beginning of the chapter may be correct, but in a more general sense it is not the way the people down below in the villages assess the *panchayat* institution and its leaders.

The views from below do convey a picture of poor men and women who do not necessarily take part in the public debates, but who do know what the public world is about, and who appear to be ready to intervene in order to defend their rights.

CHAPTER 12

The Rural Discourse on Child Labour and Education

In recent year, the debate on child labour has caught the attention. In this chapter, I intend to investigate the conditions surrounding child labour in two adjacent villages in Uttar Pradesh, and relate this investigation to two discussions that have been at the centre of the debate, namely the magnitude of child labour in India and the relationship between (high) fertility and the reproduction of (child) labour.

It is widely argued and accepted that that the phenomenon of working children is associated with poverty. The highest incidence of child labour is said to be found in the poorest countries of the world, and in the poorest regions of those countries. Conventional macro-statistics, for example by the International Labour Organization (ILO) and by the World Bank, confirm the prevalence of child labour in those areas. Child labour participation is supposed to be as high as 32.9 per cent in Eastern Africa, 24.2 per cent in Western Africa, 20.0 per cent in East Asia, 14.0 per cent in South Asia, 12.8 per cent in South America, 11.1 per cent in South-East Asia, etc. (Fallon and Tzannatos 1998: Annex). Globalization, and the collateral indebtedness and widening income gap between the rich OECD countries and the countries in the Third World, may have exacerbated the problem. Poverty continues to increase, and quite a number of countries, particularly in Eastern Europe and Africa have actually witnessed a sharp decline in incomes and in social security arrangements. The structural adjustment policies, which have come along with globalization, in many developing countries have reduced the spending on basic services such as education. This may lead to an increase in child labour.

In this introductory statement, we have assumed the definition of child labour to be unproblematic, but neither the 'child' nor the nature of 'labour' in the context of child labour has been well-defined. A crucial distinction could be made between child labour and child work. Child work should be used as the generic term, and should refer to any type of work being done in any mode of employment relationship. The concept of work should then serve as a description of the physical (or mental) involvement in a job. It is an activity which, rather than being harmful may be beneficial to the child in its formative socialization. The concept of labour on the other hand should be restricted to the production and services which interfere with the normative development of children as defined in the UN Convention. The nature of the labour relation (paid-unpaid, hired or self-employed, full-time or part-time) is immaterial to the definition. A useful definition is the one delineated by Stein and Davies (1940: 112–13) and referred to occasionally: 'any work by children that interferes with their full-physical development, the opportunities for a desirable minimum of education and of their needed recreation'.[1]

The mundane feeling is that quite a lot of what has been subsumed under child labour, and as such has entered the statistics of ILO, UNICEF, World Bank and many other organizations, is work performed during a standard process of socialization and not associated with labour exploitation or interfering with the quality of development which the child in the given circumstances could expect. Because of the definitional confusion and because of its association with poverty, the extent of child labour can easily be blown up out of proportions, as has happened in the case of India.

The General Parameters of Child Labour in India

The knowledge that India is one of the poorest countries in the world reinforces the idea that it must have a high incidence of child labour. The correlation between regional poverty and child labour, however, is inconclusive. Some of the poorer states, probably for different reasons, have a lower child labour count, and some of the richer states have a higher count.[2]

---

[1] Such a definition would be in alignment with the UN Declaration and with the ILO strategy of targeting the intolerable forms of child labour, the 'worst forms' as referred to, but hardly defined, in Convention 182 of June 1998. The UN 1989 *Convention on the Rights of the Child* does not contain a blanket statement against employment of children, but rather recognizes: 'the right of the child to be protected from economic exploitation and from performing any work that is likely to be hazardous or to interfere with the child's education, or to be harmful to the child's health or physical, mental, spiritual, moral or social development' (Article 32.1).

[2] The highest number of working children is to be found in Andhra Pradesh (around two million in 1981, or 16.6 per cent of the child population), Madhya

Many scholars and activists have suggested that the problem is much more rampant than the government is willing to concede in its official statistics. The guesstimates on the number of working children in India indeed has suffered from exaggeration.[3] The Population Census of India and the National Sample Survey, which are fairly reliable instruments, have counted around 13–16 million child labourers in the 1980s and 10–13 million in the 1990s. The enumeration in government surveys is based on a clear definition of what is meant by child labour. Work, in the instruction manuals to the census enumerators is to be understood as 'participation in any economically productive activity' (Census 1981, Vol. 22, Part IV-A: 13). Many activities which children, and women, may be undertaking and which are necessary inputs in the (economic) management of the household will not be included under the heading 'work'.

Many more children than those registered as 'working' indeed are not attending school, and many of them may be engaged in work. It is an argument that by many observers and institutions has been used in a brazen fashion. Children not in the school system have then been assumed to be working children. This is one of the reasons why the estimates by Government Census operations have not found much credence with western government as well as NGO institutions in the arena of child labour. More credibility has been given to the 1983 findings of the Operational Research Group—a research institute in Baroda commissioned by the Government of India to assess the extent of child labour (Khatu 1983). Its figure of 44 million has been invested with a high degree of reliability. Rudi Rothier (1995), inclusive of the increase in population, extrapolated a figure close to 60 million, of which 10 million '*child slaves*', by the mid-1990s. Other estimates mention 3 million slaves, many more than the 350,000 which the Government of India is

---

Pradesh and Karnataka (both 13.9 per cent labour participation rate), Maharashtra (12.9 per cent), Tamil Nadu (10.8 per cent), Orissa (10.5 per cent), Rajasthan (9.9 per cent) and Gujarat (8.8 per cent). At the other side of the scale, we find, in ascending order, Kerala, Tripura, West Bengal, Uttar Pradesh, Punjab, Haryana, and Bihar. See also Naidu (1988: 160) for the inter-district trend in Maharashtra. Educationally and economically backward states like Bihar and Uttar Pradesh have a relative low child labour ratio because of a failing demand for labour.

[3] Exaggerated figures may be associated with political and institutional considerations: generally to portraying of the other (developing countries) as lacking in good government and high ethics, the usefulness in Western attempts at trade sanctions and the NGO self-interest in having more finances earmarked for their work (see Lieten 2001d).

willing to admit (ILO World Labour Report 1993: 12). The ICFTU makes a difference between bonded labour and other child labour, but they also do adopt the fairly high number of 50 million working children (Dorai 1994). The Dutch Ministry of Social Affairs, in its policy paper subsequent to the February 1997 Amsterdam Child Labour Conference, after referring to the discrepancy between the different sets if figures, seemed to suggest that India had 55 to 60 million *bonded child labourers*, a figure based on the claims of the South Asia Coalition against Child Slavery (SZW 1997: 7). The International Confederation of Free Trade Unions, in its major 1996 study (*Child Labour. No Time To Play: child workers in a global economy*) knows for sure that the official figures are underestimates and adds that 'independent studies reckon the figures to range from 44 million to 100 million'.

Allowing for undercount and overcount, this chapter proceeds on the assumption that probably between 10 and 15 million children in India are working, in one form or the other which does engage them in such a way that it interferes with their physical development, with their possibility to go to school and with their need for recreation (cf. Stein and Davies above). In that case, we are discussing around 5 per cent of the children in the 0–14 age-cohort who can be classified as labourers as per the Census definition. The working child in fact is very much a rural phenomenon, in self-employment on the family farm or joining the family work force unit during the crop season as agricultural labourer.[4] In India, with around 30 per cent of the population urbanized, urban child labour accounts for only 5.5 per cent of the entire child labour in the country. In the household industry, construction and mining, the sectors where, more than in agriculture, the physical and mental well-being of the child may be at risk, in absolute figures, we are referring to a total labour force of 1,5 million (Singh and Mahanty 1993: 17). It is possible, and quite probably that (many) more children are incidentally 'working' in one way or the other, but this at the most could be classified as a gray area, and not as child labour in the strict sense.

Micro-studies confirm that the incidence of child labour is closer to the 5 per cent mark than to the much higher counts.[5] We intend do

[4] Many of these activities are relatively light in nature and, most of the time, have limited working hours. The activities, apart from transplanting, weeding and crop collection on the family farm or, usually with their parents, as agricultural labourers, include grazing and washing of cattle, catching of fish, collection of grass and fruits, collection and carrying of firewood, etc.

[5] A.N. Singh in a study of 19 villages in the Sewapuri area of Varanasi district,

such a micro-study, in one district in the northern state Uttar Pradesh, but not in the first place to determine the labour participation rate. We rather shall be interested in the mode of thinking on the meaning of children and the work done by children in the household. The question will be asked whether children are primarily seen as an economic asset, a potential work force benefiting the household income, as a number of studies in the past has maintained, and whether procreation is a conscious activity in that context.

Some Considerations on Fertility and Child Labour

Child labour, in the mainstream perception, is associated with poverty and illiteracy on the one hand and with high fertility levels on the other hand. To an extent, child labour, it has been argued, could even be ascribed to a willful strategy of the parents. In the theoretical debate in the 1970s, sparked by Mamdani's seminal contribution, it was argued that birth control would remain a myth since high fertility made good economic sense in peasant societies. Mamdani (1972), in his study of the Green Revolution impact in the Punjab, had stressed that the need for labour in rural areas had increased the demand for children. The argument was extended in sociological and demographic studies in which it was asserted that peasant families were behaving rationally in the realm of fertility: the minimal costs of upbringing were more than compensated by the income contribution of the siblings. Children can be called in to assist in the rather simple and time-consuming tasks, particularly in the seasonal peaks of high demand for labour. A high fertility regime is thus seen as a rational strategy in families with low labour incomes.

The explanatory framework to explain for high fertility begs the question why fertility is high in some places, and among some classes of people. Mamdani's theorem in the debate was challenged and contested (see e.g. Vlassoff 1979), and in the changing circumstances may have lost much of its validity. Tim Dyson (1991), while critically assessing the net economic benefit and the intergenerational wealth flows (from children to the parents) has argued that the real question is not why many peasant families have many children, but rather why fertility

---

one of the centres of carpet weaving, counted 9.3 per cent of the children as working; more than half of them were in the 13–15 years' age group, and, interestingly as an indication of the social context, more than half of the working children were married (A.N. Singh 1990: 84 and 89).

is low in some populations. In traditional societies, children do perform many useful household jobs, and peasants tend to stress the utility that children also have, but 'there seems only little room for any purely economic rationale' (Dyson 1991: 96). He argues that in fact: 'children work because people have children, rather than people have children because children have work. . . . Thus child labour resulted from fertility rather than the reverse' (Dyson 1991: 95, 97).

This view proclaims that high fertility may cause child labour, but high fertility as such is rather related to a natural process of sexual intercourse in which the regulating ideas of family planning have not adjusted to the changing social and economic conditions (longevity, lower child mortality, land scarcity, proletarinization, etc.). The opposite view that poor people produce children in order to make them work remains unmitigated. In the authoritative view of Myron Weiner (1991: 186):

It is well-known that many poor parents bear children in order to enhance family income. As economists say, children are viewed as economic assets, not as economic liabilities. . . . Government officials in other countries have reasoned that parents ought not be allowed to use children to increase their own income. To permit otherwise is to view the child as the property of the parents, to be used as the parent sees fit, a conception that comes periously close to slavery. Such a policy, it has been noted by demographers, is also an inducement to a high fertility rate. (italics added)

Some of these notions will be addressed in the context of a rural district (Faizabad in Uttar Pradesh) where questions will be asked related to child labour, education and fertility.[6] We may get some idea of the extent of work done by children, but the questions, and answers, will be more of a normative nature: how do parents see the costs and benefits of children, and how do they intend to cope with fertility? These questions will be addressed in a discursive mode during a field study of two adjacent villages.

---

[6] The original reason why we went for fieldwork to Milkipur in Faizabad district was its location close to and along one of the main roads to Ayodhya, a road which in the early 1990s carried many frenzied Hindu pilgrims on their way to dispossess and ultimately destroy the historic Babur mosque. We had intended to study the ideological impact of the events on the world view of the villagers (see also Chapter 10). The area offered an interesting environment for studying the childhood issues as well.

Uttar Pradesh: Dismal HDI Performance

Uttar Pradesh is one of the states in India that has become famous for the preponderance of child labour.[7] Uttar Pradesh as a matter of fact, in terms of most human development indices has an abysmally bad record. The rural child mortality rate, 126 per thousand in 1990 was actually the highest of all Indian states. Since it is often assumed that fertility rates are related to the child mortality rates and survival chances, it is reasonable to expect that the birth rates also will remain high. In line with the national pattern, they have tended to come down over the last two decades, but they indeed remain among the highest of all Indian states. Educational levels also have remained among the lowest in India. Rural literacy rates (i.e. effective 7+ rates) for males and females in 1991 remained as low as 52.0 per cent and 19.0 per cent respectively. The latter figure was appreciably up from 11.8 per cent in 1981, but it was still dramatically low in comparison with the 30.6 per cent national average. Among women of the lowest castes, the SC group, literacy remained as low as 8.5 per cent. The total fertility rate in the state was also exceptionally high (see Table 12.1).

Particularly important for the issue under investigation, fertility and child labour, is the unfavourable gender balance. It is remarkable that

Table 12.1: Literacy and Fertility Rate of Some Selected States, 1991

State	Literacy	Rural literacy	Rural SC female literacy	Gender literacy gap (age 10–14, 1988)	Fertility rate (1992)
India	52.2	44.7	19.5	−21	
UP	41.63	36.7	8.5	−29	4.8
Kerala	89.8	88.9	73.1	0	2.0
Bihar	38.5	33.8	5.5	−25	4.0
Punjab	58.5	52.8	29.2	−7	2.9
West Bengal	57.7	50.5	26.3	−8	2.9

Source: Chakrabarty and Pal (1995: 40 ff.); World Bank (1997a: 52, 120).

[7] Many of the studies on child labour in India have been conducted in the local carpet industry, the glass bangle industry, the leather industry or the brass industry (Singh 1990; Singh 1992; Singh and Mahanty 1993; Kulshreshtra 1994) or draw in their analysis heavily on evidence from the state (Gupta and Voll 1987; Burra 1995; Chandrasekhar 1997; Anker and Barge 1998).

this gender imbalance does not appear to have narrowed down among the younger generation, at least not until the early 1990s. Unlike most other states in India, gender disparity have remained at the traditional levels.[8] A stark indication, in addition to the lower educational level, the lower work participation ratio, and the lower longevity of women are the exceedingly low female-male ratios in all regions of the state, particularly in the western districts. If lowering fertility levels is associated with increasing literacy levels and autonomy of women, as the current approach suggests, Uttar Pradesh still has a long way to go.

Faizabad, the district that we selected as well as its sub-division Milkipur, are almost purely agricultural. The urban population since Independence has remained stable at around 10 per cent of the population. Industry mainly consists of handloom weaving in the household sector, and of the sundry brick kilns, rice and flour mills, cold storage and engineering repair shops. The soil is generally clayish and allows for a good yield, especially in the rainy season *(kharif)*. Irrigation has extended the cultivation into the dry season between January and June. Wheat and gram are grown in the *rabi* season and rice, sugar cane, potato and *arhar dal* in the *kharif* season.

Cultivation, despite the extension of irrigation and the availability of high-yielding inputs, generally continues to be carried on along traditional lines. The region has a landownership structure typical of all ex-*taluqdari* areas. The ex-*taluqdars*, the revenue collecting landlords who generally used to belong to the upper castes, continue to be the dominant land owning class. The majority of the peasant families own only small parcels of land, often insufficient to invest in modern agricultural practices. The bulk of the holdings is of size less than 1 acre, and agriculture by and large rests on family labour.

We have earlier referred to the low literacy rates in the state, suggesting continuing low levels of enrollment in elementary schools. The Census figures relating to 1981 (see Tables 12.2 and 12.3) may have been overtaken by higher levels of enrollment. Going around the villages in the late 1990s, the apparent change is that children are attending schools in high numbers. If that is the case, then the percentage of working children, as officially recorded, may have come down. Tables 12.2 and 12.3 give a year-wise enumeration of the activities of respectively

---

[8] Female literacy was still 29 per cent points below male literacy in the school-age cohort as it was in the entire population (see World Bank 1997a: 120). In the case of Punjab and West Bengal for example, the comparable gap figures were −7 per cent and −14 per cent (Punjab) and −8 per cent and −20 per cent (West Bengal).

Table 12.2: Age-wise Work and School Involvement of Boys (%), District Faizabad, 1981

Age	School	Working	Both	Neither
6	25.61	0.37		74.02
7	39.92	0.97	0.02	59.62
8	48.78	0.69	0.02	50.48
9	70.22	0.93		37.62
10	59.46	2.73	0.03	37.79
11	69.93	4.80	0.23	25.03
12	61.87	10.54	0.15	27.44
13	67.37	13.86	0.20	18.57
14	61.40	21.86	0.46	16.26

Source: Calculated from Census of India 1981, Vol. 22, Part IV-A. Social and Cultural Tables: 884–5.

Table 12.3: Age-wise Work and School Involvement of Girls (%), District Faizabad, 1981

Age	School	Working	Both	Neither
6	15.09	0.09		84.92
7	20.87	0.21		79.92
8	24.22	0.31		75.47
9	30.47	0.52		69.01
10	25.81	1.40	0.02	72.77
11	31.48	2.34		66.18
12	23.31	3.80	0.04	72.49
13	22.23	5.19	0.04	72.54
14	16.66	6.95	0.03	76.36

Source: Calculated from Census of India 1981, Vol. 22, Part IV-A. Social and Cultural Tables: 884–5.

boys and girls in the district in which our two sample villages are located. The figures suggest that around 60 per cent of the boys, and around 25 per cent of the girls, go to school.[9] Only a few of them are also registered as working. The data also suggest that involvement in child labour, as it is officially defined, starts from around age 12 years onwards

[9] It is common to contest the official figures on various counts. One forceful criticism is that many of the children may have been registered as enrolled in the school, but are actually not attending school. That very well may be the case on any

in the case of boys, and that in the case of girls, it remains rather limited even at that age.

Can it be assumed that the children who are not attending school are working? The automatic assumption that children-out-of-school are children-in-work, however, is only warranted when it can be shown that the non-enrollment is because of the work they necessarily have to perform. If for other reasons children are not going to school, which is the case especially with girls, it may logically be expected that they do contribute some work in the household or in the field. It may be difficult to classify this spending of childhood time as child labour. We are left then with the Census figures of the district which indicate that effective child labour remains limited and basically starts at puberty.[10]

Interviews in Polarized Villages

In the previous section, we have put the child labour discussion in India in the context of two debates, the debate on the magnitude of 'child labour' and the debate on the rationale behind high fertility. We shall now look at the field reality in two adjacent villages in the Faizabad district of Uttar Pradesh. Like most other rural areas in the state, it has rather dismal human development indicators, a severe gender gap and an almost exclusive concentration on agriculture.

Two adjacent villages were selected in Bikapur Tahsil in Milkipur Block in Faizabad district: Upadhyaypur and Dhanaicha. Upadhyaypur, the smallest village, consisting of two *purwas* (hamlets), had 993 inhabitants in 132 households. The female literacy (27.8 per cent) is distinctly below the male literacy (62.6 per cent), but is relatively high by UP state and district standards. In comparison: female literacy in the district was as low as 3.4 per cent in 1961 and 6.05 per cent in 1971, and then

---

particular day, but the figures on the other hand are not entirely spurious. It is a statement by the parents on behalf of the children, and not the school statistics on which the government finances are based. The parents apparently have taken care to tell which of their children, most of the time, are attending school: boys by and large twice and three times as frequently as girls in the younger and older age groups respectively.

[10] It may be interesting, for the proper perspective on childhood, to bring in some other statistics. It is found that of the Scheduled Caste girls, the girls most likely to be involved in labour, almost two-thirds in the 10–14 age category were married. In the same group, 97.6 per cent was illiterate. Of the SC boys in the same age group, 78.3 per cent was illiterate; around half of them were married (Census 1991, Series 22. Part IX [VI] and Part IX [VII], Special Tables for SCs).

increased to 12.1 per cent in 1981 (UPDG Faizabad 1987: 73; Census of India 1981). The high (male) literacy is associated with a dominant Brahmin population. Brahmins account for close to 40 per cent of the households, and close to 50 per cent of the population. The rest of the villagers are SCs and OBCs. There are few Muslim households.

The population of Dhanaicha, spread over three *purwas*, is bigger (1,323 inhabitants in 224 households), and has appreciably lower levels of schooling: literacy rates for females and males were 11.3 per cent and 46.5 per cent respectively. Not a single Brahmin, Thakur, or other upper caste family is found in this village. One of the three *purwas* is inhabited by Muslims only. Another *purwa* is inhabited by Pasis. The third *purwa* has a mixed population with Yadavs dominating.

In our two villages, a majority of the households owned less than 1 acre of land. The bigger landowners reside in Upadhyaypur. In Danaicha, the other village, only 4.8 per cent of the families owns more than 1 acre of land. There is a typically strong correlation between land ownership and caste. Whereas SCs, and Muslims, are dominant among the landless and marginal land owning families, rich peasants are almost exclusively Brahmins. Particularly in the Brahmin-dominated village, inter-caste inequalities are markedly high: whereas the ownership per individual Brahmin was as high as 1.90 *bigha*, OBC individuals had to do with 0.69 *bigha* and SCs on an average with just 0.3 *bigha* of land.

Agriculture appears to dominate economic life in both the villages. In terms of occupation, 226 of the 362 households could be classified as poor peasant households, and a further 29 and 20 households respectively were middle and rich peasants respectively. In addition, 39 families derived their income from agricultural labour and 27 households were active as artisans. The occupational classification reflects the agrarian orientation of both the villages. However, a significant part of the income also derives from labour migration.[11]

The extra income from migration in addition to a reasonably fertile land has helped most families to improve their economic condition. In Upadhyaypur, the more literate village from where more migration has

---

[11] This was the case particularly with the richer households who supplemented already substantial agrarian incomes with income from migration. In Upadhyaypur (132 households), for example, as many as 106 persons were spending most of the time in far-flung places like New Delhi, Mumbai, Surat, Pune and in the agricultural fields of Punjab and Haryana. Sons of the Brahmin families in many cases had migrated as teachers and civil servants to important cities within Uttar Pradesh.

taken place, more than two-thirds of the respondent families considered their economic position as having improved. In Dhanaicha, on the other hand, less than half of the families were of the opinion that they had experienced material progress. However, not much should be made of this. Apart from 4 families with a TV set, 3 families with a motorbike and 1 family with a jeep, consumer durables and means of transport are restricted to cycles.

On the basis of the assets (house, vehicles, agricultural equipment, durable goods) in combination with land ownership and the occupational diversification, we have divided the households in the two adjacent villages over five status groups, ranging from very poor to very rich. Almost two-thirds of the very poor were SC; the poor were almost exclusively OBC, SC and Muslim. None of the rich families were SC. Together with some OBC families and some Ashraf Muslims, the upper castes account for the rich and very rich families in both the villages.[12]

In order to get a detailed view of the mores and attitude, we had detailed discussions with the parents in forty households, and occasionally also with the children. Since we were interested in the debate on child labour/child education, we selected from the two village Census records those families who had at least three children between the age of 6 and 14. Since, moreover, we assumed that children of middle and rich households went to school, we concentrated on the poor households. The interviews were preferably conducted with one of the family adults, but the exclusion of other family members and even of outsiders could not always be prevented. In the interviews, we entered very sensitive ground. We not only discussed the 'use value' of children, an exploitative relationship between parents and their offspring ostensibly born out of love, but also fertility which is intimately related to sex. Since the issue at stake is highly contested and politicized, ambivalence and contradictory stands may dominate, alternating between emotional intuition and politically correct judgement. The researcher shall continuously be aware of the ambivalence.[13] In most cases, we came home

---

[12] It is convenient to stress the class analogy of caste. Caste hierarchy, after all, has an economic content. Substituting caste for class, however, obfuscates the sharp economic differences which have emerged within the *jati*. The economic status, the class position within the agrarian system, is likely to have a more poignant effect on household management and development vision than the ascriptive caste position as such.

[13] The relatively short stay in the villages and the fairly formal visiting pattern should be kept in mind when 'deconstructing' the spoken words. Patricia Jeffery and

with the feeling that, with due awareness of the ambivalence, the encounter had been open and earnest, and that the language and the meanings had been similar and universalisable. There was no misunderstanding opposing and separating 'western' observer and the 'oriental' other. Jeffery and Jeffery (1996: 13) who have documented the private histories of dozens or women take a similar position which I like to borrow: 'An overdrawn dichotomy between India and the West tends to "other" people in India by suggesting that their social contexts are so "other" that radically different types of personhood are created within them.'

God as an Apology

Everything around her expressed poverty: the dilapidated house, the dirt on the porch, the squalor around, the cluster of emaciated and half-naked children, her own haggard appearance, the broken cycle-rickshaw in the corner. Even her name did not have an identity on its own; it was encoded in a possessive mode: the rickshaw-puller's wife. Her identity as the wife of somebody was linked to her identity as the mother of a bunch of children. One of her children had died, one was on its way into the world, and seven were still alive: S1 (17), D1 (14), D2 (12), D3 (10), S2 (9), D4 (4), and D5 (2). One of the children (S2) was going to school, and although he was already nearly ten years old, he was still in class I and could not even read. *Dikkat* and *pareshan* (both meaning 'difficult', 'trouble') are the words that run as the signifiers through her story. She is also behaves in a respectful and compliant way with the interviewer: she agrees that the *chhota pariwar* (small family), the norm of the outside *babus* (gentlemen), is absolutely necessary. Big families are *pareshan*, and do not bring any advantage. She exhibits a knowledge of the argument in favour of family planning, but apparently has failed to implement it. One basic conviction underlies her life practice: 'Whatever we do, many children or few children, we will not be able to improve our position anyway.'

Could this be the clue to understanding the high fertility rates? If life has been continuing in abject poverty, and if some of the small families around—their fertility constrained by natural causes—had not been

---

Roger Jeffery, in their methodological reflections on fieldwork in another area of Uttar Pradesh in a lucid manner have brought up the issue of mixed messages, an interpretation of local parameters and the induction of non-local readings of views expressed by the respondents who, like the researcher, 'constantly interpret and reinterpret, order and reorder' (Jeffery and Jeffery 1996: 23).

able to escape from their dire circumstances, would it then indeed not be reasonable to assume that a couple of mouths more to be fed at minimal levels of calorie intake and a couple of bodies more to be scantily dressed would not make that much of a difference? If life experience has established that one cannot improve one's position anyway, would it then not be normal to let the children come into the world, discursively as a gift of God?

When husband and wife say that the children are a gift of God, in a deconstructionist sense it can be construed as having a number of meanings. One meaning apparently is that it is a great gift, and is to be treated and cherished as such. It does not mean to say that the couples involved assume that God has miraculously planted a baby in the womb of the mother. People are well aware that '*admi khud dia he*' (people themselves are doing it), and that at a certain age the time of 'producing' is over.

It is a gift of *Allah*, that is what Ibrahim and Rehmulmisa say initially, but they also add that it happens between one man and one woman, and that if they had decided to do so, it could be stopped: 'But even if we had two children, poverty would remain'. They have 4 daughters and 2 sons. The additional children in their case have coincided with social progress: whereas the first 3 children are illiterate, the youngest 3 children are attending school. Since the parents had more children, the last children to arrive have been in a better position (in terms of being able to go to school) and if they get *naukri* (employment), they may be better placed to look after them in old age.

All solutions have an inherent degree of ambivalence. A reduction in the number of children may not open new opportunities; more births may not entail extra costs. Additional children, while not entailing extra costs, may not bring extra benefits either. But even if they do not—more on this later—the unnatural process of reducing the number of births is dependent on the social structures they live in. As an unnatural process,[14] the outcome depends on the infrastructural and cognitive environment: the means to and the knowledge of pregnancy prevention. For a majority of women in India, Mukhopadhyay and Savithri (1998: 20) have stated, the gendered socialization process determines

---

[14] I call it an unnatural process because in distinction with the natural process, even the instinctive process of love making, the prevention of conception involves the planning of precautionary measures. It involves an extra process beyond the libido.

the health-seeking and reproductive behaviour of women. Patriarchal norms and values, in combination with grinding poverty and inaccessibility of public health institutions, have pre-empted the possibility of a reproductive choice. The socialization process is informed not only by gender, but also by class and by the material conditions surrounding the families.

In the absence of this possibility of choice more children are born and men and women explicate their behaviour in terms of the ultimate legitimator. Behind the reference to God (*Bhagwan* or *Allah*) as the one who provides the couples with children, a reference which comes easily and is foremost in any talk on procreation, lies the perception of powerful social structures: 'They cannot ignore them. Thus women's resistance was conditioned and limited by the power structures to which it was a response. It was channelled by women's understanding that they acted within largely unalterable structures' (Jeffery and Jeffery 1996: 16).

God serves as a handy apology for something people appear to know of namely that the making of children is directly related to sex. Whether frequent or occasional, once the deed is over, and conception has occurred, an apology, a justification, an alibi has to be provided. Procreation, Malthus argued two centuries ago in his *Essay on the Principle of Population*, was the result of the 'passion between the sexes', and could never be overridden by rational self-interest for the 'pleasures of pure love will bear the contemplation of the most improved reason' (quote in Cowen and Sheldon 1996: 18).

A discussion on family planning and the benefit (*labh*) or disadvantage (*nuksan*) of having many children could start from the anguish that we have noticed in the case of the wife of the rickshaw-puller. The scholarly arguments on opportunity benefits of children—the Mamdami thesis—have disregarded one aspect of procreation: the longing for and the absolute delight one can find in sex. Children are also a natural product of love and intimacy and a source of joy and self-realization. I assume that these psychological traits are not limited to (reserved for) the Western and Western-oriented parents, but that they have a universal spread. The conclusion then would be that the child will remain the natural product of sexual intercourse unless and until acceptable and utilizable pregnancy prevention methods have come within reach of the couple. It is therefore questionable whether children are put on the world deliberately in order to augment labour power and income.

Child Labour

Some among the poor take pride in having produced a large number of offspring. Mohammed Rashid, the father of one boy and five girls, is a bit unhappy with having so many girls, who will hardly bring in any earnings and who will cost dearly in terms of dowry. With the help of *Allah*, he would have liked to have more boys. He suggests that it has been his *kismat* to have had so many children, but when we turn to his love for sex, he also agrees that his libido was involved. He claims that now he is 'strong' and refrains from having sex since he does not want to have another daughter, although he would like to have many more sons. Indeed sons, once they are around ten years old, do contribute to the family income and give him status in the eyes of the people in the neighbourhood. His only son, who is 7 years old only, appears to have understood this sign of the message: he has torn his books and his bag and has stopped going to school. He now assists his father as a hairdresser. Mohammad Rashid's story fits the traditional life cycle: children, while growing up, are socialized into learning the occupational skills of their family, in this case a craft in which still there is scope for many hands to be involved, and then start adding income to the family.

On this expectation of an intergenerational income transfer, initially from the parents to the children, afterwards from the children to the middle-aged and old-aged parents, the idea of children as assets has been constructed. The next question to be asked is how many families answer to this expectation.

The idea that sons will help to run the family business—a shop, a farm, a craft—has all but disappeared from the village discourse. The family plots are usually too small to engage more than one adult male, and are only occasionally assisted by family labour for odd chores. The daily routine of cutting the fodder and feeding it to the cows and looking after the cattle are among the contributions which have been set apart for children, irrespective of whether they go to school or not. They definitely help to ease the workload of the mother, who otherwise would have been involved in this household routine, but, since the mother economically active, they can hardly be seen as adding to economic gain and as an impetus for getting more children.

This argument also applies to the work done by girls, schoolgoing or not. We notice that girls are just staying around the house (when the mother is away so that the house can remain protected from intruders), collect fodder, and help in making the dung cakes. Also, like their brothers, they look after toddlers, and also assist in preparing the meals. All these sundry jobs can be classified as *sahara* (service, assistance). They can also be understood in a process of socialization as the parents instil in the children the practical knowledge needed to run a household, a farm, or a craft.

This applies particularly to the relationship between mother and daughter. Girls can lend a helpful hand. Their rearing does not involve opportunity costs. Prospective husbands and prospective family-in-laws, who by and large will belong to a similar socio-economic milieu, will not expect the bride to have received much schooling. The girl should have learned to be a good housewife. The apprenticeship is helpful to the mother since it alleviates many of the burdens of the mother. In the process of socialization, advantages accrue to the household, but it would be unfounded if one were to conclude that such advantages constitute the reason behind the high fertility pattern.

The feelings of parents who see their children as *labh* (advantageous) are almost never unambiguous in saying so. The very same parents who do enumerate the advantages of having children often also associate it with sacrifices: *dikkat* and *pareshan* are two of the words which are regularly used. The encumbrance does not lie in the in the social rearing of the children as such, but in the circumstances which go against big families: lack of land, small houses and deficient incomes. The saying 'a small family is a happy family' (*chhoto pariwar sukkhi pariwar*), which is much more often used than its antonymous 'big families are happy families', tells it all. It is usually an ex-post reflection which brings the mothers and fathers to the realization that the more the number of children, the more difficult will be the conditions. While children are growing up, it is realized that they are a burden, and do not contribute to the household, not now and possibly not in the future: one idle child is better than many of them, it was said.

To the suggestion that children can also be a support (*sahara*), derision is sometimes the answer. Support could be helpful if the family had sufficient land to productively involve many family hands, but since the land at their disposal is usually insufficient to provide a living for a big family, the children are not very useful and will remain idle for most of the day and most of the season. The saying is that a peasant who receives support is a happy peasant. My inference is that this saying was applicable in the olden days. Today, a happy peasant is also somebody who can afford the opportunity costs of sending the children to school, i.e. to a private school. The prospect of profiting from growing-up children by hiring them out as agricultural labourers is hardly attractive, as wages are abysmally low and employment opportunities are limited anyway since farm activities are mostly based on family labour.

Direct income generation, i.e. the sale of child labour power, we noticed in the case of only two families. In one Pasi family, with three sons and five daughters, the preference, the father stated with sadness, would have been for continuation schooling, but the 13 years' old son has started working as an agricultural labourer in addition to the work, together with his younger brother, on the one acre of their own land. In another family, the 12 years' old son is going along with his father as a mason. Earlier he had gone to school. Now he works and he states to be proud of the income he brings home for his 2 brothers and 4 sisters. He is stated to earn Rs 30–40 a day, which is roughly four times higher than the then prevailing agricultural wages for kids and women (Rs 8–10). His mother claims that they could not any longer afford the expenses associated with school going—an argument which is often heard—and that the five years he spent in school earlier were anyway a waste of time, an argument which also is often heard.

In addition to the wage labour, there were three families with boys who are full-time engaged on the farm or in the family profession. Two sons (of age 12 years and 14) help their respective fathers. Whereas the first one is assisting in carpenting, and is said to be as uninterested in learning the trade as he was in his studies when in school, the second one, who had never gone to school, has developed a great zeal and interest in his work as an apprentice barber. One 13 years old boy whose father is working in Delhi looks after the cattle and the small plot of land. The three boys have one thing in common: despite beating by the parents, they refused to go to school. A critical feature common to the five families who have working children not attending school is the family size: they have between six and eight home-living children.

Child labour, it appears, is not the mechanism which keeps the children out of school. At a more general level, comparing 12 villages in two other districts, villages with either a high or a low literacy rate, Srivastava (1997: 32) attributes non-enrollment or discontinuation of boy children to the involvement in work in only 3.1 per cent to 7.6 per cent of the cases. The poverty of the household (even government schools involve cash expenditure), the characteristics of the child (unwilling to submit to the pedagogical regime), and the general dissatisfaction with the school's performance turned out to be the more important reasons for the boys staying home and not going to school. Girls were kept home for more or less the same reasons. In around 12 per cent to 15 per cent of the cases education was also not considered useful.

The Imperative of Schooling

Raju, the son of a small Maurya peasant (and vegetable vendor), is an eleven years old boy who could easily enter the statistics as a child labourer. After he gets up in the morning, he goes into the fields and to the roadsides to cut grass for the two cows. He does some other jobs, and in the evening regularly go to sell vegetables in the market. Like his three years older brother, who studies in class IX, Raju in between also goes to school and does his homework, and that is where he thinks his future lies: in *naukri*, i.e. (government) service.

The children of many of the other poor families do work in the household and on the farm, and sometimes even get engaged as agricultural labourers, but only so after school hours or during the holidays. Some of them have high hopes for the future. Education is perceived as an instrument of social mobility: it should lead the boys along the road which will give access to *naukri*. But since it is realized more often than not that government service or private service turns out to be an illusion, especially since very few boys make it beyond class X, for the poor families schools lose much of the attraction which they continue to have for rich and middle peasant families.

Yet, overwhelmingly, the stand is that children should go to school and should then build their own future. If the family income is sufficient to support education, then the children should continue as long as possible (and get *naukri*); if the income is insufficient and the grown-up children (have to) start working, it is not to be regarded as an income-earning asset to be tapped by the parents. When asked whether children, rather than going to school, should join the labour market and contribute to the household earnings, it was often said, also by craftsmen: *sachai ke bad nahi* (not a correct position) and *thik nahi* (not good).

Children ought to be attending school. This normative understanding has percolated down to the village level. It is something which in the past has been the prerogative of the village elite and which the subject classes, particularly the subject castes, were not to aspire to imitate. Among the higher castes, and the wealthier families, school education has become a universal norm. Lower castes may have been aspiring for the same partaking in 'modernization' but the village elite tends to discourage universal education. In general, the conclusion by S.C. Dube (1958: 144) is still valid. In his study of the village development programmes in the 1950s, he was struck by a series of paradoxes:

> The higher castes want their children to have modern education so that they may equip themselves to face the changing conditions of the modern world and acquire modern urban skills to help their parents in *maintaining their privileged status* and position. But there is also the fear that lower caste children may use their education to break away from tradition and *may thus bring about a disintegration* of the traditional social organization. (italics added)

School attendance by children from the poorer classes in this view has been disabled by the village elite. The gradual shift in the power balance and the emancipation from below have brought the school within reach of the children of poor households as well. Gender and class continue to affect attendance, but as a norm it is realized that education is a right for all. With very few exceptions, all the boys are attending school. School attendance among the girls of the poorest families is mixed. Around one-third of them were not attending school, but non-attendance was mainly in the age group from 10 years onwards. As an explanation for keeping children out of school, expenses involved in education is more often used for girls than for boys. It is usually assumed that the underlying reason is that expenses should lead to returns. The returns of educational investment in a daughter would be low since she will get married and will leave the household. Boys at least will remain associated with the parents, and, if through education, find a better job, will be of benefit later.

The former is a standard explanation which alludes that the parents (of the poor!) have egoistic economic motives in the rearing of their children. There, however, are other considerations for keeping the girls home. The contribution of the girls to the household work is both that of a companion, giving emotional sustenance to the mother, and that of a maid servant, doing all the odd little jobs and errands. A number of these girls had been attending school for quite a few years, roughly until the beginning of puberty, but they had never progressed beyond class I. It is not unusual for a 10 years old girl, and for many boys of a similar age, to be still in the first form.[15]

---

[15] A look at the village school explains why so many of them have not progressed beyond the first form, despite many years of schooling. Spread over the big school playground groups of boys and girls are keeping each other busy with activities which are not related to learning. A few of these groups are centred around a teacher

The children of the better-off families are not affected by the substandard village schools. They are sent to the so-called nurseries, private schools which charge a fee and which maintain better teaching standards. The emergence of private schools, accessible only to a minority of the children, has had a negative impact on the services provided by the government schools: 'To the extent that the requirements of the rural elite is met by the private schools, the pressure on the functioning of government schools declines' (Srivastava 1997: 41–2). In this sense, the observation by Dube above is still valid: (good) education remains the reserve of the village elites. It appears to be associated with class, and not with any religion.

Ambivalence in the attitude of the poor parents is the outcome of the conviction that the child, in any case the son, should go to school, and the realization, on the other hand, that 'hardly any teaching is being done'. Many children drop out, and the parents, although they argue that they have given the child many beatings, may have considered it inopportune to insist on attendance. Hira Lal, a father of 6 children, has this to say about his children and their school:

We are poor, but not so poor that we cannot send our children to school. There should be no limits to the studies, and if the child wants to continue, that should be made possible. But how is it possible for them to continue? They don't learn anything here. We had to spend so much money on the books, and then the teacher is sitting so far away from the children that absolutely nothing is learned there. Everybody thinks so about the teachers. The only thing they can do is to beat up the children. So when Raju came home, and I kept telling him everyday to go to school, he just burned his books. I of course have given him a good thrashing, but what can I do about it. The nursery is too expensive.

Hira Lal is one of the many who agree that one should leave the age of ignorance behind and that also poor people should be able to read and to write letters. The facilities, which the government has started providing are helpful, but the crucial problem is that of a deficient teaching staff. If children hardly learn anything, and if whatever they learn will not help them in social mobility, then why should they be coerced to go and attend classes. The complaint that the children hardly learn anything is an exaggerated assessment. It applies to some of the children

---

who does some teaching to the selected few. The government school, which is practically free, and which during the last years even had a system of paying small amounts of scholarships (Rs 300) to SC boys and girls, has a distinct reputation for malfunctioning and bad teaching.

more than others. Indeed, the 12 years' old boys or girls who are still in class III testify to a wastage of resources and human aspirations. It also scotches the potential of imbibing what some of the parents call *gun buddhi* (mental development). Schools in many villages may not be stimulating this development.

Some of the parents realize the importance of education for mental development, for escaping from the world of darkness. Most of the parents have understood that education has an instrumental value. It is important for the kids, also for the girls, to learn to read and to write. The extension of the modern state, and particularly the labour migration to distant towns, has made communication dependent on the written word. Command over that written word has become imperative. Poor parents have come to realize the usefulness of education in this respect.

Family Planning

Awareness of family planning may be assumed to have dawned in a dramatic way during the Emergency period in the mid-1970s. During 1976–7, as many as 19,504 cases of vasectomy and 3,685 cases of tubectomy were registered in the district, to be followed by a dramatic fall to just 9 and 144 cases respectively in the following year (UPDG Faizabad 1987: 82). The Emergency was unique in more than one aspect: unlike all other attempts at family planning, it targeted men as receptacles of contraceptive policy (Mukhopadhyay and Savithri 1998: 15).

It is not surprising that all the women know about family planning. The word 'operation' has found a place in their local dialect. The evidence collated in Table 12.4 does, however, indicate that the practice of family planning in the state lags far behind the levels reached in the other Indian states. Even when couples have produced three children, only 28 per cent are recorded to be engaged in family planning of one form or the other. This compares very unfavourably with the Indian average of 58.9 per cent and with other north-Indian states with comparable family systems such as Punjab (74.1 per cent) and West Bengal (74.2 per cent). UP appears to be in the same league, though lagging behind, with Bihar, Madhya Pradesh, and Rajasthan, states which neither had the capitalist dynamism in agriculture, as in the Punjab, nor the poor peasant-based political upturn, as in West Bengal. The findings indicate that most of the couples will not practice family planning even if they have three sons.

Table 12.4: Current Use of Contraceptives by
Number of Living Children (% of Married Couples)
in Selected States

Number of children	India	UP	Punjab	Bihar	West Bengal
None	4.2	1.8	2.3	1.7	19.8
One	19.3	7.8	28.9	7.9	49.5
Two	46.1	18.6	61.1	24.7	66.4
2 sons	55.0	26.9	70.2	34.5	74.8
1 son	46.4	17.1	61.5	23.1	67.0
0 son	31.5	9.7	34.8	14.7	52.7
Three	58.9	28.1	74.1	34.3	74.2
3 sons	64.9	35.6	85.7	38.0	82.3
2 sons	68.0	35.3	82.3	46.9	78.0
1 son	51.2	19.0	65.9	24.7	72.0
0 son	31.7	14.8	29.8	14.0	53.2

Source: Irudaya Rajan as reproduced from Mukhopadhyay and Savithri (1998:31).

'Operation' appears to be all that family planning is about. The programme, unlike during the Emergency when Indira and Sanjay Gandhi directed their forceful sterilization at the males (vasectomy), is unambiguously directed at women as the target group. At regular intervals, the family planning people, assisted by the *dai* (midwife) visit the villages, and try to convince males and females to go in for the operation. The family planning message is explained, supporting it with arguments describing the individual benefits and the national benefits that would result from smaller families. The *dai* spreads her message so that all the women, and many of the men, know about it, but it is only a one line message: family planning is a question of operation and nothing else. The women listen and make up their mind. They have decided that the idea is not bad, but they also know that they have to work, in the household and in the field, and that the operation may effect their health.

Evidence of ill-effects is difficult to come by. Some do refer to a specific case, but usually it is from hearsay. The health is said to go down after the operation, and since there are insufficient medicines and insufficient high-energy food, it is explained as risky. If there is hardly any medical evidence to support the opposition to vasectomy, then there possibly are other reasons which are hidden behind the public discourse.

The argument that the health may get affected actually seems to lose its force of conviction at a stage when the family has around five living children. Arguments which are used to object to the operation, including the argument that the husband is opposed to it, then ultimately do not appear to stand in the way. Nankuna for example had the operation done, against the wishes of her husband, when her fifth child was 2 years old. Her argument was that only now she had become aware of the issue. Underlying the discursive statement at this stage was probably the fact that the survival of the progeny had been assured. This may still be the general attitude: in the face of uncertain health conditions—massive death rates are still in the collective memory system—no risks should be taken by producing only the government child norm. Even if one realizes that the infants' chances of survival have increased dramatically, there still are too many risks around. A better and, in any case, accessible public health system would help to remove those risks. The following critique at the government family planning programme by one of the women we interviewed suggests that the programme should come as a comprehensive intervention: 'It is all-right for the government to set a norm, but the government does not do anything to help us with that norm.'

Do they really want to restrict the size of the families or just shift the blame on government? Not initially, it appears. The women do have varying opinions on how many children they should have: e.g. 5 is enough, 2 sons is enough, 3 is enough, 2 is the best. When the number which they considered optimal had been produced, they, however, did not necessarily stop. The explanation often given for having more children is: *rokth nehi sahi* (I cannot stop it). Another explanation is that the optimal number of children should have reached a certain age (beyond the mortality-prone age), and that by that time more children had been born. Finally, however, when they have more than five children, the arguments against operation appear to lose much of their force. Since the operation is an unalterable intervention, one would not like to have it done immediately when the ideal number of children has been reached.

The wife of one of the carpenters in the village has given birth to eleven children: 4 sons and 5 daughters are surviving. She claims that earlier she was not aware of all this: 'When I got married, children started coming until it dried up. Then when my husband told me, I came to know that it could be stopped. He is aware of the talk which goes around in the world. Then also I got it from the neighbours, and when the *dai* came here I agreed.Two sons is the best.Then all the requirements are fulfilled.' Her daughters, unlike her sons, have remained illiterate. Presently, her youngest daughters (8 and 10 years old) are both in class I, repeating the cycle of non-learning; they are needed in the household where they do part of the cooking, the cleaning, and the washing.

When more children are born, reference to God may serve as an apology in the face of ambivalent thinking on restricting the number of children. This reference to God as the ultimate referee is common among Hindu as well as Muslim men and women. An ideological argument against family planning, however, is found more often among the Muslim families. They have been told by the *maulvi* that the Koran and the Hadi have instructed the believer to go and multiply and not to interfere with the body. Moreover, *Allah* will look after his people's well-being.

Not all Muslims are in agreement, and in general they have as many children as their class equals.[16] Ahmad, who has only three children (it may be added, three sons) argues that the Koran does not allow operation, at least that is what the *maulvi* has said, but on the issue of other forms of family planning, the Koran does not give guidelines, and there are two opposite camps:

We have to find our own way. *Kudra* will look after all of us if we respect him, but that does not mean we should be with as many as possible. In earlier days, the word of the *maulvi* did carry some weight. Many children were not a big problem. Many of them died anyway. Six of my nine brothers died, and the rest could help in the fields, which we then still had. Now things have changed, and whatever the *maulvi* says about *Kudra's* wishes, people have their own wishes.

Ahmad's account illustrates how religious discourse develops in a changing context. As long as many children was not a real issue, 'many of them died anyway', and there was still some land left for tilling and for housing, the natural process of sexual intercourse, conception, and

[16] The assumption of higher fertility among Muslims, it should be added, is not confirmed by aggregate data at the all-India level. In the propaganda stories of Hindu organizations, Muslims are painted as a pampered minority whose appeasement allows it retain polygamous practices with an unrestricted production of siblings. It is indeed true that the Muslim population is growing at a faster rate than the Hindu population (2.71 per cent *versus* 2.19 per cent from 1971 to 1981, and similar rates from 1981 to 1991). The difference, however, is associated with poverty levels: Muslims, like the SC and ST population, generally belong to the poorer and less-educated echelons of society (NSS, 43rd Round, 1990).

childbirth continued to be underwritten by religious scriptures or by a general reference to the omnipotent power. Nowadays, the context has changed, and 'people have there own wishes'. What, however, has not radically changed, is the restricted access to and knowledge of pregnancy prevention methods.

Conclusions

We have covered some ground in confronting a common view that children in the rural hinterland are considered as an economic asset. Such a view has led to the assumption that child labour and high fertility are two sides of one coin. Poor parents are said to generate more children in order to tap their labour power and thus bear responsibility for the prevalence of child labour.

Child labour has become associated with poverty and with developing countries. The number of children living and being exploited in India as 'child labourers' has been blown up to bizarre proportions. A careful look at empirical evidence suggests that in India many millions of children are possibly working in one way or the other. The Census data indicate that 'child labour' is mainly limited to agriculture. The fieldwork in two villages would suggest that the aggregate picture (available from official sources) that labour market participation by children is rather limited is by and large correct.

We are aware that Uttar Pradesh, despite the common impression, may have a low child labour participation ratio, as statistics suggest, and that child labour in other regions of India may be more prevalent. The major point we had wanted to establish was that the economic rationale of parents behind the adherence to high fertility levels is questionable. These alleged strategies of parents to have many children and send them to add the family income, now and later, is an accepted notion in much upper-class commonsensical commentary on high fertility levels of the poor. It has also found its way into scholarly work. Such an association of fertility with economic design has to be cautioned against. Parents do acknowledge that ideally, in the long run, there are advantages associated with having a smaller family. Not only did most of the parents scoff at the idea that a large number of children would constitute an advantage from which they themselves later would benefit. Rather, it has been suggested, they do realize that lesser children would be advantageous. The parents apparently are judging between two alternative probabilities. It is possible that the sons stay with them, but it is also possible that they will abandon them and go their own way, as the daughters anyway will do.

The problem then boils down to the possibility of choice: pregnancy prevention methods other than 'operation', have not been brought within reach of the village female poor. Operation is a very serious intervention. It is unalterable to start with. Such an intervention becomes a realistic option only when the number of issues has passed a certain threshold. This threshold is higher than the ideal norm.

Another point that this chapter has tried to establish was that access to education is a general wish among parents and children, but that the access remains limited to the ill-equipped and ill-functioning government schools. The appropriation of child labour power to augment family income is generally rejected. Children should be sent to school, but dissatisfaction with the functioning of the schools may induce the child and the parents to forego 'education' and to start working. The drop out from schooling is more likely to be associated with push factors internal to the school system than to a pull factor emanating from the labour market. If the public school is often experienced as a place where one hardly learns anything, and if it is realized that it does not help to further the chances on the labour market, and possibly even entails missing out on the labour market, then parents may not be insisting upon children going to school and children may also not be anxious to do so. Hanging around the farmyard and doing some work in the bargain will be the consequence.

Glossary

acchut	untouchable
adharmik	non-religious
admi	people, person
aman	traditional rice (July–December season)
anparh	blind
aasmaan	heaven
ashraf	upper segments among Muslims
asuraksha	insecurity
aus	traditional winter rice
avatar	re-incarnation
babu	mister
bahajut	majority
bakwash	stupid fool
bania	trader
bargadar	sharecropper
begar	useless, jobless
besarkar	non-government
bhadrolok (bhodrolok)	gentlemen
bhaichara	traditional community-owned land cultivation system in western UP
bharat	India
bhoy	fear
bigha	one-third of an acre; in some areas one-fifth of an acre
biradari	community, agnate group
boktrita	lecturing, speech
boro	new (dry season) rice variety
boshomo	command performance

GLOSSARY

buggy	cart
charpoy	string bed
Chhatra Parishad	Student Union
chhota	small
chhotolok	small people
chinta	worries
chor	thief
chowkidar	watchman
dahej	dowry
dai	midwife
dalal	middleman
Dalit	activist name for ex-untouchables
danga	trouble, violence
dapoth	suppression, exertion
doab	land between two rivers
fatafat	fast
garam	hot
garib	poor
ghooskhor	bribe taker
golpo	gossiping
gona (gauna)	marriage
goonda-gardi	muscle-power, banditry
gotra	lineage, ancestral reference group
gram	village
granthshala	library
gulam	slave
guzara	subsistence allowance
gyan	knowledge
halwai	sweets
harijan	name give to the ex-untouchable castes
hat	weekly market
hijra	eunuch
Hindutva	Hindu-ness, the ideology of Hindu nationalism

GLOSSARY

hookah	water-pipe
imam	Muslim priest
imamdari	honesty
izzat	honour
jajmani	traditional Hindu-system of reciprocal services
jatha	procession
jat-pat	casteism
jenmi	heriditary landlord (in Kerala)
jenmon	birth rigth
jhamela	disturbance, conflict
jhumidar	land owner
jotdar	landowners, usually used negatively for landlords (in Bengal)
juta	shoe
kaliyug	dark, bad
kamdila	weak hearted
kanamdar	substantial tenant (Kerala)
karangi	brickstone
karma	predestination, assigned behaviour
karshak	agriculturalist (Kerala)
katha	one-tenth of an acre
khandsari	sugar mill
khap	area
kharif	rainy season crop
khomota	influence, capacity
khudkast	self-cultivation
khul	quality
khutni	toiling
kirtan	morning prayer songs
kisan (krishak)	peasant
kismat	fate, (bad) luck
kudikidappukar	hutment dwellers
kudra	God

labh	advantage
lathi	rod, stick
lota	brass vessel
malik	master
manik	master
masjid	mosque
maulvi	Muslim priest
mofussil	provincial, rural
moksha	release from bodily existence
morol	defamatory name for jotedars, landlords
morrum	gravel
munish	servant, dependent worker
nadia	river bed
namke lije	namesake
nari	women
naukri	employment
nuksan	disadvantage, damage
nyaya	justice
onchal	administrative cluster of adjoining villages (West Bengal)
pakka	good, concrete, confirmed, stable
panchayati raj	village government
panchayat	village council
pandit	teacher
para	ward, quarter
parampara	tradition
paramshakti	custom, inertia
pardha (pordah)	seclusion
pareshan	trouble, difficult
parivartan	change
pariwar	family
pradhan (prodhan)	mayor

GLOSSARY

protha	custom
punjipatti	wealthy person, capitalist
purwa	small settlement
rabi	dry season crop
raj	rule
sabha	assembly, organization
Sabhapati	the president of the district council (West Bengal)
sadhu	renouncer, holy man in Hinduism
sahara	support
samiti	council, association
sansad	parliament
sarkar	government
sasural	in-laws house
satiyug	the era of truth
shantipriyo	peace loving
sharabi	drunkard
shubidabadar	opportunist
shlokas	*mantra* prayers
shramdan (shromdan)	voluntary work
shudra	low-caste
taluqdar	feudal revenue collector, landlord
tanatani	tension
tarawad	family residence (Kerala)
tari	a hamlet (para) in North-Bengal
tebhaga	3-parts movement (of sharecroppers) claiming two-thirds of the crop
thok	lineage
toshon niti	conciliatory politics
unnoti	improvement
upopradhan	vice-chairman of the village council
varna	the main divisions of the Hindu caste system
veerompattadar	tenants-at-will (Kerala)

GLOSSARY

vimochana samaran	liberation movement
wallah	person
yatra	journey, travel
zabardasti	coerced
zameen	earth
zamindar	landowner, feudal landlord
zila	district
zimmadar	trustworthy person
zulum	coercion

Bibliography

AERC (1970),'Agricultural Enterprise in Burdwan District. Preliminary Findings of Sample Survey', *Economic and Political Weekly*, Vol. V, No. 33, pp. 1383–6.

Ahluwalia, Montek S. (2000), 'Economic Performance of States in Post-Reform Period', *Economic and Political Weekly*, Vol. XXXV, No. 19, pp. 1637–58.

Ahmed, Iftikhar (1999),'Getting Rid of Child Labour', *Economic and Political Weekly*, Vol. XXXIV, No. 27, pp. 1815–22.

Alam, Javed (1989),'Political Articulation of Mass Consciousness in Present-day India', in Zoya Hasan et al., *The State, Political Processes and Identity, Reflections on Modern India*, New Delhi: Sage.

——— (1993), 'Democracy and Rights in India in the Wake of Ayodhya', *Social Scientist*, Nos. 242–3, pp. 49–62.

Anderson, Benedict (1993), *Imagined Communities: Reflection on the Origin and Spread of Nationalism*, London: Verso.

Anker, R. and S. Barge (1998), *Economics of Child Labour in Indian Industries*, Geneva: ILO.

Atkinson, Edwin T. (1876), *Statistical, Descriptive and Historical Account of the Muzaffar Nagar District*, Allahabad.

AVARD (1962), *Panchayati Raj—As The Basis of Indian Polity*, New Delhi: Association of Voluntary Agencies for Rural Development.

Bagchi, A.K. (1998), 'Studies on the Economy of West Bengal since Independence', *Economic and Political Weekly*, Vol. XXIII, No. 47/48, pp. 2973–8.

Bandyopadhyay, D. (1988), 'Direct Intervention Programmes for Poverty Alleviation', *Economic and Political Weekly*, Vol. II, No. 15, pp. A77–87.

——— (1993), 'Fourth General Elections of Panchayats in West Bengal', *Mainstream*, 26 June, pp. 15–21.

——— (2000),'Land Reform in West Bengal: Remembering Hare Krishna Konar and Benoy Chowdhury', *Economic and Political Weekly*, Vol. XXV, No. 21/22, pp. 1795–7.

Bandyopadhyaya, Nripen (1988),'The Story of Land Reforms in Indian Planning', in A.K. Bagchi (ed.), *Economy, Society and Polity*, Calcutta: Oxford University Press.

Bandyopadhyay, S. (1990), *Caste, Politics and the Raj 1872–1937*, Calcutta: K.P. Bagchi.

Bardhan, Pranab (1984), *Land, Labour and Rural Poverty: Essays in Development Economics*, Delhi: Oxford University Press.

────── (1997), 'The State Against Society: The Great Divide in Indian Social Science Discourse', in Sugata Bose and Ayesha Jalal, *Nationalism, Democracy and Development*, Delhi: Oxford University Press, pp. 184–95.

Baruah, Sanjib (1990), 'The End of the Road in Land Reforms? Limits to Redistribution in West Bengal', *Development and Change*, Vol. XI, pp. 119–46.

Basu, Jyoti (ed.) (1997), *People's Power in Practice: 20 Years of Left Front in West Bengal*, Calcutta: National Book Agency.

Basu, Tapan et al. (1993), *Khaki Shorts and Saffron Flags: A Critique of the Hindu Right*, New Delhi: Orient Longman.

Baxter Craig (1975), 'The Rise and Fall of the Bharatiya Kranti Dal in Uttar Pradesh', in Myron Weiner and John Osgood Field (eds.), *Electoral Politics in Indian States*, Vol. IV, pp. 113–42, New Delhi: Manohar.

Bergman, Theodor (1984), *Agrarian Reform in India: With Special Reference to Kerala, Karnataka, Andhra Pradesh and West Bengal*, New Delhi: Agricole.

Berreman, Gerald D. (1979), *Caste and Other Inequities, Essays on Inequality*, Meerut: Folklore Institute.

Bhargava, B.S. (1979), *Panchayati Raj System and Political Parties*, New Delhi: Ashish.

Bhat, P.N. Mari and S. Irudaya Rajan (1990), 'Demographic Transition in Kerala Revisited', *Economic and Political Weekly*, Vol. XV, Nos. 35–6, pp. 1957–80.

Bhattacharya, Mohit (1977), 'West Bengal', in G. Ram Reddy, *Patterns of Panchayati Raj in India*, New Delhi: Macmillan.

Bhaumik, S.K. (1993), *Tenancy Relations and Agrarian Development: A Study of West Bengal*, New Delhi/London: Sage Publications.

Blunt, E.A.H. (1931), *The Caste System of Northern India*, Lucknow: SC Publishers.

Boyce, James (1987), *Agrarian Impasse in West Bengal: Institutional Constraints to Technical Change*, Oxford: Oxford University Press.

Brass, Paul (1965), *Factional Politics in an Indian State: The Congress Party in Uttar Pradesh*, Berkeley: University of California Press.

────── (1985a), *Caste, Faction and Party in Indian Politics*, Vol. One: *Faction and Party*, Delhi: Chanakya.

────── (1985b), *Caste, Faction and Party in Indian Politics*, Vol. Two: *Election Studies*, Delhi: Chanakya.

────── (1992), *The New Cambridge History of India*, Vol. IV, Part I: *The Politics of India since Independence*, New Delhi: Cambridge University Press.

────── (1997), 'General Elections 1996 in Uttar Pradesh: Divisive Struggles Influence Outcome', *Economic and Political Weekly*, Vol. XXII, No. 38, pp. 2403–21.

Brass, Tom (1990), 'Class Struggle and the Deproletarianisation of Agricultural Labour in Haryana (India)', *Journal of Peasant Studies*, Vol. 18, No. 1, pp. 36–67.

Burra, Meera (1995), *Born to Work: Child Labour in India*, New Delhi: Oxford University Press.

Census (1981), *Uttar Pradesh: Primary Census Abstract. District Census Hand Book: Part XIII-B: District Faizabad*, Lucknow: Government Press.

Census Jalpaiguri (1951), *West Bengal Districts Handbook: Jalpaiguri*, Calcutta: Government Press.

Census of India (1951), *District Census Handbook Uttar Pradesh, No. 42, Rae Bareli*, Allahabad: Government Press.

——— (1891), *District Census Statistics, Muzaffar Nagar*, Allahabad: Government Press.

——— (1921), Vol. XVI, *United Provinces Agra and Oudh*, Part 1 (Report) and Part II (Imperial Tables), by E.H.H. Edye, Allahabad: Government Press.

——— (1931), *United Provinces of Agra and Oudh*, Vol. XVIII, Part I (Report), Allahabad: Government Press.

——— (1981), *Uttar Pradesh District Census Handbook, Part XIII-B, Rae Bareli*, Lucknow: Government Press.

Cernea, M. (ed.) (1991), *Putting People First: Sociological Variables in Rural Development*, 2nd edn., Oxford: OUP for the World Bank.

Chakrabarty, G. and S.P. Pal (1995), *Human Development Profile of Indian States*, New Delhi: NCAER, Working Paper, No. 52.

Chambers, Robert (1983), *Rural Development: Putting the Last First*, Harlow: Longman.

Chandhoke, Neera (1998), 'The Assertion of Civil Society Against the State: The Case of the Post-Colonial World', in Manoranjan Mohanty et al. (eds.), *People's Rights: Social Movements And The State In The Third World*, New Delhi: Sage Publications, pp. 29–44.

Chandrasekhar, C.P. (1993), 'Agrarian Change and Occupational Diversification: Non-agricultural employment and rural development in West Bengal', *The Journal of Peasant Studies*, Vol. XX, No. 2, pp. 205–70.

Chatterjee, Biswajit (1998), 'Poverty in West Bengal: What have we learnt?', *Economic and Political Weekly*, Vol. XXXIII, No. 47/48, pp. 3003–14.

Chattopadhyay, S.N. (1992), 'Historical Context of Political Change in Rural West Bengal: A Study of Seven Villages in Barddhaman', *Economic and Political Weekly*, Vol. XXVII, No. 13, pp. 647–58.

Chenery, Hollis B. (1975), 'The Structuralist Approach to Development Policy', *The American Economic Review*, 65, pp. 310–16.

Chenery, Hollis B. et al. (1974), *Redistribution with Growth*, London: Oxford University Press.

Chew, Sing and Robert Denemark (eds.) (1996), *The Underdevelopment of Development: Essays in Honour of Andre Gunder Frank*, Thousand Oaks: Sage Publications.

Chief Ministers Conference (1969), 'Notes of Agenda', Chief Ministers Conference on Land Reforms, 28–9 August 1969, New Delhi: Department of Agriculture, mimeo.

Chopra, Suneet (1985), 'Bondage in a Green Revolution Area: A Study of Brick Kiln Workers in Muzaffarnagar District', in Utsa Patnaik and Manjari Dingwaney: *Chains of Servitude, Bondage and Slavery in India*, Hyderabad: Sangam Books, pp. 162–86.

Chowdhury, Khorshed (1993), 'Food And Hunger Nexus: Availability and Entitlement Hypothesis Reconsidered: Evidence from Bangladesh Data', *Journal of Developing Societies*, Vol. IX, pp. 88–104.

Clift, Charles (1977), '*Progress of Irrigation in Uttar Pradesh*, East-West difference', *Economic and Political Weekly*, Vol. 12, No. 29, pp. A83–A90.

Constituent Assembly, *Official Reports of the Constituent Assembly Proceedings*, New Delhi: Government of India.

Cooper, Adrienne (1988), *Sharecropping and Sharecroppers' Struggles in West Bengal, 1930–1950*, Calcutta: K.P. Bagchi.

Cowen, M.P. and R.W. Shenton (1996), *Doctrines of Development*, London: Routledge.

Crooke, William (1989), *A Glossary of North Indian Peasant Life*, ed. Shahid Amin, Delhi: Oxford University Press.

Danda, Ajit and Dipali Danda (1971), *Development and Change in Basudha*, Hyderabad: National Institute of Community Development.

Das Gupta, Ranajit (1992), *Economy, Society and Politics in Bengal: Jalpaiguri 1869–1947*, Delhi: Oxford University Press.

Datta Ray, S. (1994), 'Agricultural Growth in West Bengal', *Economic and Political Weekly*, Vol. XIX, No. 29, pp. 1883–4.

Datta, Prabhat (1992), *The Second Generation Panchayats in India*, Calcutta: Calcutta Book House.

District Gazetteer Muzaffar Nagar (1980), *Uttar Pradesh District Gazetteers, Muzaffarnagar*, Lucknow: Department of District Gazetteers.

District Magistrate (1993), *A Report on the Floods of July 1993 in Jalpaiguri District*, Jalpaiguri, mimeo report.

Dorai, P.T. (1994), *Women in Industrial Relations*, Brussels: ICFTU/APRO.

Drèze, Jean and Amartya Sen (1995), *India: Economic Development and Social Opportunity*, Oxford/Delhi: Oxford University Press.

Drèze, Jean and Haris Gazdar (1997), 'Uttar Pradesh: The Burden of Inertia', in Jean Drèze and Amartya Sen, *Indian Development: Selected Regional Indicators*, Delhi: Oxford University Press.

Dube, S.C. (1958), *India's Changing Villages: Human Factors in Community Development*, London: Routledge and Kegan Paul.

BIBLIOGRAPHY

Dutt, N.K. (1965), *Origin and Growth of Caste in India*, Vol. II, *Caste in Bengal*, Calcutta: KLM.

Dyson, Tim (1991), 'Child Labour and Fertility: An Overview, an Assessment, and an Alternative Framework', in Ramesh Kanbargi, *Child Labour in the Indian Subcontinent: Dimensions and Implications*, New Delhi/London: Sage, pp. 81–100.

Eashvaraiah, P. (1993), *The Communist Parties in Power and Agrarian Reforms in India*, Delhi: Academic Foundation.

Engineer, Ali Asghar (1989), *Communalism and Communal Violence in India: An Analytical Approach to Hindu-Muslim Conflict*, Delhi: Ajanta Publications.

Escobar, Arturo (1995), *Encountering Development: The Making and Unmaking of the Third World*. Princeton, NY: Princeton University Press.

Esteva, Gustavo (1992), 'Development', in Wolfgang Sachs, *The Development Dictionary: A Guide to Knowledge as Power*, London: Zed Books.

Etienne, Gilbert (1968), *Studies in Indian Agriculture: The Art of the Possible*, Bombay: Oxford University Press.

Fallon, Peter and Zafiris Tzannatos (1998), *Child Labor: Issues and Directions for the World Bank*, Washington: The World Bank.

Fan, Shenggen, Peter Hazell and Sukhadeo Thorat (1999), *Linkages between Government Spending, Growth, and Poverty in Rural India*, Washington: International Food Policy Research Institute.

Field, John and Marcus Franda (1974), *Electoral Politics in Indian States: The Communist Parties of West Bengal*, New Delhi: Manohar.

Frank, Francine (1971), *India's Green Revolution: Economic Gains and Political Costs*, Bombay: Oxford University Press.

Franke, Richard W. and Barbara H. Chasin (1992), *Kerala: Development Through Radical Reform*, Delhi: Promilla and Co.

Frankel, Francine (1978), *India's Political Economy, 1947–1977: The Gradual Revolution*, Delhi: Oxford University Press.

FS Report Muzaffarnagar (1931), *Final Settlement Report, Muzaffar Nagar District*, Allahabad: Government Press.

Fukuyama, Francis (1989), *The End of History*, Avon Books.

Fyfe, Alec (1989), *Child Labour*, Cambridge: Polity Press.

Gardner, Katy and David Lewis (1996), *Anthropology, Development and the Post-Modern Challenge*, London/Chicago: Pluto Press.

George, Susan (1992), *The Debt Boomerang*, London: Pluto Press.

Ghatak, Maltreesh and Maitreya Ghatak (2002), 'Recent Reforms in the Panchayat System in West Bengal: Towards Greater Participatory Governance?', *Economic and Political Weekly*, Vol. XXVII, No. 1, pp. 45–58.

Ghose, A.K. (ed.) (1983), *Agrarian Reform in Contemporary Developing Countries*, London: Croom Helm.

Ghose, Buddhaded (1971), 'People and Panchayati Raj', *Kurukshetra*, Vol. IX, No. 23.

Ghosh, Buddhadeb and Prabir De (1998), 'Role of Infrastructure in Regional Development', *Economic and Political Weekly*, Vol. XXIII, No. 47/48, pp. 3039–48.

Ghosh, Madhusudan (1998), 'Agricultural Development, Agrarian Structure and Rural Poverty in West Bengal', *Economic and Political Weekly*, Vol. XXIII, No. 47/48, pp. 2987–95.

Gill, Sucha Singh and Ranjit Singh Guman (2001), 'Changing Agrarian Relations in India: Some Reflections on Recent data', *The Indian Journal of Labour Economics*, Vol. XXXIIII, No. 4, pp. 809–26.

Gould, Harold A. (1962), 'Traditionalism and Modernity', *Economic Weekly*, 18 August.

Gould, Harold A. (1967), 'Changing Political Behaviour in Rural Indian Society', *Economic and Political Weekly*, Vol. II, No. 33, pp. 1515–24.

Goulet, Dennis (1971), *Development Ethics: The Cruel Choice: A New Concept in the Theory of Development*, New York: Athen.

Government of West Bengal (yearly), *Economic Survey*, Calcutta.

Gupta, Dipankar (1992), 'Peasant Unionism in Uttar Pradesh: Against the Rural Mentality Thesis', *Journal of Contemporary Asia*, Vol. XII, No. 2, pp. 155–66.

Gupta, Dipankar (1988), 'Country-Town Nexus and Agrarian Mobilisation: Bhartiya Kisan Union as an Instance', *Economic and Political Weekly*, Vol. XVII, No. 51, pp. 2688–96.

Gupta, M. and K. Voll (eds.) (1987), *Young Hands at Work: Child Labour in India*, New Delhi: Atma Ram.

Gumaste, V.M. et al. (1987), *Intervention and Poverty*, Madras: Institute for Financial Management and Research.

Hanumantha Rao, C.H. (1989), 'Decentralised Planning: An Overview of Experiences and Prospects', *Economic and Political Weekly*, 25 February, pp. 411–16.

——— (1992), 'Integrating Poverty Alleviation Programmes with Development Strategies: Indian Experience', *Economic and Political Weekly*, Vol. XVII, No. 48, pp. 2603–8.

Harriss, John (1983), 'Making Out on Limited Resources: Or, What Happened to Semi-feudalism in a Bengal District', *Cressida Transactions*, Vol. II, No. 1/2, pp. 16–76.

——— (1993), 'What is Happening in Rural West Bengal? Agrarian Reform, Growth and Distribution', *Economic and Political Weekly*, Vol. XVIII, No. 24, pp. 1237–47.

Herring, Ronald J. (1983), *Land to the Tiller: The Political Economy of Agrarian Reform in South Asia*, Delhi: Oxford University Press.

Hettne, Bjorn (1991), *Development Theory and the Three Worlds*, Burnt Mill: Longman.

BIBLIOGRAPHY

Hobart, M. (ed.) (1993), *An Anthropological Critique of Development: The Growth of Ignorance*, London: Routledge.
Hulme, David and Paul Mosley (1996), *Finance Against Poverty*, 2 vols., London/New York: Routledge.
ILO (yearly), *World Labour Report*, Geneva: ILO.
—— (1996), *Child Labour: Targeting the Intolerable*, Geneva: ILO, 86th Session 1998, Report VI (1).
Jain, L.C. (1985), *Grass without Roots: Rural Development under Government Auspices*, New Delhi: Sage.
Jeffery, Patricia and Roger Jeffery (1996), *Don't Marry me to a Ploughman!*, New Delhi: Vistaar.
Jeffery, Roger and Patricia Jeffery (1994), 'The Bijnor Riots, October 1990: Collapse of a mythical special relationship?', *Economic and Political Weekly*, Vol. XIX, No. 10, pp. 551–8.
Jha, Raghbendra (2000), 'Growth, Inequality and Poverty in India: Spatial and Temporal Characteristics', *Economic and Political Weekly*, 11 March, pp. 921–8.
Johnston, B.F. and Kilby, P. (1975), *Agriculture and Structural Transformation*, New York: Oxford University Press.
Jose, A.V. (1984), 'Poverty and Inequality: The Case of Kerala', in A. Khan and E. Lee, *Poverty in Rural Asia*, Bangkok: ILO.
Joshi, P.C. (1975), *Land Reforms in India*, Bombay: Allied Publishers.
—— (1979), 'Fieldwork Experience: Relived and Reconsidered: Rural Uttar Pradesh', in M.N. Srinivas, A.M. Shah and E.A. Ramaswamy, *The Fieldworker and the Field*, Delhi: Oxford University Press, pp. 73–99.
Kanbargi, Ramesh (ed.) (1991), *Child Labour in the Indian Subcontinent: Dimensions and Implications*, New Delhi: Sage.
Kantowsky, Detlev (1970), *Dorfentwicklung Und Dorfdemokratie, Formen und Wirkungen von Community Development und Panchayati Raj*, Bielefeld: Bertelsmann Universitätsverlag.
Khanna, B.S. (1994), *Panchayati Raj in India (Rural Local Self-Government), National Perspective and State Studies*, New Delhi: Deep and Deep.
Khare, R.S. (1984), *The Untouchable as Himself: Ideology, Identity and Pragmatism among Lucknow Chamars*, Cambridge: CUP.
Khasnabis, Ratan (1981), 'Operation Barga: Limits to Social Democratic Reformism', *Economic and Political Weekly*, Vol. VI, No. 25/26, pp. A43–8.
Khatu, K.K. (1983), *Working Children in India*, Baroda: Operations Research group.
Kitching, Gavin (1989), *Development and Underdevelopment in Historical Perspective*, London: Routledge.
Kohli, Atul (1987), *The State And Poverty In India, The Politics of Reform*, Bombay: Orient Longman.

Kolenda, Pauline (1983), *Caste, Cult and Hierarchy, Essays on the Culture of India*, Meerut: Folklore Institute.

—— (1989), 'Micro-Ideology and Micro-Utopia in Khalapur: Changes in the Discourse on Caste over Thirty Years', *Economic and Political Weekly*, Vol. XXIV, No. 32, pp. 1831–7.

Kolodner, Eric (1995), 'The Political Economy of the Rise and Fall (?) of Hindu Nationalism', *Journal of Contemporary Asia*, Vol. XV, No. 2, pp. 233–53.

Konar, Harekrishna (1977), *Selected Works*, Calcutta: Saha.

Korten, David (1990), *Getting to the 21st Century: Voluntary Action and the Global Agenda*, West Harford: Kumarian.

Kothari, Rajni (1989), 'Decentralization: The Real Issue', *Seminar*, No. 360, pp. 14–19.

Krishnan, T.N. (1976), 'Demographic Transition in Kerala: Facts and Factors', *Economic and Political Weekly*, Vol. I, No. 31/33, pp. 1203–24.

Kulshreshtra, Jinesh C. (1994), *Indian Child Labour*, New Delhi: Uppal Publishing House.

Kumar, A.K. Shiva (1996), 'UNDP's Gender-Related Development Index; Computation for Indian Sates', *Economic and Political Weekly*, 6 April, pp. 887–95.

Kurian, N.J. (2000), 'Widening Regional Disparities in India', *Economic and Political Weekly*, Vol. XXXV, 12 February, pp. 538–50.

Kurien, John (2000), 'The Kerala Model: Its Central Tendency and the Outlier', in Govindan Parayil, *Kerala: The Development Experience*, London: Zed Books.

Kuttikrishnan, A.C. (1994), 'Educational Development in Kerala', in B.A. Prakash 1994, pp. 349–67.

Lehman, D. (ed.) (1974), *Agrarian Reform and Agrarian Reformism*, London: Faber.

Lerche, Jens (1995), 'Is Bonded Labour a Bound Category? Reconceptualising Agrarian Conflict in India', *Journal of Peasant Studies*, Vol. 22, No. 3, pp. 484–515.

Lewis, Oscar (1958), *Village Life in Northern India*, Urbana: University of Illinois Press.

Lieten, G.K. (1977a), 'Land Reforms: Failure even in Kerala', *Economic and Political Weekly*, Vol. XII, 9 March, pp. 415–17.

—— (1977b), 'Education, Ideology and Politics in Kerala', *Social Scientist*, September.

—— (1982), *The First Communist Ministry in Kerala, 1957–9*, Calcutta: K.P. Bagchi.

—— (1988), 'Panchayat Leadership in a West Bengal District', *Economic and Political Weekly*, Vol. XIII, No. 40, pp. 2069–73.

—— (1990), 'Depeasantisation Discontinued: Land Reforms in West Bengal', *Economic and Political Weekly*, Vol. XV, No. 35, pp. 2265–71.

—— (1992a), *Continuity and Change in Rural West Bengal*, New Delhi/London: Sage Publications.

—— (1992b), 'Caste, Gender and Class in Panchayats: Case of Barddhaman', *Economic and Political Weekly*, Vol. XVII, No. 29, pp. 1567–74.

—— (1993), 'Village Councils in a Static Mould: The Case of Coastal Medinipur', The Hague: IDPAD OP&R, 1993–4.

—— (1994a), 'The North Indian Kulak Farmer and His Deficient Democracy', New Delhi/The Hague: IDPAD OP&R, 1994, No. 4.

—— (1994b), 'On Casteism and Communalism in Uttar Pradesh', *Economic and Political Weekly*, Vol. XIX, No. 14, pp. 777–81.

—— (1994c), 'Rural Development in West Bengal: Views from Below', *Journal of Contemporary Asia*, Vol. XIV, No. 4, pp. 515–30.

—— (1996a), *Development, Devolution and Democracy: Village Discourse in West Bengal*, New Delhi/London: Sage.

—— (1996b), 'Hindu Communalism: Between Caste and Class', *Journal of Contemporary Asia*, Vol. XVI, No. 2, pp. 236–52.

—— (1996c), 'Land Reforms at Centre Stage: The Evidence on West Bengal', *Development and Change*, Vol. XVII, pp. 111–30.

—— (2000a), 'Decentralisation in India', IDPAD Newsletter, No. 8, November, pp. 4–8.

—— (2000b), 'Child Work and Education', *Economic and Political Weekly*, Vol. XV, No. 24, pp. 2037–43 and, No. 25, pp. 2171–81.

—— (2001a), *State and People in South Asia: Village Views on Development in India and Pakistan*, Report for the UNRISD, Geneva.

—— (2001b), 'The Human Development Puzzle in Kerala', *Journal of Contemporary Asia*, No. 4, pp. 47–68.

—— (2001c), 'Decentralisation in India: Learning from Old and New Histories', *Cahier du Gemdev*, Paris, Cahier 27, pp. 161–78.

—— (2001d), 'Key Issues of the Conference', inaugural address to the IDPAD Conference on Child Labour in South Asia, New Delhi, 13–15 October 2001.

——, (2002a), 'Development Priorities: Views from Below', in R. Jeffery and Jens Lerche, *Dynamics of Rural Development in Northern India*, New Delhi: Manohar.

——, and Ravi Srivastava (1999), *Unequal Partners: Power Relations, Devolution and Development in Uttar Pradesh*, New Delhi/London: Sage.

Linlithgow (1928), *Royal Commission on Agriculture in India*, Appendix to the Report, Bombay: Government Central Press.

Lipton, Michael (1993), 'Land Reform as Commenced Business: the evidence against stoppage', *World Development*, Vol. XI, No. 4, pp. 641–57.

Maddick, Henry (1970), *Panchayati Raj, A Study of Rural Local Government in India*, London: Longman.

Mahadevan, K. and M. Sumangala (1987), *Social Development, Cultural Change and Fertility Decline: A Study of Fertility Change in Kerala*, New Delhi: Sage.
Maheshwari, S.R. (1994), *Local Government in India*, Agra: L.N. Agarwal.
Malaviya, H.D. (1959), *A Report to the Nation*, New Delhi: People's Publishing House.
Mallick, Ross (1993), *Development Policy of a Communist Government: West Bengal Since 1977*, Cambridge: Cambridge University Press.
Mamdani, M. (1972), *The Myth of Population Control*, New York: Monthly Review Press.
Manor, James (1993), 'Panchayati Raj and Early Warnings of Disasters', *Economic and Political Weekly*, Vol. XVIII, No. 21, pp. 1019–20.
Marriott, McKim (1969), *Village India: Studies in the Little Commmunity*, Chicago: University of Chicago Press.
Mathew, E.T. (1999), 'Growth of Literacy in Kerala. State Intervention, Missionary Initiatives and Social Movements', *Economic and Political Weekly*, Vol. XXIV, No. 39, pp. 2811–20.
Matthai, John (1915), *Village Government in British India*, 1993 rpt., London: T. Fisher Unwin.
Mehta, Asoka (1978), *Report of the Committee on Panchayati Raj Institutions*, New Delhi: Ministry of Agriculture and Irrigation.
Mehta, Balvantray (1957), *Report of the Team for the Study of Community Projects and National Extension Service*, Vol. I, New Delhi: Planning Commission.
Mehta, Niranjan et al. (1977), 'Towards a Theory of Rural Development', *Development Dialogue*, No. 2, pp. 11–67.
Mencher, Joan (1980), 'The Lessons and, non-Lessons of Kerala: Agricultural Labourers and Poverty', *Economic and Political Weekly*, Vol. V, Nos. 41–3, pp. 1781–1802.
Mertin, Joachim (1962), *Das Dorfsentwicklungsprogramm als Methode des Wirtschaftsausbau fur das landlichen Indien*, Stuttgart: Gustav Fischer Verlag.
Mishra, G.P. and P.N. Pande (1996), *Child Labour in the Glass Industry*, New Delhi: Nangia.
Moore, Barrington (1969), *The Social Origins of Democracy and Dictatorship*, Harmondsworth: Penguin.
Morris-Jones, W.H. (1971), *The Government and Politics of India*, London: Hutchinson University Library.
Mueller, E. (1976), 'Economic Value of Children in Peasant Agriculture', in R.G. Ridken, *Population and Development: The Search for Selective Interventions*, Baltimore/London: University of John Hopkins Press.
Mukarji, Nirmal and D. Bandyopadhyay (1993), 'New Horizons for West Bengal's Panchayats: A report for the Government of West Bengal', New Delhi, report.
Mukherjee, Subrata Kumar (1974), *Local Self-Government in West-Bengal*, Calcutta.

Mukherji, Nirmal (1993), 'The Third Stratum', *Economic and Political Weekly*, Vol. XVIII, No. 18, pp. 859–62.
Mukhopadhyay, Swapna and R. Savithri (1998), *Poverty, Gender and Reproductive Choice: An Analysis of Linkages*, New Delhi: Manohar.
Mukhopadhyaya, Ashok (1977), *The Panchayat Administration in West-Bengal*, Calcutta.
Namboodiripad, E.M.S. (1984), *Kerala Society and Politics: An Historical Survey*, New Delhi: National Book Centre.
Nandy, Ashish (1987), *Tradition, Tyranny, and Utopias*, Delhi: Oxford University Press.
────── (1992), 'State', in Wolfgang Sachs (ed.), *The Development Dictionary*, London: Zed Publications.
Nicholson, L. (ed.) (1990), *Feminism/Post Modernism*, London: Routledge.
Nossiter, T.J. (1982), *Communism in Kerala: A Study in Political Adaptation*, Delhi: Oxford University Press.
Oommen, M.A. (1994), 'Land Reform and Economic Change: Experiences and Lessons from Kerala', in B.A. Prakash (1994), *Kerala's Economy: Performance, Problems, Prospects*, New Delhi: Sage Publications, pp. 117–40.
────── (ed.) (1995), *Panchayati Raj Development Report*, New Delhi: Institute of Social Sciences.
Osmani, S.R. (1991), 'Social Security in South Asia', in E. Ahmad at al. (eds.), *Social Security in Developing Countries*, Oxford: Clarendon Press.
Pai, Sudha (1988), *Changing Agrarian Relations in U.P: A study of the North-Eastern Areas*, New Delhi: Inter-India.
────── (1994), 'Caste and Communal Mobilisation in Electoral Politics in Uttar Pradesh', *Indian Journal of Political Science*, Vol. LV, No. 3, pp. 307–20.
────── (2001a), 'From Harijans to Dalits: Identity Formation, Political Consciousness and Electoral Mobilisation of the Scheduled Caste in Uttar Pradesh', in Ghanshyam Shah (ed.), *Dalit Identity and Politics*, New Delhi: Sage.
────── (2001b), 'The State, Social Justice and the Dalit Movement: The BSP in Uttar Pradesh', in N.P. Jayal and Sudha Pai (eds.), *Democratic Governance in India*, New Delhi: Sage.
Palmer-Jones, R.W. (1992), 'Sustaining Serendipity? Groundwater, irrigation, growth of agricultural production, and poverty in Bangladesh', *Economic and Political Weekly*, Vol. XVII, No. 39, pp. A128–A140.
Panikar, P.G.K. and C.R. Soman (1984), *Health Status of Kerala: The Paradox of Economic Backwardness and Health Development*, Trivandrum: Centre of Development Studies.
Panikkar, K.N. (ed.) (1991), *Communalism in India: History, Politics and Culture*, New Delhi: Manohar.

——— (1999), *Rethinking Development: Kerala's Development Experience*, New Delhi: Concept Publishing House.

Planning Commission (1952), *First Five Year Plan*, New Delhi: Government of India.

Prabhu, Seeta (1998), 'Social Sectors During Economic Reforms: The Indian Experience', The Hague: IDPAD Occasional Papers.

Pradhan, M.C. (1966), *The Political System of the Jats in North India*, London: Oxford University Press.

Prakash, B.A. (1994), *Kerala's Economy: Performance, Problems, Prospects*, New Delhi: Sage Publications.

Preston, P.W. (1996), *Discourses of Development: State, Market and Polity in the Analysis of Complex Change*, Aldershot: Avebury.

Radakrishnan, P. (1989), *Peasant Struggles, Land Reforms and Social Change: Malabar 1936–82*, New Delhi: Sage Publications.

Radwan, Samir (1977), *Agrarian Reform and Rural Poverty: Egypt 1952–1975*, Geneva: ILO.

——— (1993), 'Outlook on Employment and Poverty: Challenges and scope for employment intensive growth strategy', Keynote address, IFPRI Policy Workshop on 'Employment for Poverty Alleviation and Food Security', Washington, October.

Rahman, Anisur (1984), *Grassroots Participation and Self-Reliance*, New Delhi: OUP.

Ramachandran, V.K. (1997), 'On Kerala's Development Achievements', in Jean Drèze and Amartya Sen, *Indian Development: Selected Regional Perspectives*, Delhi: Oxford University Press, pp. 205–356.

Rao, V.M. (1992), 'Land Reform Experiences: Perspective for Strategy and Programmes', *Economic and Political Weekly*, Vol. XXVII, No. 26, pp. A50–A64.

Rawal, Vikas and Madhura Swaminathan (1998), 'Changing Trajectories: Agricultural Growth in West Bengal, 1950 to 1996', *Economic and Political Weekly*, Vol. XXIII, No. 40, pp. 2595–602.

Ray, G.L. and Sagar Mondal (1993), *Gram Panchayat Organisation: Effective Management for Rural Development*, Calcutta: Naya Prokash.

Riad El Ghonemy, M. (1990), *The Political Economy of Rural Poverty: the Case for Land Reforms*, London: Routledge.

Rist, Gilbert (1997), *The History of Development: From Western Origins to Global Faith*, London: Zed Books.

Rogaly, Ben (1998), 'Containing Conflict and Reaping Votes: Management of Rural Labour Relations in West Bengal', *Economic and Political Weekly*, Vol. XXIII, No. 42/43, pp. 2729–39.

Rogaly, Ben, Barbara Harriss-White and Sugata Bose (eds.) (1999), *Sonar Bangla? Agricultural Growth and Agrarian Change in West Bengal and Bangladesh*, New Delhi: Sage Publications.

Roszak, Theodore (1969), *The Making of A Counter Culture*, New York: Anchor Books.
Rothier, Rudy (1995), *Kinderen van deKrokodil*, Leuven: Atlas.
Rudolph, Susanne Hoeber (2000), 'Civil Society and the Realm of Freedom', *Economic and Political Weekly*, Vol. XXXV, 13 May, pp. 1762–8.
Rudra, Ashok (1981), 'One Step Forward, Two Steps Backward', *Economic and Political Weekly*, Vol. VI, No. 25/26
――― (1992), *Political Economy of Indian Agriculture*, Calcutta: K.P. Bagchi.
Saha, Anamitra and Madhura Swaminathan (1994), 'Agricultural Growth in West Bengal in the 1980s: A Disaggregation by Districts and Crops', *Economic and Political Weekly*, Vol. XIX, No. 13, pp. A2–A11.
Said, Edward (1993), *Culture and Imperialism*, London: Vintage Books.
Saith, Ashwani and Ajay Thankha (1972), 'Agrarian Transition and the Differentiation of the Peasantry: A Study of a West UP Village', *Economic and Political Weekly*, VII, No. 14, pp. 707–24.
――― (1992), 'Longitudinal Analysis of Structural Change in a north Indian Village: 1970-1987: Some preliminary findings', The Hague, ISS: Working Paper Series, No. 128.
Salmen, Lawrence F. (1987), *Listen to the People: Participant-Observer Evaluation of Development Projects*, New York: Oxford University Press for the World Bank
Sanyal, Manoj Kumar, P.K. Biswas and S. Bardhan (1998), 'Institutional Change and Output Growth in West Bengal Agriculture: End of Impasse', *Economic and Political Weekly*, Vol. XXIII, No. 47/48, pp. 2979–86.
Saradamoni, K. (1999), 'Kerala Model: Time for Rethinking', in M.A. Oommen, 1999, pp. 159–74.
Sen Gupta, Bhabani (1979), *CPIM: Promises, Prospects, Problems*, New Delhi: Young Asia Publications.
Sen, Amartya (1993), 'The Threats to Secular India', *Social Scientist*, Nos. 238–9, pp. 5–23.
――― (1997), 'Radical Needs and Moderate Reforms', in Jean Drèze and Amartya Sen, *Indian Development: Selected Regional Perspectives*, Delhi: Oxford University Press, pp. 1–32.
Sen, Amartya (1999), *Development as Freedom*, Delhi: Oxford University Press.
Sen, Gita (1992), 'Social Needs and Public Accountability: The Case of Kerala', in Marc Wuyts, M. Macintosch and T. Hewitt, *Development Policy and Public Action*, Oxford: Oxford University Press in association with The Open University, pp. 253–77.
Sen, Sunil (1972), *Agrarian Struggle in Bengal, 1946–47*, New Delhi: People's Publishing House.
Sengupta, Sunil (1981), 'West Bengal Land Reforms and the Agrarian Scene', *Economic and Political Weekly*, Vol. VI, No. 25/26, pp. A62–A75.

———, and Haris Gazdar (1997), 'Agrarian Politics and Rural Development in West Bengal', in Jean Drèze and Amartya Sen, *Indian Development: Selected Regional Perspectives*, Delhi: Oxford University Press, pp. 129–204.

Sharma, Indradeo et al. (1993), 'Child Labour in India: An Anatomy', in B. Singh and S. Mahanty, 1993, pp. 13–26.

Sharma, Miriam (1979), *The Politics of Inequality: Competition and Control in an Indian Village*, Hawaii: The University Press of Hawaii.

——— (1985), 'Caste, Class and Gender: Production and Reproduction in North India', *Journal of Peasant Studies*, Vol. XII, No. 4, pp. 57–88.

Singh, A.N. (1990), *Child Labour in India: Socio-economic Perspective*, New Delhi: Shipra.

Singh, Bhagwan P. and Shukla Mahanty (1993), *Children at Work: Problems and Policy Options*, Delhi: B.R.

Singh, H.N. (1986), 'Caste, Land and Power: A Study of Dhobi Block in Jaunpur District of Uttar Pradesh', in K.L. Sharma (ed.), *Social Stratification in India*, New Delhi: Manohar.

Singh, I.S. (1992), *Child Labour in India*, New Delhi: Oxford and IBH.

Singh, Jagpal (1992), *Capitalism and Dependence: Agrarian Politics in Western Uttar Pradesh, 1951–1991*, Delhi: Manohar.

Singh, Yogendra (1961), 'The Changing Power Structure of Village Community: A Caste Study of Six Villages in Eastern UP', in A.R. Desai, *Rural Sociology in India*, Bombay: Popular Prakashan, pp. 668–85.

Sobhan, Rehman (1993), *Agrarian Reform and Social Transformation: Pre-Condition for Development*, London: Zed Books.

Srivastava, Ravi S. (1994), 'Planning and Regional Disparities in India: The Uneven Record of Change and Growth', in T.J. Byres (ed.), *The State and Development Planning in India*, Delhi: Oxford University Press, pp. 147–219.

Srivastava, Ravi S. (1997), 'Accounting for Disparities in Access to Elementary Education', working paper, Department of Economics, University of Allahabad,.

Srivastava, Sushil (1991), *The Disputed Mosque: A Historical Inquiry*, New Delhi: Vistaar Publications.

Stein, E. and J. Davis (eds.) (1940), *Labour Problem in America*, New York: Farraer and Richer.

Surjeet, Harkrishan Singh (1992), *Land Reforms in India: Promises and performance*, New Delhi: National Book Centre.

SZW (1997), 'Kinderarbeid. Beleidsnotitie', The Hague: Ministry of Social Affairs and Employment.

Tharamangalam, Joseph (1981), *Agrarian Class Conflict: The Political Mobilization of Agricultural Labourers in Kuttanad, South India*, Vancouver: University of British Columbia Press.

——— (1999), 'The Social Roots of Kerala's Development Debacle', in M.A. Oommen, 1999, pp. 175–97.
Tessier, Stephane, ed. (1998), *A La Recherche des Enfants des Rues*, Paris: Karthala.
Thorner, Alice (1981), 'Nehru, Albert Mayer, and Origins of Community Projects', *Economic and Political Weekly*, Vol. VI, No. 4, pp. 117–20.
Todaro, Michael T. (1992), *Economics for a Developing World: An Introduction to Principles, Problems and Policies for Development*, London/New York: Longman.
Tornquist, Olle (1991), 'Communists and Democracy: Two Indian Cases and One Debate', *Journal of Concerned Asian Studies*, Vol. XI, No.1, pp. 63–76.
Toye, John (1987), *Dilemmas of Development: Reflections on the Counter-revolution in Development Theory and Policy*, Oxford: Basil Blackwell.
Turner, Terence (1997), 'Human Rights, Human Difference: Anthropology's Contribution to an Emancipatory Cultural Politics', *Journal of Anthropological Research*, Vol. 53, No. 3, pp. 273–91.
Turner, Victor (1979), *Process, Performance and Pilgrimage: A Study in Comparative Symbology*, New Delhi: Concept Publishing Company.
UNDP (1992), *Human Development Report*, New Delhi: OUP.
UPDG (1987), *Uttar Pradesh District Gazetteer*, Faizabad, Lucknow: Government Press.
Vlassoff, M. (1979), 'Labour Demand and the Economic Utility of Children: A Case Study of Rural India', *Population Studies*, Vol. XXIII, No. 3, pp. 415–28.
Warriner, Doreen (1969), *Land Reforms: Theory and Practice*, Oxford: Oxford University Press.
Washbrook, David (1997), 'From Contemporary Sociology to Global History', *Journal of the Economic and Social History of the Orient*, pp. 410–28.
Webster, Neil (1990), 'Agrarian Relations in Burdwan District, West Bengal: From the Economics of Green Revolution to the Politics of Panchayati Raj', *Journal of Contemporary Asia*, Vol. X, No. 2, pp. 177–211.
Webster, Neil (1992), *Panchayati Raj and the Decentralisation of Development Planning in West Bengal: A Case Study*, Calcutta: K.P. Bagchi.
Weiner, Myron (1991), *The Child and the State in India: Child Labour and Education Policy in Comparative Perspective*, Princeton: Princeton University Press.
Weiner, Myron and John Osgood Field (1975), *Electoral Politics in Indian States: Party Systems and Cleavages*, Delhi: Manohar.
Wertheim, W.F. (1976), *De Lange Mars der Emancipatie*, Amsterdam: Van Gennep.
Westergaard, Kirsten (1987), 'Marxist Government and People's Participation: The Case of West Bengal', *Journal of Social Studies*, No. 38, pp. 95–113.
Whitcombe, Elisabeth (1972), *Agrarian Conditions in Northern India, Vol. 1: The United Provinces under British Rule 1860–1900*, Berkeley: University of California Press.

White, Ben (1976), 'Population, Involution and Employment in a Javanese Village', *Development and Change*, VII, No. 1, pp. 267–90.

Whitehead, Judy (1982), 'The Mirror of Inequality: A Reinterpretation of Homo Hierarchicus', *Social Scientist*, No. 114, pp. 33–49.

World Bank (1997a), *Development in Practice: Primary Education in India*, Washington: The World Bank/New Delhi: Allied Publishers.

——— (1997b), *India: Achievements and Challenges in Reducing Poverty*, Washington: The World Bank (also as Report No. 16483-IN, 27 May 1997).

——— (2000), *India: Reducing Poverty, Accelerating Development: A World Bank Country Study*, New Delhi: Oxford University Press.

Zaidi, S. Akbar (1999), *The New Development Paradigm: Papers on Institutions, NGOs, Gender and Local Government*, Karachi: Oxford University Press.

Zamora, Mario D. (1990), *The Panchayat Traditions: A North Indian Village Council in Transition, 1947–1962*, New Delhi: Reliance.

Index

Advani, L.K. 193
agrarian growth in West Bengal 117–21
agriculture, advances in 35
Ahluwalia, Montek S. 91, 129
Alam, Javeed 185, 204
Ambedkar, B.R. 20–1, 26
Ananda Bazar Patrika 80
Ananda Marg 86
Anderson, Benedict 189
Arya Samaj 68
Asoka, Mehta Committee 23–4
Atkinson, Edwin T. 58, 167

Bag, Pratimo 224
Bagchi, Amiya Kumar 119
Bahujan Socialist Party (BSP) 173, 197
Bandyopadhyay, B. 80, 93
Bandyopadhyay, D. 80, 209–10, 226
Bandyopadhyaya, N. 34
Bardhan, Pranab 160
Barman, Pradip Kumar 15
Baruah, Sanjib 36
Basu, Jyoti 112, 127
Basu, Tapan 200
Basu, Uday 79–80
Baxter, Craig 57
Beidelman 173
belief systems 184–5, 195
Bell, Clive 91
Bergman, Theodor 115
Berreman, Gerald D. 22
Bhabha, Homi 151
bhaichara land system 165
Bharat Sevashram 86
Bharatiya Janata Party (BJP) 57, 81, 83–4, 86, 170–2, 188, 191, 193–5, 198–9, 203–8, 211, 219
Bharatiya Kisan Union (BKU) 68
Bhargava, B.S. 20
Bhat, Marti 134–5
Bhattacharya, M. 34
Bhattacharyya, Dwaipayan 114
Blunt, E.A.H. 59
bonded child labour 230
Boyce, James 94, 105, 109, 111, 118
Brass, Paul 74
Breman, Jan 15

capitalism 149
caste system in Uttar Pradesh 173–80, 185
Chakrabarty, G. 134, 233
Chambers, Robert 82, 159, 162
Chandrasekhar, C.P. 95
Chasin, Barbara H. 134–5
Chatterjee, Biswajit 122
Chenery, Hollis 91
Chew, Sing 149
child labour,
    age-wise work and schooling of 234–5
    definition of 227
    fertility and 231–3
    in India 228–31
    parameters of 228–31
    studies on 229–30
    villagers view of 236–41
Child Labour, No Time To Play 230
child slaves 229
Chopra, Suneet 74
Chowdhury, Benoy 101
Chowdhury, Khorshed 109

civil society 17–19, 25, 29, 150,
    154–5, 159
  bewilderment in 171–3
  class struggle, to institutional
    management shift 36–8
  communalism, see, Hindu
    communalism
Communist Party of India (CPI)
  92–3, 112, 116, 135–6, 139–41,
  144, 197
Communist Party of India (Marxist)
  33–4, 39–40, 44, 46–50, 52–4,
  57, 81, 83–4, 88, 93, 100,
  113–14, 127, 140, 210–12, 214,
  220–1, 223, 226
Community Development
  Programme 18, 21
  failure of 21–5
Comprehensive Rural Development
  Programme 55
Congress party 57, 83–4, 92, 172
Constitution of India,
  73rd Amendment 18–19, 24
  Article 40 20
Cooper, Adrienne 92
Cowen, M.P. 148, 241

Dag Hammarskjöld Foundation 57
dahej (dowry), practice of 180–1
Danda, A. 46
Danda, D. 46
Das Gupta, Biplab 15
Dasgupta, Asim 102
Datta, Devipriya 15
Davies, J. 228, 230
De, Prabir 118
decentralization,
  civil society and 17–19, 25, 29,
    31–2
  early approaches to 20–1
  failure of community development
    21–5
  in India 17–32
  new push and new questions to
    25–7
  that works 27–31

Denemark, Robert 149
Department of Rural Development
  51
development,
  class-wise priorities 160–1
  concepts of 152–3
  definition of 148
  in villages of Uttar Pradesh
    155–64
  modernization and 149
  of underdevelopment 149
  post-modernist assumptions
    147–54
  pre-modernist assumptions 147–64
  priorities 160–4
  state and 158–60
  Western civilization and 149
dharma, significance of 174, 176,
  179
Dorai, P.T. 230
Drèze, Jean 133
Dube, S.C. 246–7
Duloy, John 91
Dumont 173
Dutta, Prabhat 15
Dyson, Tim 231–2

Eashvaraiah, P. 140–1
Economic and Political Weekly 39
Economic Review 102, 108
El Subdesarrollo del Desarrollo 149
Engineer, Ali Asghar 190
Enlightenment objective 153
Escobar, Arturo 150, 152
Essay on the Principle of Population 241
Esteva, Gustava 151, 153
European Enlightenment 149

Fallon, Peter 227
family planning 232, 241, 248–53
Fan, Shenggen 119
fertility,
  child labour and 231–3
  gender imbalance and 233–4
  literacy and 233–4
Field, John 39

INDEX

floods in Jalpaiguri, West Bengal,
   after-effects 87–9
   local assessment 81–7
   reporting on 79–81
Franda, Marcus 39
Frank, Andre Gunter 149–50
Franke, Richard W. 134–5
Frankel, Francine 34, 39
free-market, process of 26
Fukuyama, Francis 148

Gandhi, Indira 23–4, 39, 72, 123, 170, 191
Gandhi, Mahatma 17, 20, 25
Gandhi, Rajiv 24
garibi hatao slogan 123
Gazdar, Haris 119, 121, 125–6, 129
Ghose, Buddhadeb 34, 118
Ghosh, Madan Gopal 15
Ghuman, Ranjit Singh 123
Gift Deeds Act of 1979 140
Gill, Sucha Singh 123
globalization 26
   predatory forces of 150
good governance 17
Gould, Harold A. 173
gram panchayat 35
gram sabha (village assembly) 24, 52–4
   in West Bengal 224–5
Green Revolution 23, 38, 57, 95, 119
   in Uttar Pradesh 165–8, 231

Harriss, John 93, 97–8, 101–3, 110
Herring, Ronald J. 139–40
Hettne, Bjorn 147
Hindu communalism,
   around Ayodhya 187–208
   between caste and class 187–208
   compensatory illusions 188–90
   contextualization of 190–4
   intra-Hindu divide 194–6
   lower castes and 196–9
   temple politics and 203–7
Hindu Mahasabha 212
Hindu nationalism 187–8

Hinduism 188–9, 195, 200
Hindutva 195, 197, 202–6, 208
human development,
   facts about 133
   fertility levels 127
   IMR 125–6, 130
   in Kerala 132–46
   in West Bengal 124–31
   literacy and 128–30
Human Development Index (HDI) 125, 133, 145
   performance in Uttar Pradesh 233–6

ICFTU 230
ILO World Labour Report 230
illusory consciousness 189–90
imagined community 189
Indian National Congress (INC) 20, 23–4, 40, 46, 167, 187, 191, 194, 197–9, 205, 207, 211
inequality and poverty in West Bengal 121–4
institutional management,
   shift from class struggle to 36–8
Integrated Rural Development Programme (IRDP) 35, 63, 161, 212, 214, 216, 223
Intensive Agricultural District Programme 39
International Labour Organization (ILO) 110, 227–8
International Monetary Fund 123, 154, 192
irrigation in West Bengal,
   expenditure on 117–21
   floods and 106–11

Jain, L.C. 18
Jan Sangh 212
Janata Dal 172, 192–3, 197–8
Janata Party 57, 171
Jeffery, Patricia 15, 170, 200, 239, 241
Jeffery, Roger 170, 200, 239, 241

Jha, Raghbendra 122, 124
Joshi, P.C. 13–14, 34

KAR Act of 1964 140
Kanshi Ram 179
karma, significance of 174, 176, 179
Karshaka Sangham 141
Kerala, human development in,
 crude death rate in 137
 demographic transition in 137
 educational reforms 142–5
 facts about 133–9
 land reforms and 139–42
 literacy in 136–9
Kerala Agricultural Relations Bill
 (KARB) 139–40, 142, 144
Kerala Education Bill 143
Kerala Land Reforms (Amendment)
 Act 1969 140
Kerala Shashtra Sahitya Parishad
 (KSSP) 136
Khare, R.S. 179
Khasnabis, Ratan 15
Khatu, K.K. 229
khudkast land 55
Kisan Sabha 50
Kitching, Gavin 147
Kohli, Atul 93, 98, 115
Kolenda, Pauline 173–5, 187
Konar, Harekrishna 50
Kooiman, Dick 15
Kothari, Rajni 19
Kumar, Nagesh 15
Kumar, Santosh 15
Kurian, N.J. 118, 127
Kuttikrishan, A.C. 142

labour market regulation 100
land reforms in Kerala 139–42
land reforms in West Bengal 92–111
 agrarian growth 117–21
 causal factors 101–3
 comprehensive intervention
  97–101
 contrasting arguments 112–17
 depeasantization 93–7

disaggregating agreement 103–6
expenditure on irrigation 107–9
fertility levels in 127
human development and 124–31
IMR 125–6, 130
inequality 121–4
irrigation and 106–11
land redistribution, technological
 inputs and productivity changes
 104–5
literacy in 128–30
polarization 93–7
poverty and 121–4
Leach 173
Leclerq, Michele 15
Left Front Government (LFG) 34,
 36–7, 39, 93–4, 98, 102–3, 109,
 112, 114–15, 125, 127–8, 131,
 209–11, 216–17, 226
Lewis, Oscar 173
liberalization 26, 192
Liberation Movement (Vimochana
 Samaram) 143
Lieten, G.K. 36, 38–9, 54, 88, 93,
 96–8, 117, 136, 140, 142–3,
 155, 198, 210
Lipton, Michael 102
literacy in West Bengal 128–30
local self-government 18
Local Self-Government Act of 1885
 33

Maddick, Henry 20
Mahanty, Shukla 230
Malaviya, H.D. 142
Mallick, Ross 93, 113, 209
Malthus 241
Mamdani, A. 231, 241
Mandal Commission 171–2, 192–3
Manor, James 78
Marriott, McKim 173
Mass Literacy Programme 128
Mathew, E.T. 135
Mathews, George 15
Matthai, John 20
McNamara, Robert 91

INDEX

Mehta, Asoka 23
Mehta, Balwantray 22, 24
Mehta, Nirajan 58, 72
Metcalfe, Charles 17, 20
Moore, Barrington 23
Morris-Jones, W.H. 22
Mukarji, Nirmal 80, 93
Mukerji, D.P. 13
Mukhopadhyay, Swapna 240, 248–9

Nair Service Society (NSS) 143–4
Namboodiripad, E.M.S. 132
Nandy, Ashis 151, 154
National Bank for Agriculture and Rural Development (NABARD) 106, 109
nation-states 26
Nehru, Jawaharlal 191
non-governmental organizations (NGOs) 18, 25, 81
North Atlanitc capitalism 147
Nossiter, T.J. 139, 142–3
nyaya panchayat 58

Oommen, M.A. 141–2
Operation Barga 122
Osmani, S.R. 93
Other Backward Castes (OBC) 178–80, 193, 197, 201–3

Padmanabhan, Mannath 144
Pal, Ravikant 69
Pal, S.P. 134, 233
Palmer-Jones, R.W. 109
Panchayat Act 1973 52
panchayat samiti 35
Panchayati Act of 1957 34
panchayati raj (PR) 20, 23–6, 34, 55, 85
panchayati raj institution 78
panchayats,
  composition of 40–54, 70
  failure of 19
  floods in Jalpaiguri and 78–90
  functioning of 58
  in Uttar Pradesh 27–31, 55–77
  in West Bengal 27–31, 33–54
  in Western Uttar Pradesh 55–77
  legislation for 22, 34
  meetings and members 58–61
  members,
    by caste 46–7
    by class and power 47–9
    by gender 43–6
    by occupation 48–9
    fear psychosis among 62–4
    marginal differences 61–2
    meetings and 58–61
    representation and control 49–54
  natural disasters and 78–90
  pradhan and 60–9, 71, 76
  public works and private corruption 64–7
  recognition in Indian Constitution 18
  significance of 37
  social void 68–71
  structure of 21–2, 59
  traditional 20
  villagers' opinion about 71
Pande, Harish 15
pardah system 183
participatory development 17–19
Planning Commission 22
post-modernism, fallacies of 151–4
poverty and inequality in West Bengal 121–4
poverty and social indicators, in Indian states 130
Pradhan, M.C. 167–8
pradhan,
  functioning of 60–9, 71, 76
Praja Socialist Party (PSP) 140
public works and private corruption 64–7

Radhakrishnan, P. 139–41
Radwan, Samir 110
Rahman, Anisur 33
Rajan, Irudaya 134–5, 249
Ramachandran, V.K. 134–5, 140–1

Ramakrishna Mission 81, 86
Rawal, Vikas 117, 120
Revolutionary Socialist Party (RSP) 80, 83–4
Rist, Gilbert 148
Rogaly, Ben 113–14, 117, 119, 209
Rotary Club 86
Rothier Rudi 229
Roy, Pronesh Chondra 15
rural development in West Bengal 209–26
  benefits of 212–14
  class relations and 216–21
  gram sabha and 224–5
  loan politics and 214–16
  social changes and 221–3
Rural Labour Employment Guarantee Programme (RLEGP) 35
Rutten, Mario 15
Ruud, Engelsen 114

Saha, Anamitra 95, 119
Said, Edward 189–90
Saith, Ashwani 15, 166, 173
Samajwadi Party 62
Sanyal, M.K. 120
Savithri, R. 240, 248–9
Seeta Prabhu 126, 128
Sen Guputa, Bhabani 35
Sen, Amartya 108, 128, 133–5, 208
Sen, Gita 134
Sen, Sukumal 15
Sen, Sunil 92
Sengupta, Sunil 98, 119, 121, 125–6, 129
Sharma, Miriam 173
Shenton, R.W. 148, 241
shramdan programme scheme 66, 72
Singh, Ajit 170
Singh, Bhagwan P. 230
Singh, Bishambhar 62
Singh, Charan 56, 170
Singh, I.S. 166
Singh, Kalyan 192
Singh, Mulayam 62

Singh, V.P. 171, 192, 198
social indicators for south Indian states 134
social movement, success of 149
socialism 149
Sonar Bangla? 113, 117
South Asia Coalition against Child Slavery 230
Srivastava, Ravi S. 15, 155, 244, 247
Srivastava, Sushil 15
state and civil society dichotomies 18, 90
Statesman 79–80, 86
Stein, E. 228, 230
Surjeet, Harkishen Singh 34
Swaminathan, Madhura 95, 117, 119–20

taluqdari estates 92
Tankha, Ajay 166, 173
tebhaga movement 92
Telegraph 80
Tikait, Mahendra Singh 55–6, 171
Tornquist, Olle 38
Tzannatos, Zafiris 227

UNDP Human Development Report 110
UNICEF 228
United Front (UF) 93, 96, 140
United Nations Development Programme (UNDP) 124, 133
Uttar Banga Sambad 80
Uttar Pradesh,
  caste and,
    class in 187–208
    religion in 165–86
    system in 173–80, 185
  caste-wise and caste-wise political preferences 198
  child labour and education in 227–53
  civil society bewilderment 171–3

INDEX

class relations in 217–18
communalism in 200–3
destruction of Ayodhya mosque 203–7
economic progress 168–71
family planning in 248–52
fertility and child labour in 231–2
green revolution area 165
HDI performance in 233–6
Hindu communalism around Ayodhya in 187–208
insecurity and criminalization in 169
labour-peasant ratio 166
literacy in 166, 233–4, 236–7
panchayats in western area 55–77
polarized villages 236–41
schooling of child labour in 245–8
see also, western Uttar Pradesh
social deterioration in life in 168–71
temple policies 203–7
women status in 180–4

van den Muyzenberg, Otto 15
village councils 26
village democracy, precondition for 23
Village Self-Government Act of 1919 33
villages of Uttar Pradesh,
conception of development priorities in 157–64
socio-economic conditions in 155–7
status groups 157
Vimochana Samaram 143–4
Vlassoff, M. 231

Warriner, Doreen 99, 102
Webster, Neil 15, 33, 36–8, 54, 93, 97, 114, 225
Weiner, Myron 232
Wertheim, W.E. 185

West Bengal,
benefits to weak in 212–14
class relations 216–21
development of weak in 209–26
gram sabha 224–5
loan politics 214–16
public space 210–12
rural development in 209–26
social changes 221–3
West Bengal panchayats,
advances in agriculture 35–6
case of Barddhaman 38–54
changing public space in 210–12
composition of 40–54
by caste 46–7
by class and power 47–9
by gender 43–6
by occupation 48–9
representation and control 49–54
socio-economic background 42–3
councillors 84
floods in Jalpaiguri and 78–90
after effects 87–9
local assessment 81–7
reporting 79–81
land reforms 36
literacy and 128–9
local power 33–5
natural disasters and 78–90
Westergaard, Kirsten 37–8, 103
Western civilization and development 149
western Uttar Pradesh,
panchayats in 55–77
composition 70
economic benefits 74–6
fear psychosis 62–4
functioning of *pradhans* 60–9, 71, 76
marginal difference 61–2
members and meetings 58–61

public works and corruption 64–7
social void 68–71
state and 74–6
villagers' opinion about 71–3
see also, Uttar Pradesh
White, Ben 16
Williams, Glyn 114
Wiser 173
Women status, in Uttar Pradesh 180–4

World Bank 18, 91, 110, 123, 154–5, 161, 228

Yadav, Mulayam Singh 179, 198

Zaidi, Akbar 26
zamindari class 34
zamindari estates 92
zamindari land 55
Zamora, Mario D. 20
zila parishad 35